Sling approved Same adapt as 12 gauge rifled slug .750 of an inch long and .715 of an inch in dia.

A National Rifle Association Library Book

THE RIFLE
Its Development for Big Game Hunting

"After all, the digest of the experience of a hundred
men—picked men, not chaps who once killed a buck in
the Adirondacks and know all about game rifles is the best
way to reach an intelligent decision."—NED CROSSMAN.

"A National Rifle Association Library Book" means a book recommended as the
standard on the subject by the National Rifle Association.

OLIVER F. WINCHESTER. SHIRT-MAKER, RIFLE MANUFACTURER,
LIEUTENANT-GOVERNOR OF CONNECTICUT.

From Mr. Arthur T. Ward.

THE RIFLE

ITS DEVELOPMENT FOR
BIG GAME HUNTING

S. R. TRUESDELL

Member, National Rifle Association

Lt. Col. Army of the United States, 1942-1945

THE MILITARY SERVICE PUBLISHING CO.

HARRISBURG, PENNSYLVANIA

1947

DEDICATED
TO ALL THE GRAND FELLOWS WHO REALLY WROTE
THIS BOOK, AND TO MY WIFE WHO THINKS THAT I DID.

TABLE OF CONTENTS

PREFACE

*F*OR some shortsighted reason we ignore the rifle when writing, teaching and thinking about American history.

So few people know or are able to appreciate the debt that all of us owe to past supremacy in the use of this most individual of weapons. Probably future histories, as in the past, will be replete with references to machine guns, a European development; the tank, an English invention; jet-bombs, which came from Germany; and atomic weapons, which, to our apparent discomfort, we know how to make, but don't seem to know what to do with. But of the rifle, which we took up and perfected beyond all other nations, there is never a word. Search as you will the modern histories of the United States written by Channing, Bryce, Fiske, McMasters, Sparks, McLaughlin, Paxson, Woodrow Wilson, Rhodes, Beard, or any others, and you will find nothing about the rifle, which by one crucial and accurate shot at Saratoga turned back the single greatest threat to victory in our War for Independence; which contributed to the decisive defeat of the British at King's Mountain and encouraged our people in their determination to fight on to victory; which against odds of 3 to 1, and the pick of Wellington's army on the Field of Chalmette, won for Jackson the Battle of New Orleans and for the United States the western continent. Not a word is there about the Henry and Spencer repeating rifles which Johnny Reb said were "loaded on Sunday and shot all the week," or of the rifles with which the doughboy and the G.I., led by such masters as York and Woodfill, won and held all battlefields in two world wars against the "Master Race." There is much of the plow, the humble log cabin, and the axe that made it, the spinning wheel and the loom, and linsey-woolsey of flax and sheep's hair, but never a word of the weapon that made it all possible; that exercised the white man's supremacy over the red; over wild animals, and against foreign foes in a hundred million episodes; the one primal advantage of the American against the world.

I say again, that there is some great defect in our processes of thought, which has left too much of the teaching of history to our women folk, who dread firearms, and to our academicians who know little or nothing of firearms, or their importance in the development of this nation. There is little doubt that we owe much to the plow, the reaper and the railroad, but pause for a moment, if you will, and picture the original settler in his clearing, felled and hewed out of the forest which furnished the material for his cabin and the wild game for his food while he built, and planted his crops. How long would he have been unmolested, in a wilderness over-run by that most savage and warlike of races, the American Indian, without the constant possession and proficient use of the rifle. Or picture again, the settlers of the Great Plains, where in addition to the brutal and predatory "horse" Indians, the country was subjected twice yearly to the migration of irresistible hordes of buffalo. Indeed without the rifle, westward migration would have been impossible, and all other elements of progress which have set this nation above all the world in industry and science, would have been unneeded and probably undeveloped.

Outside of toughness of body and soul, the American pioneer was equipped with an axe and a rifle, in the use of both of which he was a past master. These were with him as he packed his family and goods on horseback over the Alleghanies, along the Wilderness Road; with him again on the seat of his wagon as he drove his ox team west across the plains, and were close by as he plowed his fields from Massachusetts to California. With the possibility of a red Indian lying out beyond a stump or a post of the lower forty, ready to pot him as he turned his team at the end of the furrow, nothing was more necessary than the rifle. The histories that do not recognize and acknowledge these facts, were written in the safe and academic atmosphere of eastern halls of learning and not in the log-cabin or sod-hut of the settler. It is one of the great failings of our otherwise rich Americana, that there is little literature of the use of the rifle on this utmost fringe of civilization, where each minute of the day was hazardous; and that, the little that was written, is now unknown to the descendants of the pioneers. If the full importance of the rifle had been known, there probably would have been more attention given to physical and military preparedness, and we would not have been subjected to the periodic drives of otherwise well-educated men and women, for the passage of legislation restricting our Constitutional rights to bear arms, or the ill advised and futile desire of some mothers to prevent a knowledge of firearms reaching their progeny, although this knowledge might later have saved their lives in an emergency. It is a well known fact among riflemen that a boy who has been well grounded and instructed in the use and care of firearms is infinitely less apt to be involved in dangerous accidents later.

The object in writing this book is the correct presentation of rifle facts, developed from the experience of prominent big game hunters throughout the world. Statements about the rifle are sometimes at variance with the truth as is illustrated by the following. In a recent book the .30-06 Springfield is represented as less well suited for big game than some of the newer "Super-dupers," that one hunter using the Springfield found that the *huge* Ovis Poli rams required a lot of shooting unless hit just right! Actually the .30-06, with 180 grain hollow-point boat-tail bullets, on these Asian bighorn in the instance referred to by the "expert" performed as follows:

"It was a very simple shot, not over fifty yards. Another was easily accounted for; two hurried shots were misses but the fifth brought down the third ram. We watched the last * * * this one had a head fully as large as the first and I was fortunately able to stop him just as he was disappearing behind the ridge. All were within a hundred and fifty yards—a rare bit of luck which gave us four excellent specimens, the best we had seen. * * *

"A careful advance, snakewise, brought us within range and a single shot, at approximately two hundred yards, bagged the prize. It was a big symmetrical head 56¾ inches around the curl, an excellent addition to the group."

Five sheep in seven shots, and one sheep for each hit is not requiring "a lot of shooting." As a matter of fact, evident from the tables presented later in this book, the Springfield is such an excellent all-round rifle that it has been used by many famous big game hunters, of all nationalities, in all parts of the world, while some of the much touted "Super-dupers" have already been forgotten, or soon will be.

And so in order to be sure of the facts, as against such poetic license, this book started from a tabulation of the experiences of these big game hunters all over the world, when they hunted, the game animals shot, and the rifles used. Around this tabulation, which was reconstructed and expanded as additional information became available, four articles were written at the suggestion of the *American Rifleman* staff, for publication in that magazine. Under the painstaking care of Mr. John Scofield, Associate Editor, this material was so interestingly presented, that it brought almost immediate offers to publish in book form. Even then, there might have been considerable misgiving as to my ability to expand the original material into the larger manuscript required for a book, had it not been for the great interest and help of all members of the *American Rifleman* staff, including Mr. C. B. Lister, General J. S. Hatcher, Capt. John Scofield, Mr. John Harper, and Mr. Al Barr whose first suggestion started the ball rolling.

But most importantly, the enthusiasm and constant help and encouragement of Mr. Richard Gordon McCloskey, Editor of The Military Service Publishing Company has been an inspiration far beyond the ordinary. Had it not been for his taking the author and the embryonic idea of this book under his immediate care; rendering valuable suggestions and criticisms; unearthing sources for material and illustrations; making seemingly impossible problems of writing and arrangement simple and feasible; the work would have been difficult to complete.

I can only hope that riflemen and others will find this book of sufficient interest to want to possess a copy, to purchase it for their friends, and to recommend its reading to all who are interested in firearms, and in knowing their major role in this country's welfare, thus justifying the editor's faith in its value.

My thanks are also due Mr. H. L. Hardy for criticism and assistance with the title, to Dr. R. L. Sutton for valuable comment and pictures of some rare old rifles, to Mr. Arthur T. Ward for his kindness in permitting the use of pictures of Winchester, Ross, Savage and Henry, to Mr. Guy Hubbard for permission to use Christian Sharps' picture, to Mr. A. D. Bissell for securing a picture of Charles Newton, and to Miss Josephine Shannon for assistance with the manuscript.

S. R. TRUESDELL,

Evanston, Illinois,
May 10, 1947.

INTRODUCTION

*I*N the past, wherever people have encroached on foreign lands it has meant war, either with the aborigines, or wild game, or both. One is led to picture the settlers' plough, the traders' beads and calico, or the missionarys' cross as the implements of civilization, but in truth, these were secondary to the pistol, sword and musket of the pioneer. Probably the first man to step on Plymouth Rock shouldered a well primed matchlock and had his hand on his pistols, rather than stepping off with a hymnal and an air of sanctimony. The latter picture is what we like to imagine, but the first is the more practical. As a means of spreading civilization, firearms, and more particularly the rifle, have been the principal but unsung tools of the white race. They have meant the difference between man's wearing skins and eating raw meat, and the cut-glass, silverware and thick steaks on our present dinner-table. Indeed, if it had not been for the rifle, the buffalo, wild deer and panther conceivably might still be roaming at will, interesting and beautiful, but a constant hazard and impediment to our existence. While we may look with a feeling of sadness at the disappearance of wild game, it was an inevitable part of the progress of civilization and one which has made it necessary now for most of us to enjoy the vicissitudes and excitement of big game hunting from the safety of our arm chairs.

Firearms were not an invention of the English or even of the Anglo Saxon race. But it is a faculty of energetic and intelligent people, formed by hardship and a fusion of pioneer races, that they are quick to adopt and perfect the inventions of others. (It is this trait which Europeans now seem to find so remarkable in the Americans of today.) Firearms and more importantly the rifle were a South European invention. The rifle seems to have first appeared in Nuremburg, Germany, about the year 1500. Some local gunsmith, by the name of Kotter or Kollner by different versions, experimenting with the idea of grooves to receive the residue from black powder and thus make the loading of a round ball from the muzzle easier, decided to make these grooves spirally, and the rifle was born.

But making a rifle barrel by hand was an expensive process, useful apparently at this time only for hunting, and so the idea of rifled firearms

spread slowly.   Certain of these Bavarian people, persecuted on account
of their religion and also perhaps for a slight disregard of kingly pre-
rogatives in the way of wild game, emigrated to Eastern Pennsylvania in
the American Colonies in 1709.   Among this group were a goodly number of gunsmiths, and these men with the advice and help of experienced
backwoodsmen, evolved the long-barrelled, small-bore Kentucky rifle
using the American invention of the patched ball.   Others, from the
Bavarian homeland, enlisted in the Hessian troops hired by King George
and fought, much to their discomfiture, with their short-barrelled large-
bored Jaeger rifle, on various American battlefields.

Although not strictly speaking its first recognition as a military weapon,
the advent of the American rifle in the Revolutionary War is described
most interestingly in the book *War Through the Ages* by Lynn Montross:

Another regiment of specialists saved the new nation the following
Autumn.   Early in 1777 Washington placed 500 picked riflemen under
the command of Colonel Daniel Morgan, recently released from captivity
at Quebec.   A cousin of Daniel Boone, this burly, self-educated Virginia
pioneer had served as a wagoner in the last war.   Now at the age of
forty-one he became a natural leader of Virginia and Pennsylvania frontiersmen whom he disciplined with a patriarchal firmness enforced by his
own hard fists.

The formation of this unit—the first of its kind in history—came just
in time to meet the greatest British threat of the war, a concerted effort
to occupy the Hudson-Lake Champlain line.   According to the original
plan, Howe's forces were to march northward from New York to meet
the army of General John Burgoyne, invading from Canada.   Such a
result would have split the colonies hopelessly, laying them open to conquest in detail.

The rifle was not a new weapon.   Even in classical time it had been
remarked that the velocity and accuracy of a projectile were increased by
the imparting of a spinning motion.   Ancient armorers tried to apply the
principle to the spears shot from war engines, and sixteenth century gunsmiths made the first experiments with spiral grooving in the bore of
wheel-locks.   They found that any gains were offset by a slow rate of fire;
for in order to prevent the escape of propelling gases, the ball had to be
driven into the grooves with a ramrod and wooden mallet.   Due to this
defect the European rifle was rejected by soldiers and used chiefly for
target or sporting purposes.

During the last war the advantages of the American rifle had been
noted by Howe and Bouquet, though it played a minor part in the out-

come. The real development of the national weapon did not begin until afterward, when the victory opened the frontier to the first great wave of westward migration.

It was a backwoods invention—a slight improvement of epochal significance—which established the superiority of the American arm over its short-barrelled counterpart of the Old World. Some unknown genius of the border discovered that a 'greased patch' could be placed over the muzzle as a temporary wrapping for a ball driven home by a few light strokes of the ramrod. This bit of lubricated linen or leather not only made the bullet fit the grooves but also cleaned out the fouling from the previous discharge and acted as a 'gas check' to utilize the full force of the explosion. The patch had thus created history's first firearm of precision.

Not until the perfection of the breechloader three generations later, was the 'long rifle' ever excelled. The speed of charging still lagged behind that of the smoothbore, but the gains in range, accuracy and penetration were impressive. At 100 yards, the battle range of the musket, tacticians expected only 40 per cent of hits, and even this average suffered from misfires. The rifle accounted for 50 per cent at 300 yards, while at two-thirds of that distance the border marksman aimed with deadly certainty for a foeman's head or heart.

American 'patch-loading' also resulted in economy of ammunition. Because of the increased gas pressure, it was found that the caliber could be reduced to .54, taking a half-ounce ball, whereas most smoothbores of the day fired a one-ounce bullet of about .70 caliber. The smaller projectile, with less air resistance to overcome, developed much more velocity and striking power.

Such gains may be traced in part to expert Pennsylvania gunmakers whose masterpieces are still cherished by collectors. Even so, the effectiveness of the rifle in Revolutionary campaigns owed to a generation of Americans who rank among the natural, warriors of history. Like the Parthians or Mongols of old, they were shaped by a daily existence of peril and hardship for the tactics which soldiers of later ages have had to learn by rote. . . .

Such warfare, of course, was alien to the farmers and villagers of the seaboard. Smoothbores were the weapons of Lexington and Bunker Hill, and not until afterwards did Congress authorize the recruiting of ten companies of riflemen from frontier districts. These units took part in the Quebec, Boston and New York campaigns, but an entirely new chapter of tactics begins in 1777 with the formation of Morgan's regiment.

Up to this time the rifleman had been considered an auxiliary to formal operations—a scout or sharpshooter whose usefulness lay chiefly in skirmishing. It was left to Morgan and his command to prove that the new weapon could also become a decisive factor on the battlefield.

The decisiveness of this new arm was particularly evident in the fighting of Morgan's riflemen at Freemans Farm, September 19, 1777, and at Bemis Heights October 7, 1777 ending in Burgoyne's surrender October 15, 1777. Charles Winthrop Sawyer in his *Firearms in American History* claims that the shot made by one Tim Murphy with a superimposed double barrel 'long rifle' which mortally wounded General Simon Fraser, 'probably was the most important shot ever fired in the United States,' leading as it did to the confusion and defeat of Burgoyne's army at a crucial moment of the second battle.

The decisive use of the Kentucky rifle used by the American backwoodsmen in the fighting at Boston, Freemans Farm, Kings Mountain and Cowpens, had a momentous result on the history of the world. Because of this, as Americans, we like to think, that it was the first use of the rifle in war, but for this "first" we will have to go back to Braddock's defeat in July, 1755. He had been saved from complete disaster by the frontiersmen—soldiers using the Kentucky rifle. In December 1755 profiting by the disastrous experience of Braddock, the 60th Royal Americans, the first rifle regiment, was formed as a part of the British Army and recruited from German and Swiss settlers in the eastern American colonies. Under Lt. Col. Henry Bouquet this unit was instructed in an open order drill with the rifle, of a type much better adapted to Colonial warfare. The regiment took part in the French and Indian War, fighting at Ticonderoga in 1758, was with General Forbes at the capture of Fort Duquesne, took part in the siege and capture of Louisburg, fought with Wolfe on the Plains of Abraham and with Lord Geoffrey Amherst at the capture of Montreal in 1759, and finally distinguished itself in the signal victory over the Indians at Bushey Run in its march to relieve the garrison at Fort Pitt in 1763. Subsequently as the Duke of York's Own Riflemen and later as the King's Royal Rifle Corps, dressed in rifleman's green with red facings, battalions of the regiment have taken part in all of the major wars of the British Empire. Under Sir John Moore and Wellington it was a part of the Rifle Brigade in the Peninsula Campaigns, was at Delhi in 1857, in Lord Roberts campaigns in Afghanistan in 1878-80, in South Africa in 1879, and again in 1899-1902, in Egypt 1882-1885, in World War I in France, and again in World War II. During the

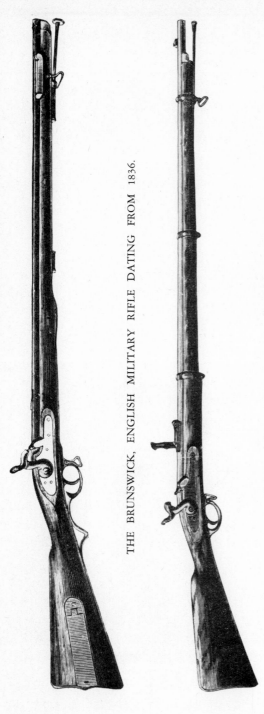

THE BRUNSWICK, ENGLISH MILITARY RIFLE DATING FROM 1836.

THE ENFIELD, ENGLISH MILITARY RIFLE OF 1855.

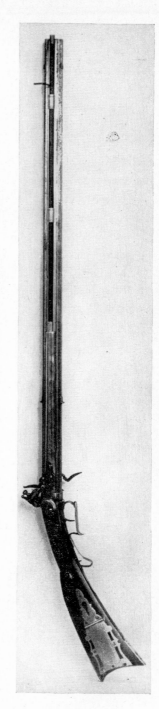

A DOUBLE BARRELED KENTUCKY RIFLE SIMILAR TO THE RIFLE USED BY TIM MURPHY.

Courtesy of the *American Rifleman*.

HENRY HOLLAND. HEAD OF
HOLLAND AND HOLLAND, ENG-
LISH RIFLE MAKERS.

From Teasdale-Buckell's *Experts on
Guns and Shooting.*

W. W. GREENER. ENGLISH MAKER
OF CUSTOM SHOTGUNS AND
RIFLES, INVENTOR, AND ONE OF
THE MOST FAMOUS AUTHORS
OF BOOKS ON WEAPONS.

From Teasdale-Buckell's *Experts on
Guns and Shooting.*

JAMES PURDEY. ENGLISH MAKER
OF CUSTOM SHOTGUNS AND
RIFLES.

From Teasdale-Buckell's *Experts on
Guns and Shooting.*

W. E. METFORD. CELEBRATED
RIFLE SHOT AND INVENTOR OF
THE METFORD RIFLING USED IN
THE LEE-METFORD MILITARY
RIFLE AND BY GIBBS IN THE
GIBBS-METFORD SINGLE SHOT
RIFLES.

From Teasdale-Buckell's *Experts on
Guns and Shooting.*

WESTLEY RICHARDS. ENGLISH
CUSTOM RIFLE AND SHOTGUN
MAKER.

From Teasdale-Buckell's *Experts on
Guns and Shooting.*

GEORGE C. GIBBS. ENGLISH GUN-
MAKER AND EXPERT RIFLE SHOT.
SPECIALIZED ON SPORTING
ADAPTATIONS OF THE
MANNLICHER RIFLE.

From Teasdale-Buckell's *Experts on
Guns and Shooting.*

JOHN RIGBY. THIS ENGLISH CUS-
TOM GUN-MAKER SPECIALIZED
IN SPORTING RIFLES MADE ON
THE MAUSER ACTION.

From Teasdale-Buckell's *Experts on
Guns and Shooting.*

THE "HASTY" SLING.

From Maj. Gen. Wm. Rice's *Indian Game*, 1884.

EARLY HUNTING FROM HORSEBACK.

From Major Leveson's (The Old Shekarry) *Sport in Many Lands.*

SIR SAMUEL W. BAKER, RAILROAD
CIVIL ENGINEER, PIONEER,
COLONIST, BIG GAME HUNTER,
EXPLORER AND AUTHOR.

From his book *Albert Nyanza and the
Nile Tributaries.*

TYLER HENRY. PIONEER INVEN-
TOR OF REPEATING RIFLES AND
CARTRIDGES.

From Mr. Arthur T. Ward.

THE LAST PORTRAIT OF WILLIAM
COTTON OSWELL, AFRICAN EX-
PLORER, BIG GAME HUNTER AND
INTIMATE FRIEND OF DAVID
LIVINGSTONE.

From W. E. Oswell's *The Life of
William Cotton Oswell.*

CHASED BY AN INFURIATED BUFFALO.

From *African Hunting* by W. C. Baldwin.

WILLIAM COTTON OSWELL'S PURDEY 10-BORE MUZZLE-LOADING DOUBLE-BARREL SMOOTH-BORE;
USED IN PREFERENCE TO A RIFLE.

From W. E. Oswell's Life of William Cotton Oswell.

SIR SAMUEL BAKER'S .577 RIFLE SHOWING STOCK REINFORCEMENT.

From Bryden's How to Buy A Gun.

American Revolution the original battalions recruited in the colonies were moved to station duty in the West Indies but a 3rd and 4th Battalion formed in England took part in the operations around Savannah.

It is not difficult, in the light of the history of this rifle regiment and the many countries to which its operations have led, to trace some of the effects that English colonization has had on the development of big game hunting.

The energy, restlessness and desire for adventure of the English race could only find an outlet overseas, since the opportunities for further adventure or advancement in their own narrow isles were limited.

As a result of their overseas activities the English became the leading big game hunters, so that in studying this sport and with it the development of the rifle, we must deal with the adventures of Englishmen or their American cousins, who perhaps because they inherit some of the same traits, have also contributed to the history of the sporting rifle. Other nationals have contributed but in much lesser degree because of their more limited spheres of activity. It is for this reason that most of the literature on the rifle and on big game hunting is in English. Even so, the record is neither complete nor continuous. The American backwoodsmen, the plainsmen and the fur traders were very largely unschooled and as a consequence the literature of that greatest of all hunting adventures, the killing of the buffalo, is very limited, although the contemporary literature on the American rifle is fairly complete.

In England, at this same time, somewhat the reverse was true. The sporting weapon at home was the shotgun, or "gun" and technical literature on the rifle was none too plentiful although the books on big-game hunting and overseas travel and adventure were numerous and well received. This was because these Englishmen were generally military men, graduates of Sandhurst or civil servants recruited from other English universities, well educated and able to write interestingly and well of their experiences. Knowing that their audience was not overly concerned with the technical side of the rifle as a weapon, little was said of this feature. It requires a good deal of search and a knowledge of conditions to get much information on the rifle from their writings.

The great game fields of the world have been in those temperate climates which have been especially inviting to white colonization. These include the continents of North America, Africa and Asia where conditions, which we have not yet determined, permitted the larger and more varied species of game, to develop and prosper.   There is strong evidence, that as in most other types of flora and fauna, Asia was the parent continent from which the sheep, elk, panther, bison, bear, and deer, but not the pachyderms, the lion or the antelope migrated to America.   Africa may or may not have received the Asian sheep, buffalo, elephant, rhino and lion, since we now know the lion was at one time a native of Persia. South America received little of this flood of species and consequently is a comparative void for big game hunting.   So it is the game of Asia, Africa and North America which are of interest in the growth of white settlement and the development of the sporting rifle since the one waited upon the other.

Little could be done with the smoothbore that was not already possible with the bow and arrow, except in warfare, where the disciplined target could be commanded to approach within range of the musket.   But against wild game, except by running down slower footed animals, on horseback, the smoothbore was ineffective.   The limitations of the smoothbore and the fact that the great game herds were in the interior of these continents makes it easier to appreciate why the history of big game hunting is comparatively recent and why the first American Colonies were confined to the narrow seaboard from 1620 until 1775, when the first trans-Alleghany settlement was made from which the Kentucky rifle got its name.   Or that, although the Dutch settled Cape Colony in 1652, it was not until 1834-37 and the Great Trek that the rifle-equipped Boer farmers settled beyond the Orange and Vaal Rivers.

In India the progress of white penetration was even later, principally because the native races were further advanced in culture and there was little need of exploration, and secondly because the process of infiltration of the white races was in this case different.   Here the hunting of game waited on political intrigue and conquest.   Most of the early hunters were officers of the British Army farmed out to the British East India Company and stationed with the native princes to train their forces in the methods of war.   Later these same officers were members of local garrisons which maintained peace and order for the British "Raj," and utilized their short leaves on hunting expeditions for tiger, elephant and Himalayan game when conditions permitted. Thus Shakespear, as Commandant of the Nagpore Irregular Force to suppress thuggery in the Dekkan, hunted only the game of Central India and devoted a large part of his book to the equipment and training of irregular cavalry.   Sir

Samuel Baker, a gentleman sportsman, went to Ceylon, which was almost the earliest English settlement in the East. The first account of Himalayan game is by Maj. Gen. MacIntyre stationed at Peshawar with the Punjab Frontier Force after the Sikh War of 1848 and the Mutiny of 1857. Littledale and Cumberland were early travelers to the Russian Pamirs after the successful Afghan Wars in 1878 and '80. Later the opening of Tibet in 1903 with the pacification of other frontier tribes made wider hunting travels possible to Tibet and Central Asia.

The history of hunting has been generally the same, with an initial period of wide and unlimited slaughter of game for skins, food, ivory or trophies. It is to the credit of the white man that, with the exception of the American buffalo and the African guagga, the effect of this accelerated attack on wild game has been recognized in time and that he has further seen the need for legislation to preserve some of the most valuable species for the future. Conservation was only possible after complete political organization of colonial territory and the setting up of a government with sufficient authority to enforce laws. The hunters' solicitude and acknowledgment of the conflict between free wild life and the encroachment of civilization are poetically stated by Rainsford in a passage from *The Land of the Lion* written in 1909:

Recalling his first buffalo hunt in 1868 in Western America:

Yes as I looked long into my African camp fire, that great day came back to me again. My rude, but hospitable hosts of long ago had vanished with the innumerable herds that fed and housed them. Towns flourish and wheat harvests wave where the buffalo streamed along in thundering flight. And I thought, will this wild land in like manner know change as momentous? May it too become a land of health and homes and plenty? It is hard to say. Prophecy is fascinating but dangerous. Certainly the black man here shows no sign of vacating his heritage, nor does the white man, as yet often give proof that he is able or willing to be in it more than an adventurer and fortune seeker. The country must of right belong at last to the men, black or white, who find in it a home.

It is probably now certain that every effort will be exerted to maintain wild species of game animals in their usual habitat as long as this habitat is not needed for the cultivation of crops to feed people. But on the other hand it must be realized that it will probably be but a short time until certain types of dangerous or predatory game will be exterminated and other species which have been greatly reduced because of their special merit for trophies, skins, or ivory will be given permanent protection. One point of view on this subject is given by Prof. N. S. Shaler, in his book *Man and the Earth* written in 1905:

It is not likely that any practicable measure of care will serve to protect the whole of our kindred mammalian species from death. The larger carnivora, the lion, tiger, etc., are too inconvenient to be spared. Certain of the herbivora, such as the African buffalo, are too ineradicably fierce to submit to the domestication of preserves. Of these unsavable forms, there are not many; perhaps not more than a twentieth part of the whole number are beyond salvation. The remainder can be preserved, provided their master is willing to be a providence to them. Some of these, need speedy care; the most can wait for a century or so before they are in imminent danger of extinction. On the whole the herbivorous mammals of Africa are the most endangered of all their kindred. That continent, by far the richest in large species of the class, remained until the last century practically untrodden by the sportsman. The human assault on the life of this land was made for food, or, in the case of the elephant and the hippopotamus, for ivory, and with the ineffective arms; now the land is the favorite range of that mighty beast the big-game hunter, who with tools vastly more effective than the natives' spear or the flint-lock gun, kills not for profit but as a dog in a sheepfold for the mere love of killing. The African elephant, several of the antelopes of that country, and other very interesting species have been brought to the verge of extinction. In the opinion of those competent to judge, certain forms plentiful a hundred years ago have already passed away. The Indian elephant because of his large place as a domesticated beast, although he does not breed freely in captivity, is apparently safe from extinction until supplanted by some kind of engine, but his African kinsman being much less domesticable, hardly fit, indeed for the service of man, is doomed to certain and speedy extinction unless sedulously guarded from the sportsman; like most other large herbivora, it cannot maintain itself as a solitary paired form; it needs the conditions of the herd for its survival. As soon as it becomes rare it will speedily pass away.

This is a somewhat pessimistic view as to the fate of the lion, tiger, buffalo, rhinoceros, elephant, hippopotamus, and in our own continent by inference the grizzly and the brown bear. There are now, however, great efforts being put forth by sportsmen to preserve these species or at least to set aside permanent refuges for them, and by rigorous control prevent their damaging settled districts. In 1905, when Prof. Shaler wrote the above comment, game laws and the idea of fully protected preserves was just beginning to have recognition. These have since grown to the extent that it would seem entirely possible that all these species will be preserved in their wild state if not for hunting at least for observation. Other sections of unreclaimable mountain waste-land or jungle which apparently can never be utilized for human occupation will remain, with properly enforced laws, as a field for big game hunting forever. The development of preserves in protecting one species which Shaler considered possible of extinction, the African elephant, is illustrated by the following from the book *Elephants in Africa* by Frank Melland published in 1938:

As for the extermination bogey: in the Uganda Report of 1923 the number of elephants in the Protectorate was put at 30,000, and Mr. Swynnerton reckoned that allowing for the killing of 1,000 head a year by man, and the loss from natural causes among the annual progeny, in thirty years the number of elephants would nevertheless have doubled. In 1936 the wastage from all causes (elephant control and license holders included) was 2300 and Capt. Pitman Warden has to report 'We are just holding our own and no more' and in the previous year he had stated that 'the Protectorate is still literally over-run with elephants—big, dangerous, destructive beasts.'

So it would seem as if there might be some game preserved for our posterity to try their rifles on, even if the need of rifled weapons for defense has been forever outlawed. In order to have some idea of the type of game which exists throughout the world and also to get an idea of their habitat and characteristics, these have been grouped by families in Appendix H with a short description of their present abundance and the type of ground frequented. This will help to explain the varying types of rifle and equipment used in jungle and hill shooting in India and the similarity of the latter to sheep and goat hunting in western North America, where the Rocky Mountain goat for instance is not a goat but a member of the mountain antelope clan, inhabiting country which is very like that of its cousins the takin of India and the serow of China. The chain of similar characteristics and hunting conditions also follows the sheep family from its ancestral home in high Asia westward to the moufflon or 'aroui' of the North African Atlas Mountains, and eastward through Siberia to the bighorn of the Alaskan, Coastal, and Rocky Mountain ranges of North America.   The Indian Gaur is sort of a half cousin of the North American buffalo in that it has the dorsal verte-brae of the hump but only thirteen pairs of ribs instead of the bisontine fourteen.

PART I

THE LARGE BORES

1834 TO 1874

CHAPTER 1

EARLY RIFLEMAKING

*A*LTHOUGH invented three centuries earlier, it was not until after 1800 that the rifle came into general use in hunting and warfare. The American backwoodsman had used it for both since about 1750 and occasional military units such as the Royal Americans had been equipped with the rifle, but the great surge of rifle development was waiting on the better knowledge and interchange of ideas on rifle performance and manufacture, on better materials, and on the insistent demand from the backwoodsmen, the pioneers, the colonists and the hunters for better weapons. Much experimenting had been carried on, however, by various persons and one of these, Benjamin Robins, in 1742 made a notable prophecy:

Whatever state shall thoroughly comprehend the nature and advantages of rifled barreled pieces and having facilitated and completed their construction, shall introduce into their armies their general use, with a dexterity in the management of them, will by this means acquire a superiority which will almost equal anything that has been done at any time by the particular excellence of any kind of arms, and will, perhaps, fall but little short of the wonderful effects which histories relate to have been formerly produced by the first inventor of firearms.

But 'facilitating' the construction of the early rifle was beset by many difficulties. Until about 1850 except in the United States rifles had been forged, rifled, and fitted by hand. Parts were not interchangeable so that a new part could not be supplied to an old model except by careful hand fitting. The interchangeability of parts which finally permitted machine manufacture of rifles started with Eli Whitney in connection with an order of 10,000 muskets for the U. S. Army in 1798 and was further perfected in the Hall breech-loading flint-lock rifle made at Harpers Ferry in 1819, but was not brought to Europe until Col. Colt was interviewed by a committee of the House of Commons in 1852. Col. Colt's testimony before the committee of Parliament was humiliating but convincing. Upon being shown a Minié rifle of the best French work-

13

manship and being asked whether the weapons manufactured in the United States were as well made, his reply was: "There are none so badly made at our armories. That arm could not pass any of our inspectors." On the strength of his testimony, American machinery for boring and turning barrels and shaping gunstocks was installed in the plant at Enfield under the supervision of engineers from the U. S. Arsenal at Harpers Ferry.

The four principal defects in muzzle loading rifles were the difficulty of loading a groove-sized ball from the muzzle, the presence of caked fouling from black powder, faulty ignition, and the poor materials available for locks and barrels.

Loading was made easier by the use of patched balls in the smaller bores from 1750 on, by the adoption of the Delvigne narrowed chamber or the tige-wedge in the chamber on which to upset the round ball with the ramrod, by the belted ball in two-grooved rifles in 1836, by the Minié hollow expanding base bullet in 1851 and finally by the gradual conversion to breechloaders between 1836 and 1867. These breech-loaders, Hall's flint-lock, Lefaucheux's break-open pin-fire double gun in 1836, Dreyse's needle-gun or "Zundnadelgewehr" in 1838, Sharp's falling block rifle in 1850, the Spencer repeating carbine in 1860 and the Snider conversion of the British Enfield in 1867, paralleling the Springfield conversion of the U. S. rifled musket in 1866, with the gradual improvement of the cartridge from a paper case to Berdan's drawn brass case of 1869 solved the major problem of using a groove-size bullet. The brass case by springing back to size cured the early extraction difficulties with the breech-loader. The various bullet developments also permitted a reduction in bore size, harder bullets, quicker twists and higher velocity and energy, completely ending the day of the round ball.

In 1807 the Reverend Forsyth's invention of fulminate of mercury for ignition, used at first in pills or tubes and after 1816 in copper covered caps for percussion lock muzzle loaders, and in the rim or central fire cartridges for breech-loading rifles, solved the problem of reliable ignition. Even this improvement was not adopted by the British Army until the Brunswick rifle in 1836 nor by the U. S. Army until its rifle model of 1842.

As bullets improved, the difficulty from powder fouling became less and was finally effectively removed by the invention of smokeless powder by Viellé, a Frenchman, in 1885.

Improved steel for barrels and locks followed the course of steelmaking, from the discovery of methods for making crucible steel in 1740, the development of better processes of iron puddling in 1783, the adoption of hot blast furnaces in 1830, the invention of the Bessemer process to furnish better gunsteel for the Crimean War in 1856, to the development of the Siemens open-hearth processes between 1861 and 1867. This latter method of steel making produced a metal of uniform quality and of any desired degree of alloy or hardness. It would not be too much to presume that the insistent demands of the firearms industry, prompted by the needs of the soldier, hunter and colonist overseas was a factor of no little importance in these improvements in steel-making, and also that some of the early mishaps and defects of firearms in the hunting field were due to the inferior quality of the metal in earlier rifles.

The various types of rifles in use around 1800 were based on the German Jaeger rifle. How this influenced the American Kentucky rifle has already been described. The backwoodsman could secure lead with great difficulty and found that the high velocity small bore used at the short ranges possible in the woods of Eastern America was sufficiently powerful for his purpose. But by 1840 the game had been driven out of the woods and mountains onto the plains and across the Mississippi where lead was again available from local sources. The buffalo and the grizzly were hardier and larger beasts than the deer and the bear of the east, and ranges were longer. A heavier bullet with more carrying power was needed in a rifle that could be carried and operated from horseback with more ease than the Kentucky rifle. This was the Plains' rifle as made by Hawkens and others from 1819 on in St. Louis and later in Denver. These gunmakers were of German descent and had emigrated west from Lancaster, Pennsylvania. Their newer product was a reversion to the shorter and larger bore Jaeger rifle which in this case was about .50 caliber weighing 8 lbs. with a 30 inch barrel and firing a round ball of 175 grains weight. When the breech-loader entered the picture they too were of this large caliber for plains hunting but at first with very short under-powered cartridges such as the .44 Winchester, the .56 Spencer and the .58 musket cartridges. Later the longer more powerful cartridges in the Sharps single-shot rifles came into use and these were the only American cartridges that equalled the English black powder express cartridges of the period.

The first European rifles for big game hunting were the Jaeger rifles and on the continent these remained the type pattern. It was not considered sporting to use a double-barrel for ibex, chamois or roedeer, and stag. In England the German rifle was copied for military arms but for sporting rifles the English gunmakers soon set off on a different path, which has since remained typically their own, the double-barrelled rifle. The Jaeger rifle was a weapon of .70 to 1 inch in caliber using round balls of 4 to 12 to the pound in a 30 inch barrel. This rifle weighed from 7 to 10 lbs. depending on the caliber, and was equipped with the short barrel to permit using the mallet on the end of the ramrod if necessary to drive the bullet home in the deeply scalloped rifling.

The first British military rifle was the Baker, made in London of .615 inch caliber, with 30 inch barrel, weighing 9½ lbs. and shooting round balls of 20 to the pound or 350 grains. This was the rifle with which the Rifle Brigade fought in the Peninsula Campaign and was the British Army Rifle until replaced by the Brunswick cap lock rifle in 1836. The Brunswick rifle by its name reverted to the Jaeger type. It was of .704 inch caliber, 30 inch barrel, using a ball of 530 grains at 1200 ft. per sec. velocity. This rifle used a belted ball to fit the two-groove rifling but as might be expected the accuracy with the belted bullet in flight was decidedly inferior. General Jacobs stationed in India experimented to improve this rifle and designed one with four grooves of .529 inch caliber using a conical bullet of 615 grains with four lugs shaped to take the rifling. With it he developed good accuracy up to 2000 yards. When offered to the Indian Government in 1846, they turned it down as too revolutionary in design. Jacobs, however, developed a double .450 bore of the same type and perfected the use of explosive bullets which became quite popular with Indian sportsmen.

After the Brunswick rifle, England, impressed by Col. Colt's display of American arms at "The Great Industrial Exhibition of London" in 1851 and particularly his testimony before the committee of the House of Commons already quoted, began consideration of various new rifle designs, resulting in the Enfield rifle, made at the new plant equipped with American rifle making machinery under the supervision of American engineers. This rifle adopted in 1855 was of .577 caliber with a 3-grooved 39 inch barrel weighing 9 lbs. and firing a 520 grain conical bullet at 1115 feet per second. When this was converted to a breech-loader in 1867 it was to an American design by Mr. Jacob Snider consisting of a receiver attached to the barrel breech with a block hinged at the right, which when opened and pulled to the rear extracted the shell. This Snider rifle's external hammer and inclined firing pin was similar to the Springfield conversion of the United States rifle described below.

The United States Army designed and manufactured an 1800 Model rifle in limited quantities but stuck generally to the French-type Charleville smooth-bore muskets of Model 1795 and 1808 until 1817 when Harpers Ferry and other independent makers started production on a new muzzle-loading flintlock rifle of .62 caliber weighing, with 36 inch barrel, 9¼ pounds firing a 220 grain round ball with greased patch at 2000 feet per second. In 1819 Mr. John Hall was given a contract to manufacture at Harpers Ferry his flintlock breech-loading rifle of .525 caliber, 33 inch barrel, weighing 10 pounds and shooting a bare lead ball of 220 grains at about 1800 feet per second. This rifle was built with fully interchangeable parts. The block carrying the pan and frizzen and containing the chamber for powder and ball was hinged at the rear of the receiver and lifted above the line of the barrel for loading. This was the first feasible breech-loader adopted by any army but was abandoned in 1842 with the adoption of a .52 caliber percussion lock muzzle loading rifle using the same bullet at about 1850 feet per second. This caliber was increased in 1860 to .58 caliber with a 500 grain Minié bullet at 850 feet per second velocity in a rifle weighing 10 lbs. This reduction in velocity had evidently been made to lessen the recoil and to obtain a rifle with the smoothbore musket characteristics. Following designs made by Mr. Allin, the superintendent of the Harpers Ferry armory, this Civil War rifle was converted in 1866 to a breech-loader, the first Springfield, by cutting off the barrel and attaching a receiver with a block hinged at the front, retaining the outside hammer to drive an inclined firing pin contained in the block.

While the Continental and American gunmakers and sportsmen stuck to the single barrel the English gunmakers having made double-barrelled shotguns for so long, were asked by the English sportsmen to make rifles to match. The soldier or traveler who intended to do some hunting overseas, generally wanted a rifle made on the same pattern and balance and as nearly of the same weight as his shotgun or if he could afford the cost, would have a battery of such rifles made to secure additional fire power and protect himself against the accidents which might, and usually did, happen to one rifle. This was the reason behind the English habit of employing gunbearers and, indeed, with all the accessories necessary for muzzle loading and the weight of the weapons themselves, this assistance was necessary. These accessories were a heavy ramrod usually carried in thimbles under the barrels, a mallet on a thong attached to the belt for driving the bullet home, a bullet pouch, a powder flask or horn, a cap box and a pick to free the nipple of powder fouling and a worm and brush to attach to the ramrod for removing charges or cleaning the barrels. The leather sling was used for carrying the rifle and also according to a picture in General Rice's *Indian Game* to steady the aim offhand, exactly in the manner we now use the 'Hasty' sling. Either horseback or afoot the use of all this paraphernalia must have been as confusing as the use of a modern camera. It is small wonder that it took from 1¼ to 2 minutes per shot or that a big game hunter, in a tight spot, felt the need of an extra weapon already loaded, right at his shoulder from the gun-bearer. The breech-loader eliminated most of this impedimenta, but the gunbearer stayed on as a necessary adjunct for the English big game hunter.

The manufacture of rifles by hand before the advent of machinery was a tedious and skilled trade and one which brought world renown to certain communities. These communities in the early history of the rifle were Albany, Lancaster and St. Louis in the United States followed later by Providence, Hartford, New Haven and Springfield; with Nuremburg, Vienna, Prague, Suhl, Steyr, Liege, Paris, St. Etienne, Oviedo and Toledo on the Continent; and London, Edinburgh, Birmingham, Bristol, Derby, Dublin, Liverpool and Nottingham in the British Isles. The processes followed in making rifles by hand were not essentially different in any of these localities nor was the quality of product notably superior at any one place. But the free field given English industry by the Napoleonic Wars, the plentiful supply of coal and iron, and the spread of the dominions and world trade resulting from the preceding two centuries colonization, coupled with the great progress of the industrial revolution in England, gave the English gunmaking industry a chance to establish a world reputation and trade. Because of this and the Englishman's preference for finely finished sporting arms, the English gunmaking industry preserved its guild form of individual craftsmen, that has resisted the inroads of machine methods, except in the quantity production of military weapons, to this day. Sporting weapons in England are still the monopoly of the individual custom-gunmakers who although they have adopted machinery to a degree, still retain many of the special practices of the original handicraft industry. Of late years this industry has suffered from the reduction of game fields and the inroads of machine made rifles from the Continent and from America but it still maintains its reputation for fine materials, superlative craftsmanship and performance, established by over one hundred years of excellence.

Since these English rifles are the weapons which, in the main, have been used in big game hunting around the world and from the written account of which we have been able to glean most of the history of rifle performance, especially in the period of large bore rifles from 1834 to 1874 the methods used in their making will be described. Later as other rifles made by hand or machine methods, in other nations of the world become important, these rifles will also be described, and more especially by the comments of the men who have hunted big game with them.

Apropos of the importance to be given to the performances of big game rifles in various parts of the world, one American authority Capt. E. C. Crossman does not allow American conditions much weight, according to the following from *The Book of the Springfield*:

Outside of the great brown bear of Alaska we have no dangerous game on this continent and not much heavy game, the moose being about the only specimen and it being heavy only in comparison with the little deer which is the average man's idea of big game.

Because of this unfortunate fact the man whose hunting has been confined to the American continent and particularly outside of Alaska, is a game hunter in only a very restricted sense. From the standpoint of reporting on the effect of big game rifles and bullets his sheep or goat or even moose is worth no more than the Michigan deer.

In size and resistance they are all about on a par. There is more to the moose—but he takes less punishment pound for pound than a scrub Catalina goat, which in turn carries off more lead than any deer that ever walked.

The American hunter who hunts only in America is not a big game hunter in the foreign sense of the word. He kills small and mild-mannered, if shy, herbivorous animals with no fight in them, with thin hides, and with little resistance to the bullet—except in the case of the Rocky Mountain goat, the hair of which often creates unpleasant surprises to parties who attempt to smack them down with inadequate rifles at the long ranges at which they are often shot.

After all, the digest of the experience of a hundred men—picked men, not chaps who once killed a buck in the Adirondacks and know all about game rifles, is the best way to reach an intelligent decision.

Whether it be the manufacture of shotguns or rifles, English custom gunmaking has always been a specialized industry employing highly skilled hand craftsmen on the various operations. There are about fifteen of these operations or processes from the raw billet to the finished rifle but some are combined under one set of craftsmen. For instance in making barrels the forging, welding, hammering, drawing, and straightening of the barrel tube is performed by the barrel maker. In the period from 1800 to 1870 barrels were made by welding wrought iron or low grade steel billets into a tube and drawing this tube out to barrel length by rolling or hammering. Figured barrels such as Damascus were formed by coiling a twisted rod around a mandrel and welding the spiral joint, and then drawing out by hammering. But there is strong probability that the gunmaker preferred not to use Damascus figures in rifle barrels. The rifle barrels were made similarly to musket barrels by wrapping a flat sheet around a mandrel and welding the longitudinal joint then hammering or rolling to size.

When the barrel was properly welded and shaped it was carefully reamed or bored to remove scale and inside irregularities. The rifling was done by a long rifling rod. At one end of the rod was a groove cutter in a longitudinal slot which could be shimmed up to make a deeper cut at each following pass of the cutter. The other end of the rifling rod was guided in a spiral motion either by a collar on a spirally grooved mandrel or by a bore plug fitting the rifling of an old barrel. The barrel to be rifled was fixed while the mandrel or guide barrel could be rotated to various quadrant points representing the number of grooves to be cut. A loose cross handle in the middle of the rifling rod was used to push the cutter backward and forward an equal number of passes for each groove so that when finished they would be of equal depth.

Many of the leading gunmakers secured their barrels already welded, forged, bored, and rifled to size. These came from Belgium, Birmingham or Sheffield. After the gunmaker had selected the proper barrels to fill an order these barrels were struck or filed by the barrel filer to proper taper and thickness and sent to the proof house where they were loaded and fired with a charge 25 to 50 per cent higher than normal. If they bulged anywhere in the barrel or around the breech plug and could be hammered

HUNTING FROM THE HOWDAH.

From Lt. Col. Wm. Gordon-Cumming's *Wild Men and Wild Beasts.*

WILLIAM CHARLES BALDWIN.

WILLIAM CHARLES BALDWIN, AFRICAN HUNTER.

From his book *African Hunting*.

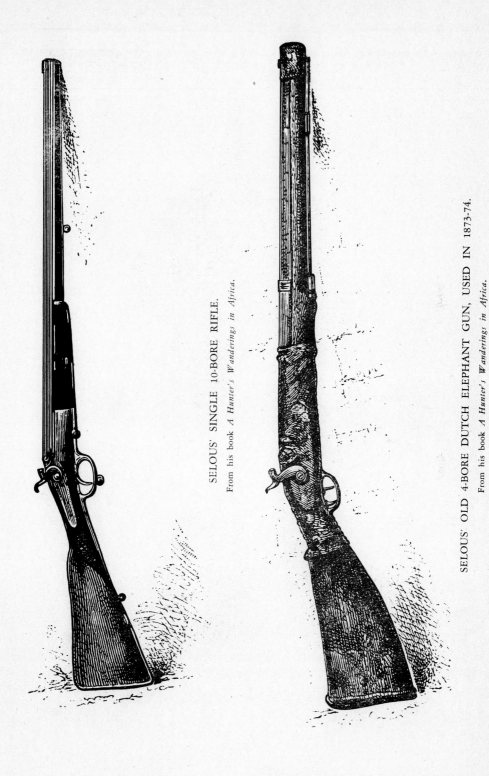

SELOUS' SINGLE 10-BORE RIFLE.

From his book *A Hunter's Wanderings in Africa.*

SELOUS' OLD 4-BORE DUTCH ELEPHANT GUN, USED IN 1873-74.

From his book *A Hunter's Wanderings in Africa.*

NATIVE GUN BEARER DRIVING AWAY A LION ATTACKING DAVID LIVINGSTONE.

ARTHUR H. NEUMANN. BIG GAME HUNTER AND AUTHOR.

From his *Elephant Hunting in East Equatorial Africa*.

CAPT. FREDERICK COURTENAY SELOUS, D.S.O., ONE OF THE MOST RE-
NOWNED BIG GAME HUNTERS OF THE WORLD.

From the biography by James G. Millais.

BUFFALO HUNTING.

From *The American Bison*, by M. S. Garretson.   Painted by J. H. Moser.

A. H. NEUMANN CAUGHT AND CRUSHED BY AN ELEPHANT.

From *Elephant Hunting in East Equatorial Africa* by Arthur H. Neumann.

back into shape and hardened to pass a second test they were approved. The barrels were then returned to the barrel filer for brazing into a double rifle and mounting the rib, lumps and standing breech, which were also brazed.

With the breech-loader, which came in about 1860-65, the fitting of barrels and breech developed another highly skilled craftsman called the action filer. This specialist's job was to bore and fit the hinge pin in the breech forging and then make the very exact fitting of the barrels and breech, the extractor mechanism, the locking bolts and the lock mortises. The locks were a specialty of the lock maker, who from various qualities of iron and steel, fashioned and mounted the hammer or tumbrel, springs, sears and cocking tumbrel to fixed standard templates. When these had been fitted and adjusted to work smoothly in the assembled rifle they were not interchangeable. As a consequence the customer generally ordered extra right and lefthand locks for field repairs.

When all metal parts of the rifle had been assembled in the white (*i.e.,* without color or ornamentation) it was turned over to the stockmaker. Selecting suitable pieces of walnut with a grain and figure depending on the quality and price of the weapon, this man carefully inlet the breech of the barrels and the locks into the wood by the cut and try method using lampblack to smudge the high spots. Then the drop, pitch, and castoff required by the particular customer were laid out and the butt plate fitted, after which the wood was shaped up ready for the percussioner who fitted and checked the hammers, at which time the rifle was ready for test and regulation of the barrels. If these did not shoot to the same mark at the specified range for hunting work, which might be 80 or 100 yards, the barrels and rib were unbrazed, adjusted, and rebrazed. When in proper register, and when tested with full loads, the rifle was brought back to finish, polish, and oil the stock, while the barrels were being given their final polish, engraved if ordered, and browned. The finished rifle was then ready for the customer's examination and to be fitted to his final satisfaction.

This procedure had one advantage and that was that the rifle was under many eyes until finished and such flaws as might exist had to be well hidden. Few defects were caused by unskilled workmanship and the customer was able to see every part used. Occasional flaws in the inferior types of steel and iron available did occur, however, and were serious handicaps to the hunter in the field. Some of these will be apparent in the narratives, quoted in the next chapter.

But before proceeding to them it would be well to have some idea of the range power and accuracy of the early hunting rifles. The figures given below are from various sources and must be considered approximate estimates in many instances since the science of ballistic measurement with the chronograph was little known and seldom used in checking early rifle performance. The variations between weapons of the same listed caliber when handmade was enough to throw these theoretical performances far off and will also explain some of the cause of irregularities, especially with bullets usually cast in the field (See table):

Of the calibers shown the first seven are muzzle loading rifles. The 8, 10 and 12 bore, and 577, 500, 450 calibers might be either muzzle or breech loading since the first breech loading cartridges used either round ball or conical bullets, with the same charges of powder, just as the hunter chose to load them. The ballistics were pretty much alike in either type of rifle.

Finally to finish this description of early English custom-made rifles the following, quoted by Professor Low in his book *Musket to Machine Gun* from Mr. W. W. Greener head of one of the oldest of these London gunmaking establishments is certainly from good authority:

A frequent and ever present danger connected with the use of the muzzle loading gun was that of accidental discharge when loading. Then again, there was the risk, with a double barreled gun, of overloading; it was no uncommon thing for the sportsman to put both charges of powder into the same barrel, sometimes with disastrous result, at least to the gun, if not to the user or his friends.

The ramrod was a constant worry, frequently breaking, and at times, when occasion arose for a rapid shot, it would be left in the barrel and fired from it by an excited sportsman. The nipple was undoubtedly the *bete noir* of the shooter of that time. If too hard it broke off, if too soft the point qickly became dubbed up and useless . . . The cleaning of the barrels was a troublesome and dirty job. They became so fouled it was frequently necessary to scour them out with boiling water, while the passing of the ramrod, when charging or cleaning, up and down the barrels dirtied the shooter's clothes. Caps were also a regular source of trouble. Many sportsmen would use the cheapest caps procurable; these often failed to explode, or split and flew about in the most dangerous fashion, and many were the shooters whose eyes were injured by this false economy . . .

The fixed breech end permitted careless workmanship to pass un-

Rifle	Date	Type	Caliber Inches	Bullet Grains	Velocity Ft. Sec.	Energy Ft. Lbs.	Sighted to Yds.
Jaeger	1700	Hunting	.75	640	800	910	150
Kentucky	1750	Hunting	.38	78	2000	690	350
Baker	1800	Military	.615	350	1200	1120	200
Hall	1819	Military	.525	219	1800	1570	500
Brunswick	1836	Military	.704	530	1200	1690	300
Jacobs	1846	Military	.529	754	850	1210	1000
Jacobs	1850	Hunting	.450	615	1000	1365	300
Springfield	1866	Military	.58	500	1300	1875	1000
Snider	1867	Military	.58	530	1200	1695	1000
.8 bore DB		Hunting	.835	862	1450	4025	100
.10 bore DB		Hunting	.775	670	1460	3170	150
.12 bore DB		Hunting	.729	549	1480	2670	200
Martini	1873	Military	.450	480	1350	1940	1000
.577 DB		Hunting	.577	480	1680	3050	220
.500 DB		Hunting	.500	505	1500	2520	300
.450 DB		Hunting	.450	480	1550	2560	500

detected. It was impossible for the inside of the barrels to be examined and even in guns of medium quality little attention was given to boring . . .

It is a curious fact that nearly all muzzle loading barrels were made too light at the breech (the ramrod weighed four to five ounces and this additional weight has been utilized in strengthening the breech ends of modern barrels). Accidents from the unnecessary weakness were of frequent occurrence . . .

The sportsman of today, with his gun and cartridges, is easily and quickly equipped; not so the sportsman of the thirties. The nipples of his gun being properly cleaned, he had to remember his ramrod, shot pouch or belt, powder flask, caps, cap charger, paper for his wadding, spare nipples and a nipple key, although the latter was useless if the nipples were rusted in.

It is well to keep the above picture in mind when reading the next chapter of the hunting adventures of Baker, Gordon-Cumming, Oswell and Selous and the difficulties they experienced in securing effective weapons for elephant, rhino, buffalo and other large game. It will also help to explain why they needed a battery of such rifles and the unusual number of shots fired at times to down these animals. If we compare their puny and ineffective weapons with the speed, power, range, and accuracy of the modern rifle, it can be appreciated what giants of the hunting field these men were, and that their accomplishments have probably never been equalled.

CHAPTER 2

EARLY BIG GAME HUNTERS

*T*HE hunting of big game has been possible for the common man only in the past 150 years. Before that firearms were too expensive and the available big game was owned by royalty or the landed gentry. We have seen that with the development of travel and the colonization of backward continents, the explorer, the soldier, the planter, and the trader carried firearms for protection. Finding immense herds of wild game in many of these lands, until then safe from the primitive weapons of the natives, these men turned to hunting for sport, to secure meat, or for the valuable hides, horns, or teeth.

Coincident with this opening of new game fields came the development of the rifle. In many cases this development centered around military weapons, but as frequently it took the form of a more modern firearm adapted to the particular game hunted and made to the individual specifications of the purchaser by a gunsmith of his home country. These early rifles were handmade, of somewhat uncertain material, and at times of very crude workmanship. For hunting from horseback, or in the forest or jungle at short range, a muzzle-loading rifle had very little superiority over a well-made smoothbore. Considering that the rifle was a much more expensive firearm to make, its development as a hunting weapon is notable, and one for which the rifleman-hunter is principally responsible. The experiments of these men on big game of all kinds during the last century has resulted in the supremely accurate hunting rifle of today. In their hands the unwieldy muzzle loader with the round ball of uncertain accuracy and poor penetration yielded to the medium bore with conical bullet for game as it became more wary and harder to kill, only in turn to give way to the high velocity small bore of light weight when the hunter was forced to go still farther afield and afoot to find his quarry.

Counter to popular belief, the modern sporting rifle did not evolve from the Kentucky rifle. As has been explained the western plainsmen used large bores for buffalo hunting and for seventy-five years the Kentucky "pea" rifle was forgotten. When the small-bore, bolt-action, high-velocity rifle came into the hands of the big-game hunter, it was made in

Europe. True, it had certain American antecedents such as the Lee magazine, the Berdan brass cartridge, and the great assistance of American machine methods in rifle making, but the bolt-action sporting rifle made no progress in this country until the Army chose a Danish small-bore and later brought out the Springfield on a Mauser pattern. It was principally in India, Asia, and Africa that the use of the modern sporting rifle grew up, and where its merit was tested on the largest and toughest big game of the world. In the discussions in this book, consequently, as already explained the comments of foreign (meaning English rather than American) riflemen and big-game hunters will predominate.

For elephant, the English in India and the Dutch in Africa, after 1800, used single-shot, muzzle-loading, four and six-bore rifles, similar to the original Jaeger rifle, with two-grooved thirty-inch barrels and a belted spherical ball. These bore sizes represented the number of such balls to the pound of lead or, in the above instance, four-ounce and two and two-thirds ounce balls, respectively. Because of the fouling resulting from 12 to 15 drams of black powder, the round ball was not always easy to load. A steel, brass, or rhino horn ramrod carried loose on a thong and a loading mallet were used to force the ball down on the powder. In a "poly-grooved rifle the mallet was also used to upset the round ball into the rifling. If rammed too hard with a dirty bore, the rifle was very likely to burst. These four and six bore single-shot rifles weighed twelve to twenty pounds and required great skill and physique to load and fire from horseback. To secure lighter rifles and more firepower, the English gunmakers supplied double eight, ten and twelve bore rifles, weighing eleven to fifteen pounds, with twenty-six to thirty-inch barrels.

This was the type of rifle used by Shakespear and Baker in India, by Harris, Oswell and Gordon Cumming in Africa before 1860, for hunting elephant, rhino, tiger, lion, bison, and all other species of big game. Probably only the skill of the hunter, the speed of his mount, the shock of the heavy ball, and the dense cloud of smoke permitted him time to retire and reload. The penetration at low velocities was slight, and the hunting was characterized by the great number of shots usually necessary to kill an animal of large size. The following account of elephant shooting from Roualeyn Gordon-Cumming in his *Five Years Hunting Adventures in Africa* (1843-1848) is typical (The parentheses are the writers):

Having fired thirty-five rounds with my two-grooved rifle (a double twelve-bore Dickson which later burst from too much fouling), I opened fire upon him with the Dutch six-pounder (six balls to the pound), and when forty bullets had perforated his hide he began for the first time to evince signs of a dilapidated constitution.

In a later instance Cumming fired thirty-five balls from a double twelve-bore Westley Richards rifle at distances of fifteen to thirty-five yards to finish another elephant. As most loads were double charged with 10 to 15 drams of black powder, the recoil even with the twelve to fifteen-pound rifles must have been terrific, and the accuracy questionable. Shakespear, hunting in India, however, does not bear this out in the following comment from his book, *Wild Sports of India* (1834-1859):

My own battery consists of two heavy double rifles and a double gun; the heaviest is a Westley-Richards weighing twelve and a quarter pounds, length of barrel twenty-six inches, poly-grooved carrying bullets ten to the pound. It is a splendid weapon, bearing a large charge of powder without recoil; that is to say, its own bullet mould full of the strongest rifle powder. This weapon with its sights folded down carried point-blank ninety-five yards, and with great force. It has two folding sights, the first being raised, the rifle throws its ball 150 yards, the second 250. However, like all poly-grooved rifles that I have seen fired with large charges, the ball describes a parabola in its flight, rising gradually on first leaving the barrel for forty or fifty yards, and at that distance has risen some five inches; the ball then descends in its flight until it reaches the target at ninety-five yards.

My other rifle is a very broad-belted, two-grooved one by Wilkinson of Pall Mall. It takes a similar quality of powder to the other and the bullet is the same weight. It does not throw its ball in the form of a parabola, but point-blank from the muzzle up to ninety yards. The folding sights are for 150, 250, and 400 yards. This rifle perhaps is the strongest shooting one of the two. Its balls have gone through and killed a full grown bear, while running at 120 yards; and on another occasion broke the backbone of a bear at eighty yards. The weight of the rifle is ten and one-half pounds, and the length of barrel thirty inches.

The ballistics in the above are somewhat peculiar. The reference to shooting "point-blank" does not mean, as some riflemen might think, that the rifle shoots "flat" to ninety yards. The original bull's-eye was white or "blanc" and a rifle shot point-blank when its curve remained within the upper and lower limits of the bull's-eye up to a certain range. However,

Shakespear's theory of one bullet's describing a parabola and the other not, cannot be explained by modern ballistics. The ten-bore rifle described, shot a 700-grain round ball at 1,200 feet per second with 8 drams of black powder, and would have a trajectory of five inches at fifty yards. In a twelve-pound rifle, the recoil would be about sixty foot-pounds or four times that of a Springfield rifle, and certainly noticeable.

Shakespear also has something to say about penetration which may be somewhat at variance with the school which thinks the entire energy of a bullet should be expended within the beast fired at:

I know many men who think that a rifle cannot be too large in the bore. I consider myself rather an authority in this matter having had made to order (or rather by mistake) a double rifle carrying bullets weighing three and three quarter ounces. It was, to look at, and for target practice, a fine weapon, but it was not nearly heavy enough; and though not heavy enough for its large bore, it was too heavy for one to carry through a summer's day in India. Having been nearly killed by a large tusk elephant with it in my hand, I sold it at the first opportunity for nine pounds less than it cost me. Now, if I were rich enough to have new rifles made by the best maker, I would have them made two grooved carrying balls twelve to the pound weighing at least eleven pounds and length of barrel thirty inches . . . It is only the heavy rifle that will take a large charge of powder without recoil. This drives the bullet through the animal, and where the bullet escapes, owing to the impetus nearly ceasing, the wound is much larger than where the bullet enters the body; consequently, the life blood flows more rapidly and the animal becomes more suddenly weak from this wound than from one caused by a ball which only enters, but does not pass through him.

Between 1864 and 1877, Mr. George P. Sanderson was in charge of elephant catching for the Indian Government in Mysore. Although breech-loading rifles had just come into use, the preference was still for large bores, as shown by the following from his book *Thirteen Years Among the Wild Beasts of India*:

I at first killed several elephants with a No. 12 spherical ball rifle, with hard bullets and 6 drams of powder, but I found it insufficient for many occasions. I then had a single-barreled center-fire No. 4 bore rifle, weighing sixteen and one-half pounds, and firing 10 drams, made to order by Lang and Sons, Cockspur Street. A cartridge of this single barrel, however, missed fire on one occasion, and nearly brought me to grief, so I gave it up and had a center-fire No. 4 smoothbore, weighing nineteen and one-half pounds, built by W. W. Greener. This I have used ever since. I ordinarily fire 12 drams of powder with it. . . . Without something of the cannon kind, game of the ponderous class cannot be brought to fighting quarters with even a moderate degree of safety or effect . . . I am decidedly opposed to the use upon buffalo, bison, and such animals of the express rifle of either .500 or .450 bore (equivalent to 38 and 50 spherical gauge). The express is essentially a rifle for soft-bodied animals and is not adapted for use on those with thick hides and massive bones.

There is small wonder that big game hunting in those days was an expensive and a strenuous sport. Rifles of the type described would cost 150 to 200 guineas or $750 to $1,000, and cartridges in India about fifty cents apiece. Sanderson was not the only one to revert from the rifle to a smoothbore. William Cotton Oswell, hunting elephants from horseback some years earlier in South Africa, started with a double twelve-bore rifle by Westley Richards and a single eight bore using belted two-ounce balls.

This last was a beast of a tool and once—I never gave it a second chance—nearly cost my life by stinging, without seriously wounding, a bull elephant. The infuriated brute charged me nine or ten times, and the number might have been doubled had I not at last got hold of the Purdey, when he fell to the first shot.

The Purdey was a smoothbore, double-barrel gun, shooting ten balls to the pound.

The accounts of the large bores are not complete without reference to Sir Samuel Baker's various rifles. His career, from the time he left a position with the Turkish railways at the age of twenty-four to found an English colony in the hills of Ceylon at Newera Ellia in 1845, through various African exploring trips between 1861 and 1873 and two round the world hunting tours between 1879 and 1888, interspersed with a long sojourn in India hunting tiger in the eighties, covered about forty-three years of hunting big game with the rifle, in a life of seventy-two years. With wealth sufficient to suit his whims he had all of his rifles made to his personal specifications. His first, which he claims introduced the rifle to Ceylon in 1845, was a muzzle-loading, twenty-one pound, four-bore single barrel, two-grooved rifle made by

Gibbs of Bristol. This used a three-ounce, belted ball, and 16 drams of black powder. As a second rifle he had a single polygrooved eight bore by Blisset, using 16 drams of powder back of a two-ounce ball. For greater speed of fire he purchased, before he left Ceylon, four double ten-bore muzzle-loading, fifteen-pound rifles from Beattie as a battery for elephant hunting.

In Africa Baker used the ten bores, but when the British Army adopted the Snider breech-loader which used a 530 grain conical bullet at 1200 feet per second, he had Holland make him a double .577 breech-loader. Later he had Holland make him a double-barrelled .577 Express using 6 drams of powder and a 648 grain conical bullet at 1,650 foot-seconds which became his favorite rifle even on deer, bear, elk, and buffalo in North America. He did finally concede to the smaller bore, lighter rifles by purchasing a double .400 Holland express for deer shooting in England and Scotland. But in *Wild Beasts and Their Ways,* written in 1891, two years before his death, he insisted that for the largest game he would want a double eight-bore with 14 drams of powder and three-ounce bullets. The Express hollow-pointed bullet of .400 to .500 bore he had no use for, and said he would not accompany any hunter if armed with such an inferior weapon in the pursuit of dangerous game.

For any who might think that big game hunting was a task for a weakling or that the sportsman of that day was not impressed with the need for powerful rifles, the following passage from Baker's book on his exploration of the Nile—*Albert Nyanza—The Great Basin of the Nile*—written in 1866 will be illuminating:

I had a powerful pair of No. 10 polygroove rifles, made by Reilly of Oxford Street; they weighed fifteen pounds and carried seven drachms of powder without a disagreeable recoil. The bullet was a blunt cone, one and a half diameter of the bore, and I used a mixture of nine-tenths lead and one-tenth quicksilver for the hardening of the projectile. This is superior to all mixtures for that purpose, as it combines hardness with extra weight; the lead must be melted in a pot by itself to a red heat, and the proportion of quicksilver must be added a ladleful at a time, and stirred quickly with a piece of iron just in sufficient quantity to make three or four bullets. If the quicksilver is subjected to a red heat in the large lead pot it will evaporate. The only successful forehead shot that I made at an African elephant was shortly after my arrival in the Abyssinian territory on the Settite river; this was in thick thorny jungle, and an elephant from the herd charged with such good intention, that had she not been stopped, she must have caught one of the party. When within about five yards of the muzzle, I killed her dead by a forehead shot with a hardened bullet as described, from a Reilly No. 10 rifle, and we subsequently recovered the bullet in the vertebrae of the neck. This extraordinary penetration led me to suppose that I should always succeed as I had done in Ceylon, and I have frequently stood the charge of an African elephant until close upon me, determining to give the forehead shot a fair trial, but I have always failed, except in the instance now mentioned; it must also be borne in mind that the elephant was a female, with a head far inferior in size and solidity to that of the male. . . .

Among other weapons, I had an extraordinary rifle that carried a half-pound percussion shell—this instrument of torture to the hunter, was not sufficiently heavy for the weight of the projectile; it only weighed twenty pounds; thus, with a charge of ten drachms of powder, behind a half pound shell, the recoil was so terrific, that I was spun round like a weathercock in a hurricane. I really dreaded my own rifle, although I had been accustomed to heavy charges of powder and severe recoil for many years. None of my own men could fire it, and it was looked upon with a species of awe, and was named "Jenna el Mootfah" (child of a cannon) by the Arabs, which being far too long a name for practice, I christened it the "Baby"; and the scream of this "Baby," loaded with a half-pound shell was always fatal. It was far too severe, and I very seldom fired it, but it is a curious fact, that I never fired a shot with that rifle without bagging; the entire practice, during several years, was confined to about twenty shots. I was afraid to use it; but now and then it was absolutely necessary that it be cleaned, after lying for months loaded. On such occasions my men had the gratification of firing it, and the explosion was always accompanied by two men falling on their backs (one having propped up the shooter) and the "Baby" flying some yards behind them. This rifle was made by Holland of Bond Street and I could highly recommend it for Goliath of Gath, but not for men of A. D. 1866.

The following is the list of weapons that Baker had with him on his trip up the Nile to Lakes Victoria and Albert Nyanza in the years 1861 to 1865, which weapons of course, were all muzzle loaders:

My little Fletcher double rifle, No. 24
One double rifle, No. 10, by Tatham
Two double rifles, No. 10, by Reilly
One double rifle, No. 10, by Beattie (one of my old Ceylon tools)

One double gun,   No. 10, by Beattie
One double gun,   No. 10, by Purdey (belonging to Mr. Oswell of S.
African celebrity)
One single rifle,   No. 8, by Manton
One single rifle,   No. 14, by Beattie
One single rifle, that carried a half-pound explosive shell, by Holland
of Bond Street.

Baker really closes the true large-bore period. Those who came after
him passed out of the picture with the large bores, or changed to the
smaller bores as they became better perfected. Of twenty-seven hunters
who were active during this "large-bore" period, eleven used only large
bores, eleven more used medium bores in their later years, and five
(Neumann, Rainsford, Mayer, Selous, and Stockley) started with the
large bores but lived to see and use the small bore. The Americans,
Mayer and Rainsford, preferred medium and small bores even on large
game, but Neumann and Selous, starting as ivory hunters, and Stockley,
a specialist on tigers, came to the small-bore by a process of elimination
from the large bore.

Mayer, in his reminiscences speaks of hunting in many lands but
never anything larger than the American Buffalo, on which he used a
.45-120 Sharps. His comments on buffalo hunting and the rifles he
used, which properly belong in a later chapter, are related here because
of the date Mayer starting hunting. These are reported by Mr. Charles B.
Roth in *Field and Stream* magazine in 1934:

The buffalo served his mission, fulfilled his destiny in the history of
the Indian by furnishing everything he needed—food, clothing, a home,
traditions, even a theology. But the buffalo didn't fit in so well with
the white man's encroaching civilization—didn't fit in at all in fact. He
could not be controlled or domesticated, and he couldn't be corralled
behind wire fences. He just didn't fit. So he had to go. . . .

Most of the runners were Western men, young in years but old in
plains experience. Among them were a few older men. In the beginning these men made the better showing; they knew how. But in time
we youngsters learned the ropes. And when the vast army of runners
learned the killing trade, the buffalo was doomed. In three short years
they were practically wiped from the earth. . . .

Shooting buffalo presented a different problem from any other shot-
ing of that day. It was all long range work. The animals were vital,

tough, hard to kill. Since the hunting was for profit, the shooter had to have one-shot kills and no wounded game. . . .

The two best buffalo rifles, which were the choice of practically all the good runners were the Remington and the Sharps. I think the Sharps was the better of the two but many preferred the Remington. . . . I bought my first Sharps from Colonel Richard Irving Dodge. There was a man! Fine sportsman, military leader, expert rifleman, skilled hunter, gentleman—to me Colonel Dodge typified everything that is best in the soldiery of the United States.

The Colonel had several Sharps, and I had none; so I set out to convince him that he should sell one of his to me. The rifle I selected was a .40-90-320, straight shell. It was a beautiful piece, with its imported walnut stock and shiny 32 inch barrel. At $125 I considered it a bargain. This Sharps weighed 12 pounds. On the barrel I mounted a full length 1-inch tube telescope made by A. Vollmer of Jena, Germany. Originally the scope, which was a 20 power, came with plain cross hairs. These I supplemented with upper and lower stadia hairs, so set that they would cover a vertical space of 30 inches at 200 yards. . . .

After a year or so, having plenty of buffalo dollars in my jeans, I decided I needed an extra rifle in reserve—so I bought two, both Sharps. One was .40-70-320 and the other was .40-90-420; both shot bottle necked cartridges. I paid $100 for the .40-70 and $115 for the heavier rifle. These were current prices for Sharps at the height of the running years, although later they declined in price, and I saw them in John Lower's gun shop in Denver at $35, $40 and $50—the same guns we runners had paid $100 for. Both my new rifles were good guns, but I soon discarded them when the bottle-necked cartridges started giving me trouble.

And then, believing that I needed more killing power, I decided that I simply had to have one of the new .45-120-550 Sharps, the "Sharps Buffalo." This was the most powerful of all the Sharps. On the barrel it was stamped "Special Old Reliable" but on the range we knew it as the "Sharps Buffalo" or the "Buffalo Sharps." . . . The Sharps Buffalo was never in common use. I have been told that only 2000 were ever made. Since they came in at the heel of the running years, the market was limited, and there was also a price barrier that kept all but the more opulent runners from buying them. I paid $237.60 for mine, a specially made rifle equipped with a 20 power scope. But it was a rifle.

Mayer's last rifle out of many was a .270 Winchester.

William S. Rainsford, Rector of St. George's Episcopal Church of New York, made many North American big-game trips and two trips to Africa. On the largest dangerous game he used a double .450 English Cordite rifle presumably made by Rigby, but does not mention it. His favorite rifle on lion and antelope was a .350 Rigby Mauser weighing eight and one-half pounds and firing a 310-grain bullet at 2,150 foot-seconds. Of this rifle he says:

Now the rifle I used to kill hundreds of animals in Africa is a .350 Rigby Mauser, a gun with many solid advantages and, of course, some disadvantages. The advantages are an unusually heavy bullet and a good charge of powder. For a repeating rifle the bullet is a good deal longer than those fired from repeating rifles generally, much longer than the bullets of a new Winchester pattern. It has not the velocity claimed for several of those new rifles that are thrust on the market by their makers almost monthly. These I dare say do shoot up to the velocity claimed for them, but be it remembered, velocity can only be won by two methods; shortening the bullet, or increasing the charge of powder. To increase the charge means to increase the weight of the gun. To shorten the bullet means inevitably to lessen its penetration, and so its killing powers.

But, of course, when speaking of the .350 Rigby we are getting out of the large bore period as this rifle was introduced sometime around 1907 as a development of the 9 m. m. Mauser cartridge. In addition, Rainsford had a .256 Mannlicher for the smaller antelope. Stockley used a .577 double rifle made by Westley-Richards on tiger and bison in India. On elephant he used a double ten bore. He was killed by a buffalo in East Africa in 1910 but details are lacking. He may have used too small a rifle, ineffectively, because of his familiarity with heavy rifles, as he had both a .303 Lee Metford and a .256 Mannlicher with him at the time.

The two greatest exponents of rifle development from the large to the smaller bores were Neumann and Selous. Arthur Neumann was one of the world's greatest elephant hunters, hunting them over South East and Central Africa for thirty-eight years, from 1868 to 1906. In his later hunting described in his book *Elephant Hunting* he used two rifles interchangeably—a double .577 Gibbs and a military .303 Lee-Metford. In addition, Neumann later purchased a double ten-bore Holland when the .577 was out of order. But he didn't care for the ten bore:

My rifles were now a Lee-Metford and a ten-bore Holland. Both had done their work well enough today; but I had not yet acquired thorough confidence in the former, and the discharge of the other was something of a shock, which though its rubber heelplate prevented from hurting the shoulder, made one's head ache and knocked one's fingers about cruelly. The volumes of smoke emitted, too, were appalling, and a source of danger, but its worst defect was that the breech invariably jammed and the empty cases stuck, so that they had to be knocked out with a stick. Altogether, I found my prejudice against big guns in no way removed, and regretted more than ever the accident to my trusty and equally effective .577.

Neumann had just killed five elephants with seven shots, using both rifles interchangeably. In 1896, the .303 missed fire and an enraged elephant caught Neumann and crushed his ribs. He was three months recovering. Later he bought a double .450 Rigby which he liked immensely. As a second rifle he used a .256 Mannlicher, of which he had this to say in a letter to his friend, J. G. Millais:

With regard to the Mannlicher, I do think, beautiful weapon as it is, that it is rather in the extreme of small in the bore for general purposes in Africa. In spite of its high velocity, it has no *great penetrative power*, owing to the bullet being so light—there is really nothing of it. I have killed all the big beasts with it (bar elephants and, of course, it would kill them, too) but another time I think I should prefer a double .400.

Probably he underrated the penetration. Compared with the .450 Rigby, using a 480-grain bullet at 2,150 foot-seconds, the 160-grain bullet of the Mannlicher probably had as much penetration, but only half the shock.

The last and greatest of the large bore graduates was Frederick Courtenay Selous. Ivory hunter, naturalist, explorer, settler, guide, and soldier, his hunting covered South, East, Central, and North Africa, Europe, Asia Minor, Norway, and four trips to North America, between 1871 and 1913. He fought as a guide and scout in the Matabele and Boer Wars in South Africa and against the Germans in Tanganyika, where he was killed in action January 4, 1917. But Selous was not a military man. Perhaps if one designation fits him best, it was that of a rifleman-hunter. In South Africa between 1871 and 1875, he killed seventy-eight elephants with a pair of Dutch "Roer" two-groove rifles, after his double twelve-

bore Reilly rifle was stolen from his wagon on his first trip.   These Dutch
four-bores were muzzle loaders, weighing twelve and one-half and fifteen
and one-half pounds respectively, firing a handful (about 16 to 18 drams)
of black powder behind a four-ounce belted bullet.   Of them he says:

They kicked most frightfully and in my case the punishment I received
from these guns has affected my nerves to such an extent as to have mate-
rially influenced my shooting ever since, and I am heartily sorry I ever
had anything to do with them.

In 1875, he tried a single-shot .450 Martini-Henry military weapon
and liked it well enough to have Gibbs build him a .450 single-shot rifle
on the Farquharson action.   This had Metford rifling and handled a
365-grain bullet at 1,700 foot-seconds velocity.   The Gibbs-Metford he
used on all African game until worn out and replaced by a .303 single
Holland Farquharson in 1897.   This was for a hunting trip to Asia
Minor and was supplemented with a .256 Mannlicher which his friends
had persuaded him to buy for Scotch deer hunting.   On his trip to America in 1897, he used both rifles interchangeably, and with equal success,
on elk, deer, and antelope. But on his second trip in 1900 to Ontario for
moose and Newfoundland for caribou, Selous brought only the .303 falling block Holland.   Again in the Yukon in 1904, he used the .303, hunting with Charles Sheldon.   But in the same territory on the upper Mac-
millan in 1906 he used a .375 Holland Farquharson single-shot on moose,
caribou, and sheep.   In a letter to a friend he stated:

I am now using a .375 bore rifle by Holland, but I don't think it is any
better for all ordinary game than my old .303 which got worn out.

At another time, in reference to the ability of small bores, although
he had killed over 100 elephants and well over a 1,000 head of big game,
he said:

Had I only had one of these rifles in my early days, I would have shot
thrice the number of elephants I did.

With twenty-seven hunters listed in this large-bore period, eighty-seven
rifles of forty-four different types were used—an average of three rifles
apiece.   These rifles were forty-nine large-bores, twenty-five medium-bores

SELOUS' .450 GIBBS-METFORD SINGLE SHOT.

From H. A. Bryden's book *How to Buy A Gun.*

FARQUHARSON .280 or .303 SINGLE SHOT AS MADE BY GIBBS, JEFFERY, LANCASTER AND OTHERS.

ELI WHITNEY, RIFLE MAKER AND INVENTOR OF THE AMERICAN
MANUFACTURING SYSTEM.

From *The Whitney Firearms* by Claude E. Fuller, Standard Publications Inc., 1946.

Prize Medals
London 1862, Paris 1867, Philadelphia 1876, Paris 1878 (Silver) Calcutta 1884 (Silver) S. Africa International 1892, 4 Gold Medals.

Directors :—A. Stanley Brookes.
          H. F. Stevens, (Managing).
          Head Office, 37, Baldwin St.
          Works   54,
BRISTOL. Shooting Range & Trial Ground
          BEDMINSTER.
          Rifle Range, WHITCHURCH.
Telegrams : " Gibbs, Gunmaker, Bristol."
          (A.B.C. Code 5th Edition).
Telephone : 24824 Bristol.
VANCOUVER, Canada.
          P.O. Box 93

GEORGE GIBBS, Limited,

ESTABLISHED 1830

Gun, Rifle & Ammunition Manufacturers,
Fishing Tackle Specialists,

51, Baldwin Street, BRISTOL, 1.

3rd March 1947

S.R.Truesdell,Esq.,

   1830 Sheridan Road,

      Evanston, Illinois U.S.A.

Dear Sir,

     We are much obliged by your letter (undated) and much
regret to say that our records were destroyed by enemy action
in 1941.   But for this we would have been only too pleased to
let you have the information you require. The only source from
which you can now obtain details of the rifles in question is
from books published by various Hunters which are still available
in many secondhand book shops.

     Regretting our inability to helpon this occasion.

       We are,

         Yours faithfully,

George Gibbs Ltd

CHRISTIAN SHARPS. INVENTOR OF THE FIRST
SUCCESSFUL BREECH LOADING RIFLE.

From Mr. Guy Hubbard, Cleveland, Ohio.

ELIPHALET REMINGTON, FOUNDER OF THE REMINGTON ARMS CO.

From *Remington Handguns* by Charles Lee Karr and Carroll Robbins Karr.

A SHARPS BUFFALO RIFLE.

From the *American Rifleman.*

WINCHESTER 45-90 MODEL 1886 HALF-MAGAZINE RIFLE.

Courtesy Winchester Repeating Arms Co.

EDOUARD FOA. FRENCH EX-
PLORER AND BIG GAME HUNTER
IN THE AFRICAN CONGO.

From *After Big Game in Central Africa.*

R. J. CUNNINGHAME. HUNTER,
GUIDE AND OUTFITTER OF NAI-
ROBI, BRITISH EAST AFRICA.
HUNTED WITH ROOSEVELT,
STEWART EDWARD WHITE AND
MANY OTHERS.

From D. D. Lyell's *African Adventure.*

TYPICAL GRIZZLY HUNTING COUNTRY.
THE CONTINENTAL DIVIDE IS ON THE LEFT.

From the *American Rifleman.*

MAJOR C. E. R. RADCLIFFE (LEFT) AND 1200 POUND ALASKAN
BROWN BEAR.

From the Country Life Library of *Big Game Shooting*.

and thirteen small-bores, ranging in size from the single four-bore of 1.05 inches to the .256 Mannlicher, with bullets from 2,500 grains down to 160 grains. As an interesting sidelight on the professions represented, eleven were army officers, six were gentlemen-hunters, seven were professional hunters, one an administrator, one a minister of the gospel, one a naturalist-scientist, and one a rancher.

The information contained in the tables at the end of each part was secured from the published writings of the men listed or from contemporary sources, and it as accurate as possible under the circumstances. In a few cases the dates and territories hunted are approximate. Because of the length of hunting careers of men such as Baker, Rainsford, Selous, Hornaday, Littledale, Loder, Roosevelt, Millais, etc., the periods overlap and this must be considered in their later choice of rifles. The favorite rifle of each hunter is indicated by an asterisk where any preference was displayed.

The following abbreviations have been used:

ML: Muzzle Loader. BL: Breech Loader. DB: Double Barrel. SS: Single Shot M: Magazine. SP: Smokeless Powder. BP: Black Powder.

APPENDIX A

The Development of the Rifle in Big Game Hunting

NAME	WHEN	WHERE
1 Capt. Henry Shakespear	1834-1859	Central India
2 Capt. Wm. Cornwallis Harris	1835-1836	South Africa
3 William Cotton Oswell	1837-1852	South Africa
4 Roualeyn Gordon-Cumming	1843-1848	South Africa
5 Sir Samuel W. Baker	1845-1855	Ceylon
""	1861-1873	Sudan
""	1880-1882	North America
""	1882-1886	India
6 Maj. Henry A. Leveson	1845-1854	India
""	1856-1869	Europe, Africa
""	1870-1871	North America
7 Lt. Col. Wm. Gordon-Cumming	1847-1871	India
8 C. J. Andersson	1850-1854	South Africa
9 Maj. Gen. William Rice	1850-1884	India
10 William C. Baldwin	1852-1860	South Africa
11 Col. F. T. Pollok	1853-1879	Burma
12 Maj. Gen. Donald Macintyre	1853-1897	Himalayas
13 Capt. J. H. Baldwin	1859-1876	India
14 Capt. James Forsyth	1861-1871	Central India
15 Sir Victor Brooke	1862-1863	India
""	1869-1881	Spain-Sardinia
16 James Inglis	1863-1878	India
17 George P. Sanderson	1864-1877	India

APPENDIX A

Part I—1834 to 1874—The Large Bores

ANIMALS HUNTED	RIFLES USED
1 Elephant, Tiger, Panther, Bison, Bear	ML 10 bore DB Westley Richards, ML 10 bore DB Wilkinson*
2 Elephant, Lion, Rhino, Buffalo, Antelope	ML 8 bore DB
3 Elephant, Lion, Rhino, Buffalo, Antelope	ML 10 bore (Smooth) DB Purdey*, ML 12 bore DB Westley-R
4 Elephant, Lion, Rhino, Buffalo, Antelope	ML 4 and 12 bore SS, ML 12 bore DB Purdey*
5 Elephant, Tiger, Sambur	ML 4 bore SS Gibbs, ML 8 bore SS Blisset, ML 10 bore DB Beattie*
Elephant, Lion, Rhino, Buffalo, Antelope	ML 8 and 10 bore DB Reilly, BL .577 DB Holland*
Bear, Buffalo, Elk	BL .577 DB Holland*
Tiger, Bear, Sambur	BL .577 DB Holland*, BL .400 DB Holland
6 Elephant, Tiger, Bear, Bison, Sambur	ML 8 bore DB Westley R, ML 10 bore DB Westley Richards
Chamois, Lion, Rhino, Buffalo, Antelope	ML 8 bore DB Westley R, ML 10 bore DB Westley Richards*
Buffalo, Bear, Elk, Deer	BL 12 bore DB Westley Richards*
7 Tiger, Panther, Bear, Bison, Sambur	ML 12 bore DB Sam Smith*, ML 14 bore DB
8 Elephant, Lion, Rhino, Buffalo, Antelope	ML 14 bore DB Powell, ML 17 bore DB
9 Tiger, Bison, Bear, Panther, Sambur	ML 18 bore DB, .577 SS Snider, BL 12 bore DB Henry*
10 Elephant, Lion, Rhino, Buffalo, Antelope	ML 7 and 9 bore DB Burrow, ML 10 bore DB Witten*
11 Elephant, Tiger, Rhino, Gaur, Bear	ML 10 bore DB Lang*, BL 8 bore DB Westley Richards
12 Bear, Sambur, Markhor, Ibex, Ammon	ML .577 SS Enfield, ML .450 DB Whitworth*, BL .360 DB Rigby
13 Elephant, Tiger, Bison, Sambur, Ammon	ML 6 bore DB, BL 12 bore DB Powell*, BL .500 DB
14 Tiger, Bear, Bison, Sambur	ML 8 and 12 bore DB, BL 12 and 14 bore, DB BL .500 SS Henry*
15 Elephant, Bison, Ibex	ML 8 bore DB Purdy*
Moufflon, Ibex, Chamois	BL .360 DB Lancaster*
16 Tiger, Bear, Deer	12 bore DB Greener, .500 DB Murcott
17 Elephant, Tiger, Bison	BL 4 bore SS Lang, BL 8 and 12 bore DB Greener, 16 bore DB Purdy, .450 DB Lang*

* The asterisk indicates the favorite rifle.

1834-1874—The Large Bores

	NAME	WHEN	WHERE
18	William Finaughty	1864-1875	Central Africa
19	Gen. Alex A. A. Kinloch	1864-1900	India-Assam
20	W. A. Baillie-Grohmann	1865-1878	Bavaria
	"	1879-1898	North America
21	William H. Drummond	1867-1875	Southeast Africa
22	Arthur H. Neumann	1868-1906	Central Africa
23	Rev. Wm. S. Rainsford	1868-1883	North America
	"	1906-1909	East Africa
24	J. M. Murphy	1870-1880	North America
25	Frank Mayer	1871-1882	North America
26	Frederick Courtenay Selous	1871-1894	South Africa
	"	1895	Asia Minor
	"	1897-1901	North America
	"	1902	Sardinia
	"	1902-1903	East Africa
	"	1904-1906	North America
	"	1907	Norway
	"	1908-1913	East Africa
27	Col. V. M. Stockley	1874-1898	India, Burma
	"	1899-1910	Africa

1834-1874—The Large Bores

ANIMALS HUNTED	RIFLES USED
18 Elephant, Lion, Rhino, Buffalo, Antelope	ML 4 bore SS, BL 12 bore DB*, .450 SS Westley Richards
19 Elephant, Tiger, Rhino, Gaur	ML 12 bore DB, BL 12 bore DB Rigby
20 Ibex, Chamois, Roedeer	ML 24, bore SS, BL .450 DB Holland*
Elk, Bear, Sheep	BL .450 DB Holland*, .450 SS Holland
21 Elephant, Lion, Rhino, Buffalo, Antelope	BL 10 bore DB, BL 6 bore SS
22 Elephant, Lion, Rhino, Buffalo, Antelope	10 bore DB Holland, .577 DB Gibbs*, .303 Lee, .450 DB Rigby*, .256 Mannlicher
23 Bear, Elk, Sheep, Deer, Buffalo	ML 8 bore DB Rigby, .50-110 Bullard*
Elephant, Lion, Rhino, Buffalo, Antelope	.450 DB Rigby, .350 M Rigby,* .256 Mannl.
24 Buffalo, Elk, Bear, Moose, Sheep, Deer	.50 SS Springfield, .500 DB Expr.,* .45-75 Winchester
25 Buffalo, Elk, Bear, Deer	.50-70 SS Sharps, .40-90 SS Sharps, .45-120 SS Sharps*
26 Elephant, Lion, Rhino, Buffalo, Antelope	ML 4 and 10 bore SS Roer, BL 450 SS Gibbs*
Moufflon, Ibex, Red Deer	.450 SS Gibbs, .256 Mannl., .303 SS Holland*
Elk, Moose, Caribou, Bear, Sheep	.303 SS Holland*, .256 Mannlicher
Moufflon	.303 SS Holland*
Elephant, Lion, Rhino, Buffalo, Antelope	.450 SS Gibbs, .303 SS Holland*
Moose, Caribou, Bear, Sheep, Goat	.303 SS Holland, .375 SS Holland*
Elk, Reindeer	.375 SS Holland*
Elephant, Lion, Rhino, Buffalo, Antelope	.375 M Holland*, .256 Mannlicher
27 Elephant, Tiger, Bison, Markhor, Ibex	8 bore DB, .577 DB Westley R.*
Ibex, Lion, Buffalo	.577 DB Westley R.,* .405 Win., .303 Lee, .256 Mannlicher

* The asterisk indicates the favorite rifle.

1834-1874—Summary of Large Bore Rifles

Large Bore Muzzle Loaders

LARGE BORES	USED BY	TOTAL
4 SS	4, 5, 18, 26	4
8 SS	5	1
10 SS	26	1
12 SS	4	1
24 SS	20	1
6 DB	13	1
7 DB	10	1
8 DB	2, 5, 6, 14, 15, 23	6
9 DB	10	1
10 DB	1, 3, 5, 6, 10, 11	6
12 DB	3, 4, 7, 14, 19	5
14 DB	7, 8	2
17 DB	8	1
18 DB	9	1
Total		32

Medium Bore Muzzle Loaders

MEDIUM BORES	USED BY	TOTAL
.577 SS	12	1
.450 DB	12	1
Total		2

Large Bore Breech Loaders

LARGE BORES	USED BY	TOTAL
4 SS	17	1
6 SS	21	1
8 DB	11, 17, 27	3
10 DB	21, 22	2
12 DB	6, 9, 13, 14, 16, 17, 18, 19	8
14 DB	14	1
16 DB	17	1
Total		17

1834-1874—Summary of Large Bore Rifles

Medium Bore Breech Loaders

MEDIUM BORES	USED BY	TOTAL
.577 DB	5, 22, 27,	3
.577 SS	9	1
.500 DB	13, 16, 24	3
.500 SS	14	1
.50 Bullard	23	1
.50 SS Spr.	24	1
.50-70 SS	25	1
.450 DB	17, 20, 22, 23	4
.450 SS	18, 20, 26	3
.45-120 SS	25	1
.45-75 M	24	1
.405 M	27	1
.400 DB	5	1
.40-90 SS	25	1
Total		23

Small Bore Breech Loaders

SMALL BORES	USED BY	TOTAL
.375 M	26	1
.375 SS	26	1
.360 DB	12, 15	2
.350 M	23	1
.303 M	22, 27	2
.303 SS	25, 26	2
.256 M	22, 23, 26, 27	4
Total		13

Summary

	ML	BL	TOTAL
Large bores	32	17	49
Medium bores	2	23	25
Small bores	—	13	13
Total			87

Hunters—27   Rifles per hunter—3.2

PART II
THE MEDIUM BORES
1875 TO 1892

CHAPTER 3

BREECHLOADING RIFLES

*A*LTHOUGH the Hall flintlock in the United States in 1819, Lefaucheux's shotgun in 1836, and Lang's breechloader in England about 1853 should have been an indication of what might be expected, the development of the breechloader waited until about 1864, and then the conversion took place in a very short space of time and largely at first as a military expedient. In 1858 according to Wilcox, outside of a few units of the Prussian Guard, some troops in Sweden and Norway, the Cent Guards of France and a few Sharps, Burnside, Merrill, and Colt rifles issued to U. S. troops as an experiment, there were no breechloading rifles in use for military purposes anywhere. On the other hand Captain Forsyth of the Indian Army writing in 1871 in his book *The Highlands of Central India* had this to say:

In the matter of guns and rifles, improvements are still so rapidly progressing that the *dicta* of one year are very likely to be upset before the next. Regarding breechloading it is sufficient to say that by the universal consent of sportsmen, the use of the muzzle-loader is now confined to exceedingly remote countries where the cartridge cases cannot be carried. No part of India answers to this description, and a muzzle-loader is now rarely seen.

The actual change over took place between the above dates of 1858 and 1871 and was due to various causes both military and competitive. The English wars in the Crimea in 1856 and in India in 1857 had shown the great advantages of the rifle but had also brought into sharp relief the disadvantages of the muzzle-loader. Sir Samuel Baker says that "it was remarked during the Crimean War that a large proportion of wounded men were struck in the right arm, which would have been raised above the head when loading the old-fashioned rifle, and was thus prominently exposed." The German and French armies had their breechloading needle guns and the Americans had experimented with the Sharps and Spencer breech-loaders in the Civil War. Sharps and Colt breech-loading weapons made by machinery had been shown to the British at the Crystal Palace in

47

1851. So it was not surprising that both of these English speaking nations went to breech-loading arms at about the same time and, peculiarly, with conversions of the same type, the Springfield in 1866, and the Snider in 1867. Greener has this to say about the change to breechloaders, tying the date into the year 1864:

Breechloaders are divided into two classes, viz., those taking the consuming cartridge, and those with the metallic cartridge case. In the former, the most noteworthy are the Chassepot and the needle-gun; in both these the power of sustaining the force of the explosion is thrown on the breech action; the consequence of this is that an escape of gas takes place at the breech joint . . . It is surprising that no serious or deliberate attempt to introduce breech-loaders for military use should have been made until about the year 1864, when the English Government invited gunmakers and others to submit propositions for converting the Enfield rifle, and to supply 1,000 rounds of the description of ammunition which they considered most suitable to their arms. About fifty different principles were submitted to the Government and were referred to a select committee. Up to this period no Continental army had adopted breech-loaders, except Prussia and some of the minor German States and the needle-gun was the chosen weapon.

But this Enfield from which the Snider rifle was adapted was never too satisfactory and the British were soon experimenting with another rifle which was an American Peabody action perfected by a Swiss named Martini, given a barrel with Henry rifling. The Martini-Henry adopted in 1873 with the Enfield cartridge case necked down to .450 caliber was the result. The advantages of this military breech-loader were very well summed up by Greener in *Modern Breech-Loaders* published in 1871:

The principle advantages gained by applying the breech loading principle to military arms are the attainment of rapidity of fire combined with facility in loading. A well constructed weapon, in this principle, can be loaded easily in any position in which the soldier may be placed—either lying, running or riding—and also gives him the advantage of the possession of three or four rifles with the inconvenience of only one. At close quarters no troops, however, brave, devoted or well disciplined, could stand with muzzle-loaders against a corresponding force armed with breech-loaders.

With the British army supplied with breech-loaders, and a general policy among the higher authorities permitting the soldiers to take part in any sport with the rifle, it was not long until the English gunmakers were called on to furnish more powerful breech-loading rifles for big game hunting. Soldiers and civilians alike found the new .577 military cartridge an improvement in everything but power which was insufficient at 1200 ft. sec. velocity to be effective on the larger animals. The first result was the manufacture of double barreled rifles of the shotgun type with reinforced breech actions and heavier barrels firing the usual round balls out of paper cartridge cases. These were definitely more powerful but their weight in order to reduce the effect of recoil was from 12 to 18 pounds and their accuracy and range was decidedly inferior to the army rifle. So it was not long until hunters like Sir Samuel Baker, Sanderson, Neumann and Selous were asking for single and double rifles with the accuracy and range of the military rifle, which they had tried and found excellent, but with sufficient powder to give them power to deal with the largest game.

And here it was another American invention which saved the day. The English paper shells were alright with ball cartridges but the conical bullets of military cartridges required better support and the Enfield plant had been manufacturing the Boxer cartridge of thin rolled and folded brass or tin. But the American arsenals had perfected the machine drawing of solid brass shells, credited by Greener to Colonel Berdan who invented the primer known by that name. These solid brass cases could be made of sufficient strength in any necessary length. Their ability to seal perfectly the breech end of the rifle by their natural springiness solved the rifle cartridge problem for all time. Supplied at first in the Snider case this was later drawn down to .500 and .450 at the neck as in the Martini cartridge. This gave rise to a British system of cartridge designation which will be found in some references, using .577/.500, .577/.450 or .500/.450 to designate a bottle-neck case where the larger dimension is that of the base and the smaller that of the bullet caliber.

After making the large and medium bore double rifles, which began to give better accounts of themselves on the heaviest game, the gunmakers impressed by the increased power from the smaller bores and higher velocity, and beset by the high velocity fanatics of their day, began to experiment with a class of rifles which they called "Expresses" a term which Fremantle in *The Book of the Rifle* credits to Mr. James Purdey. Mr. Purdey had been impressed by the high velocity small bore rifles, being used so accurately by the American riflemen, and sought to equal their performance by utilizing deep hollow points in the English bores to lighten the bullet and increase the speed. The theory was that such a bullet would spread on impact, rendering a more disabling wound. While these "Express" loads were highly accurate and the trajectory and killing range was greatly extended, the light express bullet of soft lead flattened out or went to pieces on thick-skinned game. Consequently the rifles were only successful on deer and antelope and as a fad soon passed out. The average ballistics of these loads was somewhat as follows:

Caliber	Bullet	Velocity	Energy
.577	480	1780	3360
.500	340	1925	2795
.450	270	1975	2336
.400	230	1850	1747
.360	200	1850	1570

Another interesting type of sporting firearm appeared at this time. This was the combined double barreled ball and shotgun called the Paradox introduced by Messrs. Holland in 1886. The idea was an invention of a Colonel Fosbery and consisted of rifling the last two or three inches of the constricted bore of a shotgun. The gun could then be used as the equivalent of a medium choke bore for shotgun purposes and as a light 7 to 8 pound second rifle for big or dangerous game. The light weight restricted the amount of powder that could be used, so that velocities were generally rather low, but the weapon was dependably accurate up to 100 yards and its ball or later conical bullet had considerable stopping power. This Holland Paradox became quite popular for the purpose stated above and was followed by other makes of the same type called Cosmos, Explora, Colindian, etc. The approximate ballistics of such weapons were:

Gauge	Bullet	Velocity	Energy
8 bore	1150	1050	2820
10 bore	850	1100	2480
12 bore	750	1150	2400
20 bore	380	1600	2150
28 bore	290	1660	1772

Because of their cheapness and quality American military rifle actions were invading Europe, the Remington in Spain, Holland, Norway and Sweden, the Peabody-Martini in Turkey and now the Snider and Martini, both American designs, in England. And the American type of cartridge case and method of manufacture had been introduced into Birmingham. But the impact of American methods on rifle manufacture and on the development of rifles for big game went beyond cartridge cases and rifle actions. Until the advent of the breech-loader the careful and painstaking manufacture and assembly of rifles by hand for sporting purposes, by the English craftsmen, had been practically unthreatened. Except in America the big-game hunters of the world used English rifles of high quality but so fashioned that if one part of the rifle went wrong an expensive weapon was out of commission until returned to the factory for repairs. No part from any other rifle would fit, and because every make of rifle was different, there were seldom any trained gunsmiths closer than London who would attempt to make repairs. This might have continued except that American industry had developed the manufacture of firearms to interchangeable standards by the use of gages and power driven machinery so that a Sharps, Colt, or Winchester model of any certain year would be exactly like any other rifle of the same model. Also by the use of this machinery and these methods the cost of manufacture was but a fraction of that of the English sporting rifle. Besides entering the competitive field with the English arms, American machine tool manufacturers had installed their machinery and methods in the Government rifle factory at Enfield and in 1873 had sold a million and a half dollars worth of machinery to the German Mauser rifle factory.

While it was still too early to notice much effect of the invasion of rifles made by American methods in the development of the big-game rifle, it is interesting to diverge for a time to consider the growth of these American methods of manufacture, the effects of which will become apparent later. Nowhere is this more interestingly described than in a recent address before the Newcomen Society, entitled *Invention and Industry—Cradled in New England* by Frederick S. Blackall, Jr., from which the following quotations are made at random. Having described the development of machine tools for manufacturing textile machinery Mr. Blackall turns to the gun making industry and the men who were responsible for revolutionizing it:

But in another industry revolutionary changes were taking place in manufacturing methods. Here again individual handicraft was giving way to the embryonic form of machine production. A hardy race of pioneers, hewing a new nation out of the wilderness needed guns, and throughout the early half of the nineteenth century much of the progress in the machine tool art was inspired by or incidental to the manufacture of *firearms* . . .

Disheartened by political intrigue and endless lawsuits, Whitney turned, in 1798, to another endeavor which was destined to have an even greater influence upon the character of the modern world and the industrial revolution which was overtaking it. Not a gunsmith in any sense of the word, he nevertheless sought a contract for the manufacture of ten thousand muskets to be produced on a system of manufacture, whereby, in his own words, he would undertake "to make the same parts of different guns, as the locks, for example, as much like each other as the successive impressions of a copper plate engraving." The tedious fitting, the selective assembly of the handicraft system were thus to be eliminated. Even inexperienced operators could be trained to perform any single operation with consummate skill. Every part of the same kind being fitted to a common standard or gage would be interchangeable with every other. It is to the credit of our government that this project, at which leading European ordnance officers and many of Whitney's compatriots scoffed, was supported through substantial advances of money and the unwavering faith of the Secretary of War, even though it took Whitney some eight years to complete his initial contract. The result was so remarkable, however, that it won immediate acclaim and Whitney's system became the standard manufacturing procedure for every other gunmaker, of which there were several in the New England area at the time. The Whitney Arms Company was carried on as a business for 90 years, until consolidated in 1880 with the Winchester Repeating Arms Co.

These muskets were smoothbore guns of the French pattern but the methods used in their manufacture were soon to become standard in all arms plants. Where metal parts had been laboriously forged and filed by hand before, they were now to be machined with lathe, shaper, and milling machine, utilizing special jigs, fixtures, and gages of the type known as "go" and "no go" or maxima and minima sizes for each part. With this type of production the training of workmen was simplified and the number of machines of each type could be so planned as to produce parts as fast as needed to meet assembly schedules. All parts were interchangeable and a musket could be assembled from various bins of the manufactured parts. It is this idea, originated by Eli Whitney, which has been the foundation of all American mass production, as Mr. Blackall goes on to say:

Thus was born the *interchangeable system* of mass production, the touchstone which converted the age old craft system into a modern in-

BEAR HUNTING IN WESTERN AMERICA.

From *Hunting American Big Game.*

THEODORE ROOSEVELT AT THE TIME OF HIS WESTERN
HUNTING ADVENTURES. THE RIFLE IS A .45-90 MODEL 1886
WINCHESTER.

Courtesy of the Theodore Roosevelt Estate.

THEODORE ROOSEVELT HUNTING WITH MERRIFIELD IN
THE ROCKY MOUNTAINS.

Used by permission of the Theodore Roosevelt Estate from
Hunting Adventures in the Far West.

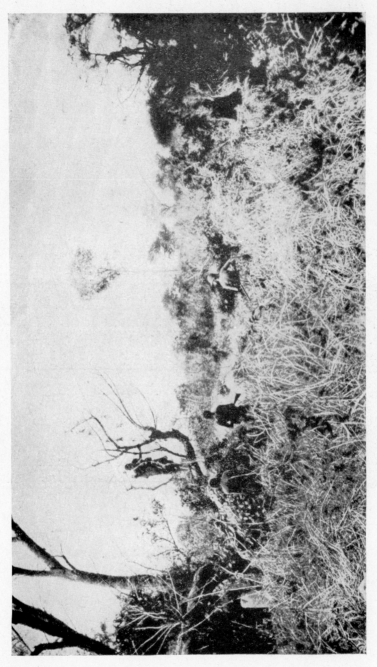

SEARCH FOR A WOUNDED LION IN THE BUSH.

From Edouard Foa's *After Big Game in Central Africa.*

INDIAN GAUR. THE HUNTER MAY BE MAJ. W. S. CUMBERLAND.

From the Country Life Library of *Big Game Shooting*.

RESULT OF A RANDOM SHOT AT NIGHT.

From Edouard Foa's *After Big Game in Central Africa.*

"K.C.A.J." AN EXTREMELY MODEST AUTHORITY ON OUTFITS FOR
HIMALAYAN HUNTING. THE RIFLE IS A .500 HENRY SINGLE
SHOT EXPRESS.

From the *Sportsman's Vade Mecum for the Himalayas.*

LIONESS PREPARING TO CHARGE.

From Edouard Foa's *After Big Game in Central Africa.*

dustrial economy, brought to the common man conveniences and a standard of living which even kings had not before enjoyed, and launched a wave of creative invention and production such as the world had never known. It was purely an American creation. While across the water, Bentham and Brunel were applying some of the principles of repetitive production and precision to the manufacture of pulley blocks, they had missed the vital element of limit gages, and Europe was to wait half a century before finally adopting the American system, as they themselves called it, first in equipping the Enfield Armory in 1855 with machine tools, jigs, fixtures, and gages, imported from the United States.

Simeon North of Berlin, Connecticut, was building muskets within a year after Whitney started. By 1813 he was employing forty or fifty men on the interchangeable system, when he built at Middletown, Connecticut, a three story brick armory costing $100,000 in which machinery, tools, and gages much like Whitney's were built and used in the production of firearms. It appears probable that some of Colonel North's equipment was of his own invention, although he certainly must have been influenced by his nearby neighbor and predecessor, Eli Whitney, whose plant was but a scant twenty miles distant.

Satterlee and Gluckman in their volume listing *American Gunmakers* say that this modernization of North's factory was done in 1808 when he received an order for 1,000 pair of "navy boarding pistols." North stuck pretty well to the manufacture of pistols until 1823 when he received an order for 6,000 flint-lock rifles and in 1828 for 5,000 Hall breech loading rifles. All in all up to 1850 North is reported to have made about 28,000 of the Hall rifles and some of his production modifications were rather upsetting to Hall the inventor, manufacturing the same rifle under contract at the Harpers Ferry Arsenal. Incidentally it was to capture this Harpers Ferry Arsenal that John Brown came east from Kansas, when he hoped to arm the slaves, and it was in one of the buildings that he was taken prisoner. The rifle making machinery was removed to Fayetteville, N. C. by the Confederates and the particular building was removed and reconstructed, brick by brick, for an exhibit at the Chicago World's Fair in 1893.

Up to the time of his death in 1826, Whitney had manufactured about 45,000 muskets for the U. S. Army and the State of New York. His son Eli, Jr., continued the manufacture of arms, delivering up to the Civil War some 30,000 of the U. S. Model 41 percussion lock rifles, as well as other military and sporting rifles.

But to continue with the history of the development of the machine production of firearms as described by Mr. Blackall:

As early as 1820, we find Thomas Blanchard producing gun stocks in a shop at Millbury, Massachusetts, on a special form of copying lathe which he had designed for the Springfield Armory. This machine later taken over by the Ames Manufacturing Company of Chicopee Falls, Massachusetts, sired a whole family of gunmaking machinery and was instrumental in spreading the fame of the American industrial system abroad. Its basic principles are still in use today. Blanchard was the father of repetitive production of parts by what we now call "tracer control" a technique which, in recent years, has assumed great importance in applications to lathes, milling machines, and profilers for the accurate duplication of dies, moulds, and other metal parts. Blanchard also was responsible to an important extent for the early mechanization of Springfield Armory, itself a pioneer in manufacture on the interchangeable system. While there, he invented or perfected more than a dozen machines for the manufacture of firearms.

It was Blanchard's machinery which was introduced first at Enfield Armory in England, an installation of 25 machines which was expected to turn out 250 gunstocks per day. With these there were other milling machines, lathes, jigs, etc., for the manufacture of locks for the new Enfield rifle. Deane in his *Manual of Fire Arms* published in London in 1858 was somewhat critical of his English brethren:

We cannot close these necessarily restricted observations on the manufacture of firearms, without adverting to the fact that with all the credit we have heard assumed, as our own, for the application of much of the new machinery now in use, in aid and in economy of handicraft labor— yet in that of the manufacture of military small fire-arms, as with many others of late years, we have been taught our best lessons by our juniors in mechanical repute, the men of the United States. The greater expense of skilled handicraft labor in the Union, induced there the resort to machinery as a more stringent necessity than with the manufacturers of Birmingham; and it there attained no less of a consequence, to a more extensive development.

The history of rifles and the machine tool industry of New England this time involves a man whose name was connected with three rifles, the Kendall, the Jennings and most famous of all, the Sharps. In Mr. Blackall's words:

We journey now to the little town of Windsor, Vermont, whose industrial history is, in relationship to its population, perhaps the most striking of any community in the United States.   There existed in Windsor during the early half of the nineteenth century a firm by the name of Robbins & Lawrence, manufacturers of rifles and machine tools, which was in many ways the most remarkable concern which ever graced the machine tool industry.   Never large, and of relatively short life, it was located in a sleepy country village miles away from a railroad.   The origins of this concern stem back to the National Hydraulic Company, founded at Windsor in 1829 for the production of a rotary fire pump, which is manufactured to this day in essentially its original form.   This device was produced from its inception on the interchangeable system and was probably the first machine in the world so built.   Like many another machine shop of our pioneering era, it was not long before National Hydraulic was making guns for our fathers of the frontier, Davy Crockett being an early devotee of their famous Kendall under-hammer lock rifle. The company also had to improvise many of the machine tools required for its manufacturing activities.   It was thus that there came to its first successor concern, N. Kendall & Company, in 1838, one Richard Lawrence, a boy of twenty one and a crack shot with a gun.   It is related that he got his first job through making a peep sight for his future boss' turkey rifle and putting three balls in a row into a 3/4 inch sap hole in a Vermont maple tree at twelve rods, or 66 yards. [This is very close to the considered maximum possible degree of accuracy, or one minute of angle per 100 yards.   Few could match this feat today with modern firearms. —S.R.T.]

Richard Lawrence was soon superintendent and a partner in the company . . . In 1851 they sent to the Crystal Palace Exposition at London a set of rifles built on the interchangeable system, which caused a revolution in European manufacturing methods as great as that which Whitney had brought about in America fifty years earlier.   The exhibit led to the appointment of a British Commission, which came to this country to study the American system and resulted in the placing of contracts with Robbins & Lawrence and the Ames Manufacturing Company for a full complement of gun machinery to be installed in the armory at Enfield near London.   It was this incident more than any other single thing which established American machine tools for the ensuing ninety-odd years as the leaders of the world.

The expansion of their rifle making activities was a natural outgrowth of such a tribute.   In 1852 Robbins & Lawrence began the manufacture under contract of the famous Sharps Carbine and with its Windsor plant operating at full capacity, agreed to erect and operate a new plant in Hartford for the Sharps Rifle Manufacturing Company.   Mr. Lawrence moved to Hartford in 1853 to superintend this work. At about the same time, the firm undertook the manufacture of 25,000 Minie rifles for the use of the British in the Crimean War. The venture was an unhappy one from the start. Robbins & Lawrence had been assured by the agent for His Majesty's Government that an order for 300,000 additional rifles would be placed with them immediately upon the completion of the initial quantity. Over the protest of Mr. Lawrence, who objected to making the heavy outlay necessary on mere promises of future business, Robbins prevailed upon his associates to undertake the commitment. The contract not only involved spending more money on special tooling than the concern would receive from the initial order, but carried a penalty clause, which was applied with damaging effect when with the abrupt ending of the Crimean War, the British agents refused to make good their promises of additional rifle contracts. Robbins & Lawrence were already embarrassed by losses in the ill-fated car-making venture and their heavy expenditures for the Sharps rifle plant in Hartford. The latest blow was too much. The firm was bankrupt, and Robbins & Lawrence passed into the ownership of the British Government, eventually to be sold at auction to a group of Windsor citizens. The Hartford plant was acquired by the Sharps Rifle Manufacturing Company.

But the English gunmakers did not yield very gracefully to machine methods as witness the following from W. W. Greener's *The Gun and Its Development*:

In short, a machine-made sporting gun is not a higher development of the shotgun, but rather a degenerate speciman. It is a *sine qua non* that all be alike; no scope is given for the fancy of workman or artist, no incentive to producing a better arm than all before turned out; and instead of being a perfectly balanced, proportionate, tastily ornamented and well built gun, it is but the assemblage of various synoforms, neither artistic nor symmetrical; in many instances a poor, and at best, only a mediocre, production.

Having seen how the American firearms industry caught up with the world's needs in the way of rifle making machinery to such an extent that we find the most conservative handicraft of England adopting its methods, some little description is needed of the types of rifles manufactured. The American sporting rifle was left in a previous chapter with the plains rifle made by Hawkens of St. Louis. No one knows just what type or make of breech-loader was the first to be carried west into the buffalo country.

It may have been a Colt with a revolving chamber using paper or cloth cartridges and the Minié ball, with each chamber covered with a nipple and cap, struck in turn by the high winged hammer. As to those rifles using metallic cartridges, it is certain that the Spencer rim and center fire cartridges have been picked up on the plains, where they probably dropped out of belts because of their short length or became lost while reloading at high speed on horseback, since the muzzle of this arm had to be depressed to feed a cartridge from the butt magazine into the chamber.

But whatever rifle started the western invasion of the buffalo ranges, two, the Springfield Army rifle in .50-70 and .45-70 caliber and the Sharps in .50, .45, .44 and .40 calibers were in at the finish. The army rifle was in the hands of every soldier, teamster, or scout connected with the army, and the Sharps, the first and only rifle that was absolutely deadly with one shot, was the favorite of the buffalo hunters. When Winchester developed the rifle of Tyler Henry, a one time employe of Robbins & Lawrence, into the Model 1873 handling the .44-40 cartridge and later into the Model 1876 adapted to the larger .45-75 bottle-neck case, this rifle was some competition as a saddle gun, but the Sharps or the Remington handling the long cases, was the main standby of the old timers for buffalo or grizzly. The first real competition in repeating rifles was the Winchester Model 1886 handling the .50-110 and the .45-90, but no American repeating rifle has ever equaled the deadly effectiveness of the Sharps and its long heavy hard lead bullet, despite the fact that modern ballistics might seem to give the lie to this statement. These various cartridges and their ballistics were about as follows:

Name	Caliber	Bullet	Velocity	Energy
Spencer Magazine	.56	380	1000	840
Springfield S. S.	.50-70	450	1240	1515
Springfield S. S.	.45-70	500	1300	1875
Sharps S. S.	.50	473	1200	1505
Sharps S. S.	.45-120	550	1400	2390
Sharps S. S.	.44-100	520	1425	2340
Sharps S. S.	.40-90	420	1500	2097
Remington S. S.	.44-90	400	1500	2000
Winchester Magazine ..	.44-40	200	1245	685
Winchester Magazine ..	.45-75	350	1344	1405
Winchester Magazine ..	.50-110	450	1383	1920
Winchester Magazine ..	.45-90	300	1480	1460

CHAPTER 4
HUNTING WITH BREECHLOADERS

*I*N a previous chapter, hunting experiences with the early large bore muzzle-and breech-loading rifles, were described, and the trend toward lighter weapons of medium bore was indicated. The present chapter continues the story of big-game rifle development in the hunting field after the advent of the breech loader, when the improvements resulting from its adoption had become fully established. To review these in brief; the problem of powder fouling, which had been an almost insuperable handicap for the smaller bores in a muzzle-loader, was now less objectionable. The bullet for the breech-loading rifle could be of full groove diameter and assist in clearing the barrel. The tighter fit of the bullet prevented the escape of gas and greater velocities were possible, even with less powder. The long, hardened bullet secured greater penetration and fewer shots were needed, if well placed, to kill the largest game.

St. George Littledale and Sir Edmund Loder were a different type of hunter from most of those described previously. They would be classed as gentlemen-sportsmen, since they hunted for pleasure and for the trophies they could secure. Men of this type with sufficient money and time generally hunted horned game and the carnivora for their skins. So, we find that neither Littledale nor Loder ever shot elephant or rhino. Loder did equip himself with a double 8 and a double 12 bore rifle battery made by Reilly of Edinburgh for hunting elephant and rhino in Sumatra, but he never used it. Both he and Littledale, however, hunted together in India for tiger, bison, sambur, and thar, a species of goat.

Littledale had already hunted sheep and elk in western North America and was on his way after markhor and ibex, the first a spiral-horned and the second a scimitar-horned goat of the Himalayas. Later he hunted much in Central Asia and was one of the first to bring out heads of the *Ovis poli,* described by Marco Polo as the father of all sheep. He hunted with a double .500 bore Henry rifle but had little to say of its performance. The Henry rifle was also an Edinburgh product. Henry's type of rifling with wide grooves and narrow lands was used also in the .450 Martini-

Henry army rifle adopted by the British Army in 1873. Littledale was one of the few hunters to have secured specimens of the bison of the Caucasus, first cousin of the American buffalo, probably now extinct.

This English or Scottish Henry rifle in single and double barrel was also the favorite weapon of Major C. S. Cumberland in India and on his trip to the Russian Pamirs for Ovis Poli, and was the rifle used by "KCAJ" described below. Sir Charles Ross did his early hunting in Scotland with Henry rifles, but they were no relative of the American Henry which later became the Winchester rifle.

Sir Edmund Loder hunted buffalo and elk in Colorado in 1875 with a double .450 Westley Richards. He rode buffalo with a .45 Colt revolver he had purchased for thirty-five dollars in New York, not having been able to secure ammunition for his English revolver. Between his round-the-world trip and a second trip to the United States in 1887, Loder made many trips to Spain and North Africa after chamois, ibex, and the wild sheep of the Atlas, the spiral-horned Barbary sheep or moufflon. Here he met A. E. Pease and C. E. Radcliffe, all gentlemen-sportsmen of his type. All of these men, Loder converted to the .256 Mannlicher in the same way he had persuaded St. George Littledale to take a cut-down Roumanian Mannlicher to Central Asia in 1895.

The ballistics of the double .450 and .500 "Express" rifles used by Littledale and Loder are shown below with the .400 and .577:

			Muzzle		
Caliber	Bullet	Powder	Velocity	Energy	Recoil
.577	591 grs.	164 grs.	1,663 f. s.	3,625 f. p.	36 f. p.
.500	444 grs.	138 grs.	1,784 f. s.	3,134 f. p.	28 f. p.
.450	322 grs.	110 grs.	1,777 f. s.	2,254 f. p.	18 f. p.
.400	209 grs.	82 grs.	1,874 f. s.	1,628 f. p.	12 f. p.

That these were the usual rifles for Indian and Himalayan game as late as 1891 is evidenced by the following quoted from *The Sportsmans Vade Mecum for the Himalayas* by K.C.A.J.:

The rifle may be either .450, .500 or magnum .500. I do not like .577; it is too large for the smaller game, and unnecessarily powerful for the larger. Just before leaving India I was corresponding with a well-known maker about a .450 magnum to take 5 drams of powder, and tomorrow I would choose that. At the time I was using a .450 made by him [Henry of Edinburgh—SRT] for 4 drams, but I used 4½, and attribute my success to the flatter trajectory even the half dram extra insured. I believe this rifle will kill all Himalayan game if handled fairly, and cannot see why a sportsman should require one that will kill everything, regardless of where it is hit . . .

So much for the bore. The next point is whether it is to be a single or double; if you can afford it, let it be the latter, but if money is an object it is better to have a really first-rate single than any second-rate double. My .450 was a single, and I never lost or missed game owing to its being so, neither was my life ever in danger from a wounded animal. It may be said I was lucky; but I think I ran little risk for I never tried shots at bears up above me! I had decided on a double .450 magnum by the same maker when duty called me out of India, and as I said before that is the weapon I would choose now."

A larger number of Americans appear in this period as it was the peak of hunting in the Great West. One of the most noted was Colonel W. D. Pickett, a Confederate veteran who settled on a ranch on the Greybull River in western Wyoming in 1876. His rifle was a single-shot .45 caliber Sharps of which he had this to say in *Hunting at High Altitudes* a book of the Boone and Crockett Club published in 1913:

I was then (1876) using the long-range .45 caliber rifle made by the Sharps Rifle Company, but by putting a double patch around the .44 caliber 275 grain Express bullet it shot as accurately from the .45 caliber rifle as from the .44. A few cartridges were sent to Major Michaelis (Ordnance officer at Springfield Arsenal) with the 275 grain Express ball and an equal number of .45 caliber Express bullets of my own design, weighing 340 grains. Into all shells 110 grains of powder were loaded, and the result as determined by the Government chronograph was that the .45 caliber bullet attained a muzzle velocity of 1,830 feet a second, while the 275 grain bullet had a muzzle velocity of 1,910 feet a second.

My conclusion was that the lighter Express bullet was not the best for game larger than deer. Later experience has convinced me that the 340 grain Express ball is sufficient for all large game of the continent. For great beasts like the Buffalo, a heavy solid bullet is the thing, but during the season of 1881, after I had become familiar with the habits of the grizzly bear, I killed, using an Express bullet with 110 grains of black powder, twenty-three of those bears of which seventeen required only a single shot.

G. O. Shields, Editor of *Recreation* magazine, did considerable hunting in the Rockies of Montana and Wyoming during the 70's and 80's. His first rifle, a .32 Stevens, was soon replaced with the then new .45-75 Winchester 1876 Model, and then later with a .45-75 single-shot Sharps. He used this successfully on buffalo, elk, and grizzly bear.

Other American hunters were: W. H. Wright, grizzly bear hunter, guide and photographer of Missoula, Montana; Theodore Roosevelt, ranchman of Medora, North Dakota; S. E. White, author, of Grand Rapids, Michigan; John B. Burnham, fish and game conservationist, New York; N. H. Roberts, of New Hampshire, old-time rifleman, author, and more recently inventor of the .257 Roberts cartridge; Bryan H. Williams, guide and game commissioner of British Columbia; B. W. Robinson, businessman-hunter of New York; and Caspar Whitney, Editor of *Outing*. At the start of their careers these men all used typical American medium bores for American game. But, lacking the heritage of the big double rifles of the elephant hunters, these rifles except for the single shots were light when compared with the English medium bores:

	Caliber	Rifle	Bullet	Velocity	Energy	Rifle Weight
Wright	.45-100	SS Winchester	600 grs.	1,300 f.s.	2,250 f.p.	12
Whitney	.40-90	SS Sharps	370	1,357 f.s.	1,515 f.p.	11½
Roosevelt & Williams	.45-90	Winchester	300	1,480 f.s.	1,460 f.p.	8½
Burnham	.40-82	Winchester	260	1,500 f.s.	1,305 f.p.	10
Roberts	.40-60	Winchester	210	1,475 f.s.	1,015 f.p.	10

Wright hunted the grizzly bear exclusively and started with a .44 which he soon discarded for the heavier rifle of which he says:

I was then using my single-shot rifle made to order for me by the Winchester people; the .45-100 in which I shot 100 grains of powder and 600 grains of lead. It was one of the guns that killed at both ends, but I liked it better than any I have ever carried. I used it for years, and I discarded it for a lighter .30-30 only when I gave up hunting with a gun and took to hunting with a camera. Personally, I could depend on this rifle for a sure three shots in twelve seconds, by holding two spare cartridges between the fingers of my right hand, and I have always thought that a hunter is apt to be much more careful if he knows that every shot must tell. I always got as close to the game as I could before shooting, and whatever I shot it generally dropped if hit, and I was usually near enough to be sure of hitting.

At one time Wright killed five grizzlies with five straight shots with the

Winchester single shot. He had discarded the .44 Winchester repeater because it would jam if he wasn't careful to "thumb" it when he pumped a shell in the chamber.

Theodore Roosevelt in his hunting in North Dakota, Montana and Wyoming between the years of 1883 and 1893 while operating a cattle ranch at Medora, North Dakota shot all types of American big-game. He had little to say about the rifles he used except the following two paragraphs, the first from *Hunting Trips of a Ranchman* written in 1885 and the second from the Appendix to his *Wilderness Hunter* written in 1893:

A word as to weapons and hunting dress. When I first came to the plains I had a heavy Sharps rifle, .45-120, shooting an ounce and a quarter of lead, and a .50 caliber, double barreled English express. Both of these especially the latter, had a vicious recoil; the former was very clumsy; and above all they were neither of them repeaters; for a repeater or magazine gun is as much superior to a single or double-barreled breech-loader as the latter is to a muzzle-loader. I threw them both aside; and have instead a .40-90 Sharps for very long range work; a .50-115 6-shot Bullard express which has the velocity, shock, and low trajectory of the English gun; and better than either a .45-75 half magazine Winchester. The Winchester which is stocked and sighted to suit myself is by all odds the best weapon I ever had, and I now use it almost exclusively, having killed every kind of game with it, from grizzly bear to big-horn. It is as handy to carry whether on foot or on horseback, and comes up to the shoulder as readily as a shotgun; it is absolutely sure, and there is no recoil to jar and disturb the aim, while it carries accurately quite as far as man can aim with any degree of certainty; and the bullet, weighing three quarters of an ounce, is plenty large enough for anything on this continent. For shooting the very large game (buffalo, elephants, etc.) of India and South Africa, much heavier rifles are undoubtedly necessary; but the Winchester is the best gun for any game to be found in the United States, for it is as deadly, accurate, and handy as any, stands very rough usage, and is unapproachable for the rapidity of its fire and the facility with which it is loaded.

And written eight years later:

There is an endless variety of opinion about rifles, and all that can be said with certainty is that any good modern rifle will do. It is the man behind the rifle that counts after the weapon has reached a certain stage of perfection. One of my friends invariably uses an old Government Springfield, a .45 caliber, with an ounce bullet. Another cares for nothing but the .40-90 Sharp's, a weapon for which I myself have much partiality. Another uses always the old .45 caliber Sharp's and yet another the .45-caliber Remington. Two of the best bear and elk hunters I know prefer the .32 and .38 caliber Marlin's with long cartridges, weapons with which I myself would not undertake to produce any good results. Yet others prefer pieces of very large caliber . . .

There seems to be no doubt, judging from the testimony of sportsmen in South Africa and in India, that very heavy caliber double-barreled rifles are best for use in the dense jungles and against the thick-hided game of those regions; but they are of very little value with us. In 1882, one of the buffalo-hunters on the Little Missouri obtained from some Englishman a double-barreled 10-bore rifle of the kind used against rhinoceros, buffalo, and elephant in the Old World; but it proved very inferior to the .40 and .45 caliber Sharp's buffalo guns when used under the conditions of American buffalo-hunting, the tremendous shock given by the bullet not compensating for the gun's relative deficiency in range and accuracy, while even the penetration was inferior at ordinary distances. It is largely also a matter of individual taste. At one time I possessed a very expensive double barrelled 500 Express, by one of the crack English makers; but I never liked the gun, and could not do as well with it as my repeater, which cost barely a sixth as much. So one day I handed it to a Scotch friend, who was manifestly ill at ease with a Winchester exactly like my own. He took to the double-barrel as naturally as I did to the repeater, and did excellent work with it. Personally, I have always preferred the Winchester. I now use a .45-90, with my old buffalo gun, a .40-90 Sharp's, as spare rifle. Both, of course, have specially tested barrels, and are stocked and sighted to suit myself.

But Roosevelt didn't object to the .450 double Holland rifle that fifty-six notable Englishmen including such sportsmen as Buxton, Loder, Littledale, Selous, Phillips-Wolley, Pike, Kinloch, Radcliffe, Pease, Millais, Jackson, Seton-Karr and Patterson, presented him with before he went to Africa. The well founded tradition that Teddy never could bear to have anyone beat him, even in a case when it might have been a matter of life and death, is illustrated by this passage of much later date from his *African Game Trails*:

Again we dismounted at a distance of two hundred yards; Tarlton telling me that now he was sure to charge. In all East Africa there is no man, not even Cunninghame himself, whom I would rather have by me than Tarlton, if in difficulties with a charging lion; on this occasion, however, I am glad to say that his rifle was badly sighted, and shot altogether too low . . . Again I knelt and fired; but the mass of hair on the lion made me think he was nearer than he was, and I undershot inflicting a flesh wound that was neither crippling nor fatal. He was already grunting savagely and tossing his tail erect, with his head held low; and at the shot the great sinewy beast came toward us with speed of a greyhound. Tarlton then, very properly, fired, for lion hunting is no child's play, and it is not good to run risks. Ordinarily it is a very mean thing to experience joy at a friend's miss; but this was not an ordinary case, and I felt *keen delight* when the bullet from the badly sighted rifle missed, striking the ground many yards short. I was sighting carefully, from my knee, and I knew I had the lion alright . . . straight through the chest . . . when he was still a hundred yards away.

The comments of some of Roosevelt's friends on his African hunting and the book which Scribner is supposed to have bought for one dollar a word, are very interesting. Millais who had the greatest respect for Roosevelt's tremendous knowledge and energy, says:

The only thing I have against Roosevelt who is a delightful man and a personal friend is that he has an abominable habit of being photographed with every zebra and kongoni he shoots for the pot as if it were some great feat. Personally, I loathe these wretched amateur photographs, and of the successful hunter posing in front of mangled corpses. It is of no earthly use or scientifically instructive and gives no correct representation of the animal, whilst it displays a cheap conceit which future generations will only laugh at, and say as in Roosevelt's case: "Here is a book dealing with the chase and habits of wild animals and there are 57 illustrations, nearly all from amateur photographs and the author appears grinning beside a carcass in 53!" I think it is deplorable.

Sir Frederick Jackson at one time governor of Kenya was no less critical of Roosevelt in his book *Early Days in East Africa* when he said:

It was, however, a matter of great regret to learn from Col. Roosevelt's own showing and from others that he was so utterly reckless in the expenditure of ammunition, and what it entailed in the matter of disturbing the country; and that he so unduly exceeded reasonable limits in certain species, and particularly the White Rhinoceros, of which he and Kermit (his son) killed nine.

As the white rhinoceros at the time was so rare as to be given complete protection by law the last criticism was probably justified. Nevertheless, Roosevelt was one of the great, big game hunters of all time, and with it all, a genuine student and lover of wild game. Probably no one man in all the world did more for wise laws and the preservation of game animals.

But, in order to analyze the trend of rifle bores at this period in big-game hunting, it is necessary to study further the rifles used in Africa and India. And note in particular the recommendations of Edouard Foa, a Frenchman hunting in the Congo, F. J. Jackson in East Africa, Swayne in Somaliland, and Fletcher and Glasfurd in India.

Foa spent twenty years hunting in French North Africa and the Congo, including a three-year hunting trip from the Cape to the Congo. But, his rifle recommendations related in his book, *After Big Game in Central Africa,* are from his later experience in the Congo:

I am still of the same opinion on the subject of large bore weapons, and if you possess neither 12 bore nor 8 bore rifles I do not advise you to buy them unless you are certain of visiting a country where elephant abound, and those countries are becoming, alas, more and more difficult to find . . . My principal weapons were two Express double barreled rifles of .577 bore. One of them had been made specially for me by M. Galand, the well-known gunsmith who had already armed me several times and according to my own indication. I had asked for an exceedingly small reduction of the bore at the top of the barrel; a small increase in the thickness of the barrels, without respect to weight; shortening of the barrels; a large pea sight; a treble lock, top lever, and a solidity equal to the severest test. This rifle, which I call my Express No. 1 is so well made that after three-and-a-half years shooting, tribulations, jolts, and handling, after having fired 600 to 700 shots, it only required cleaning upon my return . . . Express No. 1 weighs eleven pounds and one ounce. No. 2 . . . was also made in the workshops of M. Galand, and with it I killed more than 300 animals during my hunting expeditions from 1891 to 1893. The barrels are a little longer, the two sights are diamond ones, and its weight is a little less than ten and one-half pounds in all. I took with me on trial and not without a little mistrust, a double-barreled English rifle of .303 bore—that is, a little smaller than the Lebel. This weapon, which had the appearance of an Express rifle very small for its bore, was one of the first examples of the Metford Express, which had appeared on the London market. It was an adaptation of the Lee Metford army weapon which fires six shots and has a single barrel. To adapt it to sporting purposes, it was supplied with two barrels, but the repeating mechanism was done away with as in ordinary rifles. The first two weapons of the kind had burst in the faces of their owners. The third, that which I took with me, had been strengthened so as to resist the action of English Army Smokeless powders, cordite, and rifleite, which put the barrels to severe tests, so that it weighed, notwithstanding its small bore, almost as much as an Express—ten pounds and one ounce. This weapon, which I shall call my .303, has proved that it was admirably built since I have fired with it nearly 1,000 cartridges without the slightest accident. A telescope adjusted on the barrel is intended to magnify and consequently to bring the quarry nearer; but I was never able to use this instrument, and I recommend you (if one is suggested to you) not to make this useless expenditure.

F. J. Jackson, already quoted elsewhere, was in favor of the largest bores for hunters coming to Africa. The following is from the Badminton Library volumes on *Big Game Shooting*:

Without entering into the details of the merits and demerits of the different rifles and their respective charges, about which so much has been written, I strongly recommend sportsmen intending to visit East Africa to arm themselves on the principle that a big beast, and more particularly a dangerous one, requires a heavy bullet and the great shock such a bullet gives to the system to disable it or kill it, and not to allow themselves to be carried away with the idea that a .450 Express bullet is good enough for anything. There is no doubt whatever that the very largest and toughest of game can be killed by a .450 or .500 Express, and there are several well known and very experienced sportsmen who use nothing else. But as it is more than probable that the majority of those men who use, and advocate the use of, small rifles for all kinds of big game used heavy rifles when they first began and while learning by experience what they now know of the habits of the beasts, their anatomy, and their most vital spots, I should recommend beginners to use what these experienced hunters began with, that is, heavy rifles for big game . . . Approaching a beast which is quite unconscious of the stalker's presence . . . is rarely, if ever, dangerous; but following the blood spoor of a wounded buffalo, rhinoceros, or elephant into places where there is little chance of seeing the beast excepting at close quarters is quite another thing. A large bore, spherical bullet driven by plenty of powder, even if it should not strike a vital spot, will inflict such a tremendous shock that the creature is far less likely to charge than when hit with a small bullet.

The following is the battery used by myself and it is one which I have found satisfactory:

A single 4 bore rifle, weighing twenty-one pounds, sighted for 50, 100 and 150 yards, shooting 12 drams of powder and a spherical bullet.

A double 8 bore rifle, weighing fifteen pounds, sighted for 100 and 200 yards, shooting 12 drams of powder and a spherical bullet.

A double .500 Express, sighted for 100 and 200 yards, bored for the long bottle-shaped cases, "Magnum" shooting 6 drams of powder and long bullets of three kinds, solid, small-hole, and copper tube.

Lt. Col. H. G. C. Swayne, when engaged in one of his exploring and surveying trips with his brother in British Somaliland in 1885 was mauled by a lioness that charged him after it had been wounded. The lioness came at him so fast and so low to the ground, that, although he was able to fire both barrels of his .577, the last at five yards, he missed with both since the triggers were so stiff that he pulled both shots beneath the charging beast. After the lioness had seized him by the shoulder and was worrying him like a cat with a rat, his brother ran up and shot her from about five yards. He used the .577 on all heavy game but was getting much interested in the .303 Lee-Metford of which he had one of the army models and had this to say about it:

When after thick-skinned game, such as elephant or rhino, I think the Lee-Metford would be a useful rifle, provided a quiet head shot could be obtained with the animal standing still, both barrels of the double eight-bore being kept in reserve for use if it should get into motion. Although I have always believed in large bore rifles, I think there is a great future in store for the very small bores of the Lee-Metford class, having a long bullet and plenty of powder. Although the section is so small, the great remaining velocity of the Lee-Metford bullet causes a considerable shock to the animal, especially if the latter has been standing end on, and the bullet has raked forward for some distance. I consider the Lee-Metford about the best rifle for oryx shooting in uninhabited country, and have in my latter trips had great success with it. I used the ordinary military cartridge.

This ordinary military cartridge may have been the so-called Dum Dum cartridge which had been made with a thin nosed envelope or metal-case by the Indiana Government at Dum-Dum Arsenal near Calcutta for use on the Afridi tribesmen because the normal metal cased bullet went through but did not stop them.

Even in India hunters adopted the medium bores reluctantly. Others trying the hollow-pointed Express bullets which flattened or flew to pieces on horns or bone went back to the heavier bores. The most interesting arguments are from F. W. F. Fletcher, a tea planter in South India, and Major Glasfurd of the Indian Army in North India. Fletcher comments about his choice of rifles:

For some time I used a .577 but I ultimately discarded it in favor of the Magnum .500. I found that the latter, though taking a lighter bullet, was quite as effective as the heavier rifle for all purposes for which an Express could be legitimately used, and in it the principle of the Express —a large charge of powder behind a light bullet—was more fully developed that in any other rifle of this class . . . For years, I used the 340 grain bullet for deer, and the 440 grain for dangerous animals, but eventually I adopted the latter for universal use as the lighter bullet propelled by the heavy powder charge flew to pieces almost on impact, and occasionally this resulted in unduly low penetration. Both my Expresses were built by Messrs. J. & W. Tolley, and better weapons of their class it would be impossible to find. The double rifle in especial was perfect in every way—very strongly built with lever-under-guard action, wonderfully accurate, and so well balanced that even with a charge of six drams and a bittock (the utmost charge the bottle necked .577-.500 case will contain) the recoil was no heavier than that of a shotgun. This rifle I have still, and after a constant and faithful service of sixteen years it is as good today in every respect as when it left the maker's hands . . . Then I bought a .450 high velocity rifle by Messrs. Westley Richards. A very short experience with this rifle convinced me that all I had heard and read of the superiority of the cordite rifle over the black powder rifle was true, and that the latter was doomed. Parting with an old and tried friend is always painful, and it was not without regret that I put my Magnum .500 permanently on the shelf; but there was no gainsaying the fact that the .450 cordite was in every way far superior to my old love. The first three shots I fired from the new purchase were at sambur stags, and a single bullet sufficed for each. Soon afterwards I had an opportunity of trying it on bison. The first bull collapsed with a bullet through the neck; but anxious to do justice to my old shooting tools I did not accept this as convincing proof of the cordite rifle's superior powers, for, I said to myself, a solid bullet from the Express and "a fortiori," a conical from the 8 bore, would have been just as deadly. But when, a day or two afterwards, a second bull hit through the body went down all of a heap, I had to confess that my black-powder rifles must take a back seat.

Encouraged by my experience with the .450, I invested in a .600 high velocity rifle by Jeffery.   Of the tremendous power of this rifle, it is scarcely possible to convey an adequate conception on paper; but some idea of its capabilities may be gained from the statement that it has a striking energy of 8,700 foot-pounds against about 7,000 in a 4 bore with fourteen drams of black powder.   Only a rash man would prophesy in these days of rapid change and incessant invention, but it is difficult to conceive that a more powerful weapon than this can ever be built to be fired from the shoulder.   In cold blood the recoil from this rifle is somewhat severe, but in the excitement of shooting it is not noticeable— certainly not deterrent even to a man of ordinary physique.   Its smashing power, by which phrase I mean its power of disabling with even a badly placed body shot, is enormous; to hit is to bag.   By its introduction, the old heavy 4 and 8 bores have been swept clean out of the field.

This .600 rifle fired a 900 grain bullet at 1,950 foot-seconds in a sixteen to seventeen-pound double rifle, with about 100 foot-pounds of recoil.   Only three hunters mentioned in this series of articles have used such a gun.   The second was a Mr. Carl Larsen of Portuguese East Africa, whose record was some fifty-two elephants with the weapon.   It must have been murder both ways to shoot five lions with seven shots as he is reported to have done on another occasion.   The third man to carry a .600 was P. H. G. Powell-Cotton on one trip to Africa.

Another Indian sportsman with interesting comment on rifles was Sir Nigel Woodyatt, for forty years an officer in the Indian Army.   He started with black powder weapons, tried and liked the .303 but ended up shooting a high velocity medium bore:

I have had many rifles both single and double-barreled as well as magazine weapons.   The first was a single .450, then a double-barrelled .500 Express, both burning black powder.   These were followed later by a D. B. .303 cordite rifle by Fraser of Edinburgh, which was the handiest weapon I ever used.   Then came high velocity nitro rifles with tremendous power, and fairly low trajectory.   Taking the case of the sportsman who can only run to one rifle, I cannot recommend anything better for general shooting than a double-barreled .400 cordite rifle by W. J. Jeffery taking his .450-.400 3 inch cartridge.

The last one I had of this make did me extraordinarily well, and I was extremely sorry to part with it.   It helped me, by the aid of some luck, to create a sort of record.   The *last eight shots I fired out of it* killed eight animals, namely, two panther, one bear, four ghoral (chamois) and one khakur (barking deer).   Its weight (10 to 10½ lbs.) is a bit heavy to carry about in the hills, but it is wonderful how one gets used to it.

It is very nice to have a single barrel smaller bore for stalking in the Himalayas, say a .360 with an aperture back-sight weighing about 7 lbs. Some sportsmen shoot with a magazine, but I do not recommend it at all, especially for a beginner. *A great deal of harm is done with the small bore magazine rifles.* Fellows lose their heads and fire an enormous number of shots. This is detrimental to their shooting, and very detrimental to the poor game. Unless a vital spot is hit, the animal may easily appear untouched, and get away. Moreover, with so small a bullet propelled with such a high velocity a very small hole is made. This means that there is very little blood indeed sometimes none at all.

Woodyatt discarded the .303 double gun when two shots from it, well placed, failed to kill a tiger, and sent it back to England to be sold and replaced by a .450-400 double rifle. He was sorry afterward since the .303 only brought three pounds when sold.

Major A. I. R. Glasfurd has some excellent comment on the medium bores in his book entitled *Rifle and Romance in the Indian Jungle,* although his experience comes rather late in the history of medium bore ascendancy:

That the new weapons, when properly constructed, can be perfectly satisfactory under Indian conditions is proved by the fact that the writer, in practice and in shikar, has fired over 600 rounds from his (.400-55-400 hammerless top snap action) under all climatic conditions of the plains of India, using it with perfect results against almost every kind of game there is to be found. The breech, action, and barrels are as true and tight as when received from the makers, and the weapon except for slight wear to the browning is not to be known from a new weapon . . . No satisfactory truly all-around rifle yet exists; after that a choice of weapon rests largely with the sportsman himself . . . If he can handle it, the bigger the bore the better for close jungle work. For ponderous game, the medium bore cordite comes in first favorite. For dangerous soft skinned game, at close ranges, the rifled ball-and-shot gun, not smaller than 12 bore if used with a really suitable bullet. For long sporting ranges, shooting at harmless game, on hill or plain, the .303 as giving rather better killing power than the smaller bores. In these three we have succeeded in reducing to the minimum a long list of weapons.

The thirty-six hunters representing the period of medium-bore rifles from 1875 to 1892 carried in their careers a total of one hundred twenty two rifles from 4-bore to .256 (this after its advent in 1893). Twenty of these were large bores from 4 to 12 bore, sixty-six were medium bores .600 down to .40 caliber, and thirty-six were small bores of .38 caliber and under, and most of these, of course, were used after 1892.

APPENDIX B

PART II—1875 to 1892—The Medium Bores

NAME	WHEN	WHERE
28 St. George Littledale	1874	North America
"	1875-1876	India
"	1887-1889	Russia-Asia
"	1890-1891	Europe
"	1892-1895	Central Asia
29 Sir Edmund Loder	1874-1875	India-Sumatra
"	1876-1877	North Africa
"	1887-1888	North America
"	1891-1896	Europe-North Africa
"	1906-1907	East Africa
30 John R. Cook	1874-1878	North America
31 S. J. Stone	1875-1895	India-Tibet
32 Theodore S. Van Dyke	1875-1902	North America
33 C. E. M. Russell	1876-1896	India
34 Wm. T. Hornaday	1876-1877	India-Malaya
"	1886-1906	United States-Canada
"	1907-1908	Mexico
35 Col. William D. Pickett	1876-1883	North America
36 Clive Phillips-Wolley	1876-1877	North America
"	1878-1886	Europe-Russia
"	1887-1893	North America
37 Sir Henry Seton-Karr	1877-1889	Europe-Asia
"	1886-1898	North America
38 George O. Shields	1878-1887	North America
39 L. L. Dyche	1879-1891	North America
40 Maj. C. S. Cumberland	1880-1910	India-Central Asia
"	1911-1912	East Africa
41 Edouard Foa	1880-1890	North Africa
"	1891-1900	Central Africa

APPENDIX B

1875 to 1892—The Medium Bores

ANIMALS HUNTED	RIFLES USED
28 Elk, Sheep, Bear, Deer	.500 DB Henry
Tiger, Bison, Sambur, Markhor,Ibex, Sheep	.500 DB Henry
Bison, Bear, Poli, Yak	.500 DB Henry
Bison, Bear, Chamois	.500 DB Henry
Yak, Sheep, Ibex	.256 Roum. Mannl.*, .256 Mannl. Schon.
29 Tiger, Rhino, Bison, Sambur, Markhor	8 bore DB Reilly, 12 bore DB Reilly*
Moufflon, Gazelle	12 bore DB Reilly, .450 DB Express*
Elk, Sheep, Goat, Buffalo	.450 DB Express
Moufflon, Chamois, Ibex, Gazelle	256 Roum Mannlicher*
Rhino, Buffalo, Antelope	.256 Mannl.
30 Buffalo, Bear, Deer, Antelope	.577 SS Enfield, .44 SS Sharps*, .44-40 Win.
31 Yak, Bear, Sheep, Markhor, Ibex	.450 SS Henry*, .500 and 450 DB Henry, .50-110 Winchester
32 Elk, Bear, Deer	.40-60 Winchester
33 Elephant, Tiger, Bison, Bear, Sambur	4 bore DB Dixon, 12 bore DB Holland*, .500 DB Holland
34 Elephant, Tiger, Bison, Sambur	Ml 8 bore DB Westley, .40-70 SS Maynard*
Buffalo, Moose, Elk, Bear, Sheep, Goat	.40-70 SS Maynard, .303 Savage, .405 Win.*
Sheep, Deer	.303 Savage, .405 Win.*
35 Bear, Elk, Sheep	.45-102 SS Sharps, .45-90 SS Sharps*
36 Elk, Sheep, Goat, Bear	12 bore DB Paradox, .450 DB Express*
Bison, Bear, Deer, Ibex, Chamois	12 bore DB Paradox, .450 DB Express*
Moose, Elk, Bear, Sheep	12 bore DB Paradox, .450 DB Express*
37 Elk, Moufflon, Goat, Antelope	.500 DB Purdey, .400 DB Purdey*
Elk, Deer, Antelope, Goat	.500 DB Purdey, .256 Mannlicher*
Buffalo, Elk, Bear, Sheep, Goat, Deer	.32-35 SS Stevens, .45-75 Win., .40-75 SS Sharps*
39 Moose, Elk, Bear, Sheep, Goat, Antelope	.45-100 SS Sharps, .40-75 SS Rem., .40-82 Winchester*
40 Tiger, Bison, Yak, Sheep, Markhor, Ibex	12 bore DB Dougal, .500 DB Henry*, .303 Lee Metford
Elephant, Lion, Antelope	.500 DB Henry*, .303 Lee Metford
41 Moufflon, Gazelle, Antelope	8 bore DB, .577 DB Galand
Elephant, Lion, Rhino, Buffalo, Antelope	.577 DB Galand, .303 DB Lee Metford*

* The asterisk indicates the favorite rifle.

1875-1892—The Medium Bores

NAME	WHEN	WHERE
42 Edward North Buxton	1881-1890	Sardinia-N. Africa
"	1891-1892	N. America
"	1893-1897	Europe, Asia Minor
"	1898-1901	North Africa
43 William H. Wright	1893-1909	N. America
44 Theodore Roosevelt	1883-1907	N. America
"	1908-1910	East Africa
"	1911-1912	N. America
"	1913-1914	S. America
45 F. Vaughan Kirby	1884-1899	S. E. Africa
"	1900-1903	Central Africa
46 Lt. Col. H. G. C. Swayne	1884-1897	Somaliland
"	1898-1927	India
47 Frederick J. Jackson	1884-1891	East Africa
48 Sir Nigel Woodyatt	1884-1922	India
49 Stewart Edward White	1884-1909	N. America
"	1909-1914	East Africa
"	1924-1925	East Africa
50 Digby Davies	1885-1915	India-Africa
51 John B. Burnham	1887-1893	N. America
"	1898-1900	Alaska
"	1905-1906	Mexico
"	1919-1921	Siberia-Alaska
52 W. S. Thom	1887-1900	Burma
53 Maj. N. H. Roberts	1887-1934	N. America
54 Bryan H. Williams	1888-1924	British Columbia
55 Warburton Pike	1889-1891	Canada
56 Richard J. Cunninghame	1889-1924	East Africa

1875-1892—The Medium Bores

ANIMALS HUNTED	RIFLES USED
42 Moufflon, Antelope	.500 DB Express
Elk, Sheep, Bear	.500 DB Express
Ibex, Chamois, Moufflon	.500 DB Express, .256 Mannlicher*
Lion, Rhino, Antelope	.500 DB Express, .256 Mannlicher*
43 Grizzly Bear	.45-100 SS Win.*, .44-40 Win., .30-30 Win.
44 Buffalo, Elk, Bear, Sheep, Deer	.40-90 SS Sharps, .45-75 Win., .45-90 Win.*, .30-30 Winchester
Elephant, Lion, Rhino, Buffalo, Antelope	.450 DB Holland, .405 Winchester*, .30-06 Springfield
Moose, Bear, Cougar, Wolves	.30-06 Springfield*
Tapir, Deer, Agouti	.30-06 Springfield*
45 Lion, Rhino, Leopard, Buffalo, Antelope	.500 SS Westley-R., .450 SS Gibbs*
Elephant, Lion, Rhino, Buffalo, Antelope	.450 SS Gibbs*
46 Lion, Elephant, Rhino, Antelope	8 and 12 bore Paradox, .577 DB Holland*, .450 Martini, .303 Lee Metford
Elephant, Tiger, Sambur	.577 DB Holland*, .303 Lee Metford
47 Elephant, Lion, Rhino, Buffalo, Antelope	8 bore DB, 10 bore DB*, .500 DB Express, .450 SS Express
48 Tiger, Bison, Bear, Panther, Markhor, Ibex	.500 DB Jeffrey, .303 DB Fraser, .400 DB Jeffrey*, .280 Ross
49 Elk, Bear, Sheep, Goat, Deer	.44-40 Win., .30-30 Win., 30-40 Win.*
Elephant, Lion, Rhino, Buffalo, Antelope	.465 DB Holland, .405 Win., .30-06 Springfield*
Lion, Buffalo	.465 DB Holland, .405 Win., .30-06 Springfield*
50 Elephant, Tiger, Lion, Bison, Bear, Antelope	10 bore DB Dickson, 10 bore Paradox, .500 DB Rigby*, .303 Lee Metford
51 Moose, Deer, Antelope	.40-82 Winchester
Moose, Bear, Caribou, Sheep	.40-65 Winchester
Sheep	.30-30 Winchester
Sheep, Walrus	.35 Newton
52 Elephant, Tiger, Rhino, Bison, Sambur	8 bore DB Westley, 12 bore DB Dickson*, .450 Martini, .303 Lee Metford
53 Moose, Caribou, Bear, Deer	.40-60 Win., .44-40 Win., .38-55 Marlin*, .30-40 Krag, 7mm Mauser
54 Moose, Caribou, Bear, Sheep, Goat	.45-90 Winchester*
55 Moose, Caribou, Muskox	12 bore Paradox, .50-95 Winchester*
56 Elephant, Lion, Rhino, Buffalo, Antelope	.465 DB Holland*, .450 DB Express, .30-06 Springfield

* The asterisk indicates the favorite rifle.

1875-1892—The Medium Bores

NAME	WHEN	WHERE
57 F. W. F. Fletcher	1890-1909	Southern India
58 Capt. Beverly W. Robinson	1891-1922	North America
59 Capt. A. I. R. Glasfurd	1891-1906	India
60 Leslie Tarlton	1891-1926	East Africa
61 Harry Storey	1891-1906	Ceylon
62 Carl Larsen	1892-1909	Portuguese East Africa
63 Caspar Whitney	1892-1895	North America
"	1903-1905	Sumatra-Malaya
"	1910-1911	South America

1875-1892—The Medium Bores

ANIMALS HUNTED	RIFLES USED
57 Elephant, Tiger, Bison, Bear, Sambur, Ibex	.500 and 400 DB Tolley, 12 Paradox, .450 DB Westley, .600 DB Jeffery*
58 Elk, Sheep, Goat, Bear, Moose, Caribou, Antelope	.45-90 Win., .30-40 Win., .30-06 Spr.*
59 Tiger, Panther, Bear, Bison, Sambur	.577 DB Holl., .450 DB Rigby, .400 DB Jeffery*, .276 Mauser; .303 Lee
60 Elephant, Lion, Rhino, Buffalo, Antelope	.465 DB Holland, .276 Rigby*, .350 Rigby, .30-06 Springfield
61 Elephant, Buffalo, Elk, Panther, Bear, Deer	12 bore Paradox, .303 SS Lee, .303 Lee M., .303 Savage*
62 Elephant, Lion, Rhino, Antelope	.600 DB Jeffery*
63 Moose, Caribou, Muskox	.45-90 Win.*
Tiger, Rhino, Seladang, Panther	12 bore DB, .50-110 Win.,* .45-90 Win.
Tapir, Jaguar, Deer, Agouti	9mm Mannlicher*

* The asterisk indicates the favorite rifle.

1875-1892—Summary of Medium Bore Rifles

LARGE BORES			USED BY	TOTAL
ML	8	DB	34	1
BL	4	DB	33	1
	8	DB	29, 41, 47, 52	4
	10	DB	47, 50	2
	12	DB	29, 33, 40, 52, 63	5
Paradox	8	DB	46	1
	10	DB	50	1
	12	DB	36, 46, 55, 57, 61	5
Total				20

MEDIUM BORES	USED BY	TOTAL
.600 DB	57, 62	2
.577 DB	41, 46, 59	3
.577 SS	30	1
.500 DB	28, 31, 33, 37, 40, 42, 47, 48, 50, 57	10
.500 SS	45	1
.50-110 Win.	31, 55, 63	3
.465 DB	49, 56, 60	3
.450 DB	29, 31, 36, 44, 56, 57, 59	7
.450 SS	31, 45, 46, 47, 52	5
.45-102 SS	35, 39, 43	3
.45-90 Win.	44, 54, 58, 63	4
.45-90 SS	35	1
.45-75 Win.	38, 44	2
.44-40 Win.	30, 43, 49, 53	4
.44 SS Sharps	30	1
.405 Win	34, 44, 49	3
.400 DB	37, 48, 57, 59	4
.40-90 SS	44	1
.40-82 Win.	39, 51	2
.40-75 SS	38, 39	2
.40-65 Win.	51	1
.40-60 Win.	32, 53	2
.40-70 Maynard	34	1
Total		66

1875-1892—Summary of Medium Bore Rifles

SMALL BORES	USED BY	TOTAL
.38-55 Marlin	53	1
9 mm	63	1
.350 Rigby	60	1
.35 Newton	51	1
.32-35 Stevens	38	1
.303 DB Lee	41, 48	2
.303 Lee	40, 46, 50, 52, 59, 61	6
.303 SS Lee	61	1
.303 Sav.	34, 61	2
.30-30 Win.	43, 44, 49, 51	4
.30-40 Krag	53	1
.30-40 Win.	49, 58	2
.30-06 Spr.	44, 49, 56, 58, 60	5
.280 Ross	48	1
7 mm Mauser	53, 59, 60	3
.256 Mannl.	28, 29, 37, 42	4
Total		36

SUMMARY

Large bores	20
Medium bores	66
Small bores	36
Total Rifles	122

Hunters—36 Rifles per hunter—3.4

PART III
THE SMALL BORES
1893 TO 1905

CHAPTER 5

SMOKELESS POWDER RIFLES

*F*ROM the time of the monk Roger Bacon in 1249 the propellant in firearms had been black powder or just 'gunpowder' made by an intimate mixture of charcoal (to burn and form gas) sulphur (to keep the heat down) and a nitrate, usually of potassium (to furnish oxygen for quick burning). The only improvements in this material in six hundred years had been in the purity of the chemicals, better charcoal from willow trees, and the size of the powder grains, small or large, to burn fast or slow. The result of ignition in black powder was a burning process in which the expansion of gas carried with it the burning grains which might or might not be consumed within the barrel. Theoretically the small-bore, long-barreled rifle of the Kentucky type was the most efficient weapon, but the bullet, which could be used from such a rifle, was too small to be effective on large game. And the fouling was so great that it required wiping after every few shots or the barrel might burst. This wiping was possible with the muzzle loader, because the ramrod was always available, but with the breech loader such frequent cleaning was impossible. The progress from the 4-bore down to the Express rifles had been all to the good, but apparently the limit of bore diameter, bullet weight, powder charge, barrel length and effective accuracy and power had been reached at .400 caliber or at what we now consider the upper limit of the small bore.

Something faster, of less bulk and weight, with very little residue, was needed in the way of a propellant for the rifle if the trend toward smaller bores was to be continued. The advantages of the cheaper manufacture of rifles, of the discovery of new game fields with the spread of civilization, and of the improvements in transportation, were now available to everyone. But the ordinary sportsman did not have the money to hunt in the grand manner, with a battery of rifles carried by gunbearers. He of necessity carried his own rifle, and in many cases his entire outfit on his back. He might be interested in 10 bore double guns, but, like the backwoodsmen, he was compelled to use the small bore of light weight using light-weight ammunition.

Smokeless powder was invented by a French government chemist, Vielle, in 1885. In England Nobel and Sir Frederick Abel were at work at the time on similar explosives derived from gun cotton, which culminated in the powder Cordite used by the English in military and sporting cartridges for years. Smokeless powder was made by the nitration of cellulose, and Cordite by the nitration of glycerine. The product in both cases was dissolved in alcohol, dried and forced into cords or cut into grains. The "nitro" powder from glycerine, such as Ballistite and Cordite, was somewhat faster, hotter, but not considered as stable, while nitrocellulose powder was slower and cooler. With later improvements, nitrocellulose powder, as used in American and Continental ammunition seems the more preferable, permitting, with certain surface retardants, a better control of pressures and heat. In order that one does not get the idea that smokeless powder was considered entirely perfect, the following from *Notes on Sporting Rifles* by Major Gerald Burrard is of interest:

Black powder rifles possess some further advantages over cordite rifles which should not be forgotten. First the case of cleaning. There is no acid fouling from nitro-powder (in the black powder rifle) to eat into the precious barrels—a great boon when one comes in dead beat in the hot weather. It is on account of this freedom from all liability to corrosion that the barrels of a second-hand black powder rifle will probably be in far better condition than those of a second-hand cordite rifle. Few sportsmen, I should imagine, would allow rust to enter the insides of their rifle barrels, the sole danger to the black-powder Express; but there are also few who really understand how to clean a cordite rifle and avoid corrosion.

Secondly the barrels are not nearly so tapered, and consequently there is no high foresight block. When sitting up in a bad light, or when taking a hurried snap, one is much more inclined to shoot high with a pair of tapered barrels than with the more gun-like barrels of an Express.

Finally, the propellant itself is more reliable in a hot climate. Cordite is greatly affected by changes of temperature, shooting high when hot; and it also deteriorates if kept. Black powder is unaffected by climate as long as it is kept dry—no great difficulty—and seems to keep forever. I once came across some old .577 Express cartridges in a gun-case belonging to an uncle. They had been there for forty years. Out of curiosity I took them to Messrs. Holland and Holland and asked them to test them. The cartridges were found to be quite alright, and gave excellent groups, but

HAMMERLESS 8-BORE ELEPHANT RIFLE WITH 22-INCH BARREL, WEIGHING 13 POUNDS. UNUSUALLY LIGHT FOR THIS CALIBER.

The illustration is evidently a Greener custom job and is from his book *The Gun and its Development*.

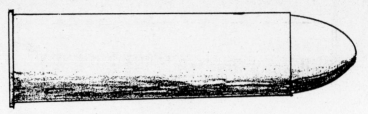

8-BORE RIFLE, BLACK POWDER.

12-BORE RIFLE, BLACK POWDER.

12-BORE PARADOX, BALL AND SHOT GUN.

.600 CORDITE EXPRESS (JEFFERY).

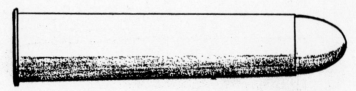

.577 BLACK POWDER OR CORDITE EXPRESS.

.500 CORDITE EXPRESS.

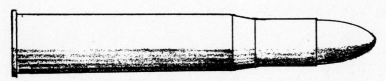

.470 CORDITE EXPRESS.

.465 NITRO EXPRESS (HOLLAND).

.450 CORDITE EXPRESS.

.416 RIGBY MAGNUM MAUSER.

.500 JEFFERY MAGNUM.

.50-110 WINCHESTER.

.45-90 WINCHESTER.

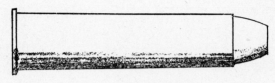

.405 WINCHESTER MODEL 1895.

.400 CORDITE EXPRESS.

FEMALE ELEPHANT ABOUT TO CHARGE.

From Edouard Foa's After Big Game in Central Africa.

FREDERICK VAUGHAN KIRBY. RANCHER, BIG GAME HUNTER AND AUTHOR.

From his book *In Haunts of Wild Game.*

9.3MM or 10.75MM MAUSER WITH 24-INCH BARREL.

From Mauser catalogue.

PAUL MAUSER, 1838-1914.
FATHER OF THE BOLT ACTION
RIFLE.

From *Mauser Rifles and Pistols*
by W. H. B. Smith.

WILHELM MAUSER 1834-1882.
SALESMAN EXTRAORDINARY.

From *Mauser Rifles and Pistols*
by W. H. B. Smith.

CHARLES M. SPENCER, FAMOUS EARLY AMERICAN
REPEATING RIFLE MAKER.

Picture discovered through courtesy of Mrs. Arline G. Maver,
Curator Connecticut State Historical Library.

I would never have used them against game in case the caps had deteriorated.

Of course, the matter of acid fouling and of powder deterioration has been a matter of research and improvement and is no longer the problem it was when smokeless was first invented. This matter of deterioration will be commented on later in connection with the actual field experiences in African hunting but one might remark that if Major Burrard "would never have used them (black powder cartridges) against game in case the caps had deteriorated," the superior permanence of black powder was not important. The real improvements due to smokeless powder were more important than these lesser evils. Its invention concurrent with the invention of the metal-cased bullet by Major Rubin of the Swiss Army in 1888 permitted the introduction of small bore rifles of high-power, for both military and sporting use. This is well presented in the following quotation from that most excellent of books on military rifle development, the *British Textbook of Small Arms*:

It was not long before the merits of the .303 inch and .256 inch cartridges became known to sportsmen, and all but the more conservative quickly became conscious of the advantages conferred by absence of smoke, light weight, and error-absorbing qualities of low trajectory at ranges outside the scope of the most efficient black powder expresses. These advantages were no less appreciated by the more progressive rifle makers, who, conscious also of limitations as regards stopping power against dangerous game, sought to make good this palpable deficiency by means other than bullet design. In place of the old 8, 10 and 12 bore rifles, .577 inch, .500 inch, .450 inch, .400 inch and .360 inch expresses now stands a range of weapons using cartridges which combine the advantages of absence of smoke, sustainable recoil, and lowness of trajectory over sporting ranges, with adequate bullet weight and enormous smashing power.

The above refers to the .303 inch Lee Metford and the .256 inch or 6.5 millimeter Dutch or Roumanian Mannlicher, but there were soon developed a host of rifles and calibers about which the same could be said. The French Lebel of 8 millimeters, the German Mauser of 7.9 millimeters, the American Winchester .30-30 and the Krag .30-40 U. S. Government cartridges were all available but it was the economical .303 English and 6.5 millimeter Dutch military rifles at about 80 shillings of $16 complete with bayonet that St. George Littledale, Sir Edmund Loder, Sir

Henry Halford and John Rigby began using on the target range and later for deer-stalking and other big game. These advantages of the smallbore and smokeless powder are somewhat differently described in the *Book of the Rifle* by T. F. Fremantle, later Lord Cottesloe, as follows:

It was not for some little time after the adoption of the .303 that the labors of Nobel, supplemented by those of Sir Frederick Abel and others, produced the smokeless explosive known as cordite, which has ever since been used in the cartridges made for the Government arm. The development of smokeless powders is a special subject which does not fall within the scheme of the present work. They are much more powerful, weight for weight, than black powder. For instance, the charge of cordite for the .303 rifle weighs from 30 to 31 grains, but it is equivalent in propelling power to the old charge of 85 grains of black powder used in the Martini-Henry rifle. Smokeless powder, too, is much smaller in bulk, and whereas the cartridge would contain no more than 70 grains of black powder even when heavily compressed into a pellet, the much more powerful charge of cordite leaves a very considerable air space behind the bullet. The use of smokeless powder, and of compound bullets with a hard envelope usually either of a mixture of nickel and copper, as in the British rifle or of steel faced with a thin plate of nickel, is general in the military arms of the present day . . . The pressure of the explosion forces it (the bullet) into the barrel under heavy stress, and it is effectually fitted to the grooving, so that the gases are sealed from escaping past it. So complete is the sealing when this principle is properly carried out that with most modern rifles of this class there seems little or no advantage in interposing a wad between the powder and the bullet. It will thus be seen that the principle of the expanding bullet, upon which so much care and invention was bestowed, and which solved the problem of accuracy and rapid loading in muzzle loaders and breech loaders has been entirely departed from in the new class of military weapons.

St. George Littledale in a letter to Denis Lyell written in 1926 described how he came to use the .256 Mannlicher rifle and his experience with this rifle in the Magnum variety which was probably the Gibbs Magnum:

In 1895 Sir Edmund Loder gave me a Mannlicher rifle, bayonet and all complete on the eve of starting for Tibet. Had only time to have sighting altered. On my protesting that I had a room full of rifles and did not want any more, all he said was try the Mannlicher, and like Lily Langtry and the soap, I have used no other since.

In my opinion the original Mannlicher was more deadly by far than either the Schonauer or the Magnum. Speaking from memory, and it is a long time ago, I got the first 40 or 50 animals I fired at without requiring a second bullet at any of them.

With the Magnum I fired at a stag at about 200 yards, it never moved and the stalker said: "You are over his shoulder." He did not move so I fired again with some irritation. The stalker said "You are over him again." So I fired with undisguised disgust. He said "over again," so I brought the rifle down and looked at the sights, making sure they must have been shifted. While looking at them the stalker said: "He's down." A half crown would have covered the three bullet holes, and what the gillie saw were the bullets striking after they had gone through the heart. The Magnum is a wonderful accurate weapon and I consider it adds a couple of hundred yards to the distance at which beasts can be shot, but is that an advantage, very questionable.

In the old days of "Express" rifles the cream of the sport was the crawl from 200 yards to one hundred. That is all over now, and so I am afraid is my big game shikar.

The most familiar type of big-game hunting in the British Isles was that of deer-stalking in Scotland, and the following quotation from *Big Game Shooting* in the *Country Life Library of Sport* published in 1905 describes the change in rifles for that sport:

It is not many years since the best weapon for deer-stalking was an Express rifle of .450 caliber firing a heavy charge of black powder. The winning rifle of this type in the Field Trials of 1884 was made by Messrs. Holland. Its bullet weighted 322 grs. and its velocity at the muzzle was 1,776 feet per second. Its striking energy was thus 2,254 foot-pounds at the beginning of the flight. At 150 yards its remaining velocity was 1,335 feet per second, giving a striking energy of 1,274 foot-pounds— amply sufficient, if expended in the right place, to do the work required. This represents a very much higher power than was available in muzzle loading rifles of similar caliber. The tendency to reduce the bore led to the development of the .400 Express while black powder was still in the ascendant. This was an excellent rifle for stalking, although it did not come very largely into use.

The adoption within the last twenty years, for military purposes, of rifles of a calibre of 8 millimeters (.315 inch) or less was made possible by the progress made in the manufacture of smokeless propellants. Thus it is that the deer-stalker of today has discarded black powder rifles in favor of such weapons as the .303, the .275 Mauser, and the .256 Mannlicher. These all have a flatter trajectory than the old Express rifle, and are, therefore, effective at a longer distance. Their accuracy is greater. Their ammunition is lighter, though this, as regards stalking in these islands, is but a small point. They have not the heavy recoil which made the express rifle so unpleasant to the firer. There is no cloud of smoke to advertise to the quarry the direction from which the shot has come or to hamper the rapid discharge of successive shots.

But all these rifles were magazine rifles which was a far cry from the English double rifle type. Their growing popularity needs some explanation. The magazine rifle was an American invention starting with the Spencer, the Henry, the Winchester and the Lee rifles. It had been adopted by France and Germany in the seventies in their tubular magazined repeating rifles of 11 millimeter bore. But Lee's box magazine appealed to the Continental military authorities in the eighties when the calibers were being reduced to 8 millimeters for the Mauser and Lebel, and this influenced its adoption by England for the Lee-Metford. The lighter weight of rifle and cartridge and the increased speed of fire permitted by the absence of smoke made a magazine possible and necessary. The cheapness of such rifles made by machinery and their improved accuracy brought them to the attention of the rifle shooting sportsmen in England. The double rifle had never been considered of any value for target work while these newer military rifles were remarkable. The reasons for this popularity are described by L. R. Tippins in his book *Modern Rifle Shooting for Peace, War and Sport* as follows:

Many men especially those who are used to a shotgun prefer a double sporting rifle. But those who are in the habit of making fine target shooting with a single rifle, find their ideas of accuracy much too advanced for many makers and sellers of double rifles. Some makers of rifles cannot make a really accurate double, but will wear out a pair of barrels trying to adjust them. Double rifles good enough to hit a foot bull at 200 yards with the same aim with each barrel are extremely scarce. Double rifles have now to compete with magazine rifles and on the whole the latter are getting the better of them for work requiring real power and great accuracy.

It follows that correctly adjusted double rifles must cost a good deal of money, and only rich men can afford the price. It is far beyond the means of a man who has to earn the money he spends.

Fremantle who has already been quoted gives additional reasons for this growing popularity of the single barrel rifle of high velocity and small bore over the double barrel rifle in the following written in 1901:

There is another reason which has aided in depriving the double rifle of its popularity. Formerly the weight necessary to control the recoil of the Express rifle was considerable, and a single rifle was almost necessarily heavier on this account than it needed to be for consideration of strength of breech action and barrel alone. The double rifle was therefore but little heavier than the single. At the present time with small caliber rifles of high velocity, the recoil is so small that the single rifle can be made much handier and lighter than the old Express, and consequently the double weapon involves proportionately more weight. It is never easy to adjust the barrels of a double rifle to shoot precisely together. The movement of recoil which begins before the bullet has left the barrel, affects the direction in which the bullet is delivered, and the barrels have to be set so as to very decidedly converge towards a point some little way in front of the muzzle, more especially when heavy charges are fired. The adjustment of the barrels is very capable of being disturbed by a blow or a strain.

He finally sums up the advantages of the small-bore as follows:

Just as with cordite, the same explosive composition is suitable for big guns or small rifles, the form into which it is being put being varied, so in these days, the same rifle and the same charge are suitable for game of very different kinds, if only the bullet be varied to suit the occasion. There is no other military rifle which has so great a penetrative power as the .256 Mannlicher, but yet if this rifle be fired with a lead-pointed bullet there is no more deadly weapon for soft skinned game of moderate size, such as deer, antelope, or mountain sheep. The .303 is almost its equal, although the trajectory is not quite so flat. The initial energy is curiously similar in the .303 and the .256, as they each give a little over 1900 foot-pounds. This energy, if it be rather less than that of the old Express rifles of larger bore than .4 is better maintained, owing to the greater comparative length of the bullet. It may be said that the development of smokeless powder and small calibres has added to the sportsman's battery an unequalled weapon for all-around work, handier to carry, quicker in loading, flatter in trajectory, and more accurate than any sporting arm before known.

Yet there were still sportsmen with a nostalgia for the black powder days and the beautiful double barreled express rifles of the seventies and eighties. This was more particularly among those at a distance from the center of rifle development and men with an investment in fine and expensive examples of the English rifle-making art. These men had long experience with their present weapons and were confident of their capability, while the newer smokeless powder rifles and more particularly the early cartridges, had been none to satisfactory in the hands of their friends. This attitude is reflected in the following statement by Major Burrard in his book already referred to:

The only real disadvantage of black powder weapons is the smoke, and this is certainly serious. All the same in hilly thorn jungle, I never noticed the smoke of my .577 firing 6 drams, although I cannot admit having fired many shots. In damp bamboo jungles the smoke would certainly be a serious drawback. This drawback has been overcome by the introduction of cartridges loaded with what is called "low pressure" cordite or axite for use in Express rifles. These cartridges are really loaded with a light charge of nitro powder. The air space in the cartridge being large, the pressure is low. The idea is neat, but is not altogether a success. The barrels of a double rifle are most carefully regulated for a certain charge of a particular propellant. If this is changed the barrels no longer shoot together. With my Holland .577 hammer rifle I could usually make a two-inch group at fifty yards when firing black powder, but the only occasion on which I tried modified cordite I failed to make a six inch group at that range.

But there were other ways in which the reduced loads of smokeless powder were not altogether successful. The reduction in pressure necessary for the barrels designed for black powder did not produce the power and accuracy expected, and, except for the absence of smoke, the black powder express rifles were still far inferior to the nitro or cordite expresses. As the latter were improved the inferiority of the older weapons became more pronounced until finally they disappeared, except as collectors items. Even in double barrel rifles the newer rifles with better steel, quicker twist, higher pressure, and velocity, were infinitely superior.

The one serious trouble with smokeless powder was that its greater heat rapidly eroded the barrel. This was far more serious in military rifles than in sporting weapons, and if coupled with lack of care could soon destroy the most perfect weapon. This danger, however, acted as a spur to further experiment with powders, steel and ignition, which have put the smokeless powder rifle far beyond any capabilities originally considered possible. These are subject matter for a later chapter and it will be sufficient here to list the early small bores and their characteristics giving as a necessary added identification, the make and date of rifle:

Make	Date	Caliber	Bullet	Velocity	Energy
Lebel	1886	8mm	231	2,073	2,200
Mauser	1888	7.9mm	227	2,000	2,020
Lee Metford	1889	.303 inch	215	1,960	1,834
Mauser	1889	7.65mm	219	2,034	2,010
Mauser	1892	7mm	173	2,288	2,010
Krag-Jorgensen	1892	.30 inch	220	2,066	2,085
Winchester	1892	.30-30	160	1,885	1,264
Mannlicher	1893	6.5mm	162	2,433	2,130
Mannlicher	1895	8mm	244	2,034	2,235
Lee	1895	.236 inch	135	2,396	1,492
Winchester	1895	.25-35	117	1,925	963
Savage	1895	.303 inch	190	1,840	1,353
Mauser	1898	7.9mm	236	2,100	1,890
Springfield	1903	.30 inch	220	2,204	2,474

CHAPTER 6

BIG GAME HUNTERS,
COLLECTORS, GUIDES

*I*T is difficult for an American to realize that although he has partici-
pated in the development of the present hunting rifle it is not an
American development. The bolt-action rifle which he uses so generally
today because of its strength and accuracy was of European origin, first
tested and tried in the game fields of Europe, Asia, and Africa. It was a
foregone conclusion that as the need arose for rifles of greater range and
accuracy than the hinged double barrel, these rifles would incorporate some
rigid-framed breech-action that would closely support the cartridge. This
was found in the single-shot falling-block action, of which we had several, and in the Mauser or Mannlicher turning bolt action, of which we
had none. Finding that the single and double rifles of 4 to 16 bore
which used round balls were greatly inferior to the medium bores which
used conical bullets, the rifleman was looking for further improvement.
This he found in the still smaller bores made possible by better steel,
smokeless powder, and jacketed bullets in the bolt- or falling-block action.

England had long had a falling-block action in the Farquharson, but
the bolt action came to them from the military weapons developed on the
Continent. In 1886 France adopted the Lebel of 8mm caliber, followed
by the German Model 88, a rifle with the Mannlicher bolt and magazine
and Mauser front lugs, and the English .303 Lee Metford in 1889. All
of these rifles were tried out on big game. The German and Austrian
rifles with the combination of the Lee box magazine and the Mauser front
locking lugs on the bolt proved most popular, especially when Mannlicher at Steyr produced a 6.5mm rifle for Holland and Roumania of this
type. Introduced to England for use on the range and at running deer
targets about 1892 by Sir Edmund Loder, Captain George Gibbs, rifle-
maker and superintendent of the government rifle factory at Enfield, and
St. George Littledale, who at Loder's insistence, had used the rifle in the
Caucasus, the Mannlicher became very popular. This was the military
type rifle using a flat full-clip magazine with 162 grain bullet at 2,400

feet per second in the cut-down twenty-five inch barrel. The rifles were reported to have cost thirty-two shillings apiece or eight to ten dollars from the factory in Steyr, or Liege, Belgium. In Austria the Schonauer type Mannlicher with short barrel and spool-type magazine was brought out about 1900 for chamois hunting, and was the model with which the American rifleman became acquainted.

Sir Alfred Pease, having hunted with Loder on several trips to the Atlas Mountains of North Africa, moved to a ranch at Nairobi, British East Africa in 1896 and took a Mannlicher along with him. His reasons for using this rifle are best stated in his *Book of the Lion*:

As to rifles I prefer to have one light handy rifle and a double-barreled ball and shotgun carried in reserve, when after lions. The rifle which has been my constant companion since 1892 is a rather short-barreled, five-shot magazine .256 Mannlicher; any apparent deficiency in size of bore and weight of bullet is compensated for in my opinion by the ease and rapidity with which it can be manipulated, the little room occupied by ammunition, the flatness of trajectory and the superiority of its striking energy over some of the larger bores. With the .256 I have killed many lions, as well as pachyderms, and antelopes from greater kudu downward, it is no weight to carry on foot or on horseback, and the mechanism is of the simplest and strongest kind; wet, sand, mud, tumbles, and croppers have never injured it, and a soft-nosed bullet or a "ratchet" hollow-point Fraser's bullet "sets up" so well that at times it makes a hole almost as big as one of nearly double its caliber. My gun bearer carries as a rule a very out of date weapon, namely, a double-barreled, 10 bore, ball and shot hammer gun, shooting black powder and a solid soft, solid hard, and hollow-point bullet; it is accurate up to 100 yards. It has always served its purpose well with me on lion, elephant and rhino and, though unwieldy, has done execution with small shot as well as with buckshot.

It would seem from the above that Sir Alfred was a two-gun man, but he speaks elsewhere of hunting with a double .400, a .303 army rifle, a .350 Rigby, and a .404 Jeffery at various times. Contemporary with Pease in East Africa were Dennis Lyell, James Sutherland, Lt. Col. J. H. Patterson of the *Maneaters of Tsavo* fame, W. D. M. Bell, Maj. C. H. Stigand, Blayney Percival, Lt. Col. J. S. Hamilton, Marcus Daly, Carl Akeley, Powell-Cotton, Kittenberger, and Frank Melland. All of these men used a small bore rifle regularly with a medium bore in reserve. Denis Lyell, author, ranchman, and student of game and hunting, has this to say in his book, *Hunting and Spoor of Central African Game*:

There were five rifles all about this weight (seven and one-quarter pounds) which did me very good service, and they were a .256 old pattern Mannlicher by Gibbs, two .275 Mausers by Rigby and Westley Richards, a 7.9mm (.311 bore) Mauser by Rigby, and a .303 falling block by Fraser. Should I be going to hunt in Africa still having the .256 I would just as soon use it as any other rifle, though according to my experience, the 7.9 was perhaps the best killing rifle of the five mentioned . . . The Mannlicher, Mannlicher Schoenauer, and Mauser bolt actions, are beautifully made, and are most ingenious mechanically, and I do not think any British bolt action can compare with any of them.

James Sutherland was an elephant hunter who did most of his hunting with a double .577 Westley-Richards, but used a .318 magazine rifle made on a Mauser action by Westley-Richards. The .577 used 100 grains of smokeless powder behind a 750 grain bullet. With this rifle he is reported to have killed 447 elephants. His comments on these weapons are as follows:

During my hunting career, I have used all kinds of rifles from the 4 bore, black powder elephant rifle downwards, but as the black powder rifle is a thing of the past, I shall confine my attention to the modern high velocity, smokeless powder rifles, which are infinitely superior to their predecessors on account of their greater range, velocity, power and lightness.

In the first place the man behind the rifle is so obviously of primary importance that the fact may be dismissed without further comment, while the great consideration in all hunting is to kill and not merely to wound the game fired at. With regard to the weapon, practically any modern rifle will kill game if the bullet penetrates a vital part such as the brain, heart or vertebrae, but under ordinary conditions, such as dense cover with sharp contrasts of light and shade, these shots are difficult, and what is requisite is a rifle with a flat trajectory, which will, should a vital spot be missed, deliver a smashing, disabling blow.

With a .303, I have killed all kinds of game from elephants downwards, but it must be remembered that the hunter who uses a weapon of such calibre against large and dangerous game at close quarters in bush country, runs considerable risk of losing his life, for the bullet has neither the requisite weight nor velocity always to prove thoroughly effectual . . .

Against small game, I have for some years used a .318 rifle, and find it, especially in conjunction with Westley Richards patent copper-capped bullets, immeasurably superior to either the .256 or .303, and one which has on account of its high velocity and ideal form of expanding bullet, all the advantages of long range and flat trajectory associated with the small bore, and a large amount of the shock-giving qualities obtained with a larger bore rifle, without the recoil inseparable from that weapon.

The elephant and rhinoceros, being in a class by themselves, require a rifle firing a much heavier bullet. After experimenting with and using all kinds of rifles, I find the most effective to be the double .577 with a 750 grain bullet and a charge in axite powder equivalent to a hundred grains of cordite. The heavier double-barreled .600 bore rifle, with a bullet weighing 900 grains, lacks the penetration of the .577, while its weight (16 lbs. against 13 lbs. of the latter) renders it a much more awkward weapon to handle. I think the superiority of the .577 over the .450 and .500 rifles will be evident when I state that I have lost elephants with these last two rifles, while I have bagged others with identically the same shots from a .577.

When using double-barrelled rifles against big and dangerous game, it is of supreme importance to have a thoroughly reliable ejecting mechanism, and I find that a single trigger is a vast improvement on the old double trigger, for, apart from eliminating the risk of a bruised finger, the single trigger is infinitely quicker, enabling a double shot to be placed almost simultaneously if necessary. I have used the single trigger for some years and would on no account go back to the double. Another factor to be considered with regard to a rifle for big game is the length of barrels. It is my opinion that they should be as short as possible, certainly not longer than twenty-six inches; for a rifle with barrels exceeding this length is extremely awkward to manipulate in bush country. The double-barrelled .577 which I have used for several years and found admirable in every detail was built for me by Westley-Richards & Co. of Bond Street. The construction of the locks is excellent and simple to a degree so that should anything go wrong with the mechanism in the bush, where you cannot take a taxi to your gunmaker, there is no difficulty in instantly detaching a lock by hand and replacing it with a duplicate. The single trigger and ejector attached to this rifle have on no occasion failed to act.

Lt. Col. Patterson, an engineer on the East African Railway, tells in *Maneaters of Tsavo* how he finally brought to bay and killed the two lions which had carried off and eaten twenty-eight workmen from his camp—this with a .303 military Lee Metford. Later when the railroad was finished, he did some general hunting in East Africa using a heavier rifle. W. D. M. Bell was another elephant hunter, having killed the prodigious bag of 1,011 elephants, most with a .276 or 7mm Rigby

Mauser using the 173 grain blunt-nosed bullet at about 2,300 foot-seconds velocity. Many of these were killed at ten to fifteen yards with a single brain shot. His opinion of the small bore is worth repeating:

Speaking personally, my greatest successes have been obtained with the 7mm Rigby-Mauser or .276 with the old round-nosed solid weighing I believe 200 grains. It seemed to show a remarkable aptitude for finding the brain of an elephant. This holding of a true course I think is due to the moderate velocity, 2,300 ft., and to the fact that the proportion of diameter to length of bullet seems to be the ideal combination. For when you come below the .276 to .256 or 6.5 mm, I found a bending of the bullet took place when fired into heavy bones . . .

I often had the opportunity of testing this extraordinary little weapon on other animals than elephant. Once, to relate one of the less bloody of its killings, I met at close range, in high grass, three bull buffalo. Having at the moment a large native following more or less on the verge of starvation, as the country was rather gameless, I had no hesitation about getting all three. One stood with head up about 10 yards away and facing me, while the others appeared as rustles in the grass behind him. Instantly ready as I always was, carrying my own rifle, I placed a .276 solid in his chest. He fell away in a forward lurch, disclosing another immediately behind him in a similar posture. He also received a .276, falling on his nose and knees. The third now became visible through the commotion, affording a chance at his neck as he barged across my front. A bullet between neck and shoulders laid him flat. All three died without further trouble, and the whole affair lasted perhaps four or five seconds.

Bell must have been a cool and accurate shot or he could not have been so successful. This is perhaps also evidenced by his having, according to his own statement, killed 23 buffalo with 23 shots from a .22 high velocity rifle, evidently a .22 Savage, although he rates the bullet as of 80 grains rather than the Savage's 70 grains standard weight. But this testimony from Bell's experience really falls in the category covered more fully in a later chapter.

Edgar Beecher Bronson hunting in East Africa in 1908-09 has this to say about Bell's elephant hunting and rifles in his book *In Closed Territory* published in 1909:

Still for the experienced and prudent elephant hunter the sport is comparatively safe. Mr. Bell an Englishman who has been for the last five or six years shooting elephant for ivory, as a business, and who has to his credit the probably unparalleled bag to one gun of over five hundred head, says he has never yet been charged. Only a fortnight ago he came into Entebbe from a four months' safari in the Congo country with the tusks of one hundred and eighty big fellows. Deducting the period of the journey in and out, this remarkable kill must have been made within no more than six weeks' actual shooting! And one day alone he bagged eighteen! No bad business with ivory at two dollars and a half a pound and an average tusk weight of probably one hundred pounds per pair.

Asked by a friend of mine how he contrived so long to come off un-scathed, Bell replied, "I never shoot until I get my big tusker right; if I find myself amid a big herd, I manage to slip out and bide my time; patience will always get you a big tusker right, and then you have it your own way," and indeed, "patience" is the watchword of every notably suc-cessful big game hunter: waiting to get them "right". . .

The heavy bores are now practically obsolete among African sportsmen, the four, eight, and twelve bores and even the .577, whose chief merit lay in the fact that they sometimes kicked you out of the way of a charg-ing beast. Few now use anything heavier than the English double-barreled .450 cordite, and I and many others find the .405 Winchester the most satisfactory of all for all-around African work, although the .30-30 is heavy enough for anything except a few of the bigger fellows, while not a few, Bell and, I understand, Selous included, prefer to trust in the higher velocity and flat trajectory of the pencil-like .256 Mann-licher for even elephant. While I have not yet tried the Mannlicher, I believe it is no more than probable its devotees are right, for such is the extraordinary vitality of all African game that the more lead you throw into them the faster and farther they run, unless you get brain, heart, or spine. I have myself in a two mile pursuit of a two hundred and seventy five pound wounded hartebeeste bull put 9 big .35 Mauser bul-lets through him before finally bringing him down . . .

Even the smaller antelope, slender and delicate though they appear, must be hit in brain, heart, or spine, no matter what the calibre of your gun, or you lose them.

Bronson is the only sportsman who reports difficulty with the .405 Winchester jamming, although Dr. Sutton remarks on this occurring with the .30-40 cartridge quoted in a later chapter. Bronson says in his book:

Frequently before my .405 had jammed in the magazine, the second or third cartridge not coming up level with the chamber—a dangerous freak I failed to fathom or correct; and I should have discarded it long before but for its superior accuracy over any other gun and its hard hitting. For a fortnight it had been working like an angel and dropping in its tracks nearly everything I pulled on, and therefore I had elected to trust it that morning.

But by every ill token, tight and fast it jammed at the first shot, compelling me to pass it down to Mataia and get the lighter Mauser, and losing me invaluable time. However, I was lucky enough to get another shot into No. 1 and one into No. 2 before they got out of range, up wind.

No. 1 elephant, finally bagged, with 4-9mm and .405 bullets in him turned out to be a one tusker, measuring 11 feet 4 inches at the withers and the third largest African elephant ever shot at the time.

Major C. H. Stigand, an officer in the King's African Rifles, also used a Mannlicher .256 because of its handiness, supported by a double .450 for the largest game. He was killed by native ambush in an uprising in the Soudan. Blayney Percival, a game ranger in British East Africa or Kenya Colony for many years, used a .256 Mannlicher supported by a .450 Rigby double rifle. In regard to the small bore he has this to say:

I shot most of my lions, say forty with the .256 I do not remember exactly, but I feel sure that two-thirds of the lions did not need a second bullet; if one did, it usually meant several more. When hunting alone I seldom fired till I had a lion just how I wanted him, and I shot to put him out of business. Soft-nosed bullets I gave up long ago except for small stuff or in heavy rifle.

Colonel J. Stevenson Hamilton, a retired Army officer and game official in East Africa, used a .303 Lee Metford in shooting lions for game protection. He is believed to have killed more lions than any other hunter in Africa, including Paul Rainey, the American who killed 150 in front of a trained pack of lion dogs, a method our English cousins did not consider exactly sporting. This and Roosevelt's game "battues" irked some of them tremendously. Marcus Daly hunting for ivory and for zoological specimens from Northern Rhodesia to the Sudan between the years 1897 and 1936 had many interesting experiences and narrow escapes recited in his book *Big Game Hunting and Adventure*. Daly's thoughts, as stated in his book, on rifles for dangerous game, especially elephant, lean toward the larger calibers in magazine rifles and to the Mauser in particular in preference to the custom made rifles:

To those who like double-barrelled guns, not too heavy, but effective and strong enough to stop a death charge, the .450 No. 2 and .475 No. 2 would take a lot of beating; they are powerful, reliable and well balanced. If the man behind the gun is as good as the gun, nothing should reach him bar accident, the possibility of which is always present.

However, I much prefer a magazine action rifle for heavy and dangerous game, such as the .416 Magnum or .404 Mauser. Both of these rifles are positively reliable against any animal . . .

Many hunters have used a small bore rifle in countries favorable to such, in tall reed country such as the Nile swamps and the Lado Enclave, using for the latter a sliding step ladder with sections so arranged that one or more can be pushed up higher and higher as required. The big bull's head showing above and through the reeds offer easy brain shots. The 7mm Mauser has been largely used for this method of shooting elephants, with solid bullets; quite all right here under those circumstances, but quite useless in heavy country. This system has been used mostly by a class of occasional hunter who goes out to collect ivory as quickly, and as safely, as possible with many photos for books and papers; but it is not big game hunting.

The 9.3 Mauser is a good, medium all-round rifle though after many tests with all dangerous game I found the 10.75 Mauser with 24-inch barrel the better gun. It is generally slightly lighter in weight or much the same and still stops a death charge of any animal, though I have never out of over a hundred elephants shot with this rifle, got a frontal-shot to penetrate right into the brain of a big bull. I never, however, failed with this rifle to drop an elephant with a frontal-shot, even charging through thick stuff, and had plenty of time to step around and put another shot in under the armpits to the heart, which invariably finished it; or to stand aside, allowing it to rise again in position to take the side brain shot; for running shots it is one of the finest rifles I have ever handled.

The super 8 mm. (.315) is a very good game rifle and a great killer in its own class, but, of course, not a big game rifle . . . The .404 Mauser, solid bullets, 84 grains powder and a 24-inch barrel, never failed to reach the brain with a frontal-shot even with the biggest elephant bull; likewise the .416 Magnum rifle. Both these rifles are absolutely reliable against anything on four legs, but the great cost of the .416 Magnum and its ammunition is a great drawback.

The medium rifles such as the .375 Magnum and the .350 Magnum as well as the .318 are giants in their class but the high cost of ammunition prevents them ever becoming very popular guns, and the metal being on the soft side, they don't last long.

The crack about hunting with the 7mm rifle, from stepladders, in the

Lado Enclave, and for pictures, is quite evidently directed at W. D. M. Bell who apparently did all of these things, yet Bell's record stands unique in all the history of big game hunting, and even then he took time off to become a major in aviation, in the First World War.

In the early nineteen hundreds a new class of big game hunters appeared. These were the collectors and scientists from the large national museums, zoological gardens and universities. Prior to this period such collections as had been made, were by the ordinary sportsmen or ivory and market hunters. In this way many notable specimens or animal groups had been contributed by Baker, Selous, Loder, Littledale and others. Major Powell-Cotton collected a number of animals including a group of giraffes for the Natural History Museum of London on his trip through Uganda in 1902-03. Powell-Cotton's battery consisted of a .600 bore double cordite express, a similar .400 bore double cordite express, both made by Jeffery of London, and a .256 Mannlicher. Except for the largest game, the Mannlicher seems to have received the most constant use as he tells in his book *In Unknown Africa*:

For those who want a heavy bore rifle that has tremendous stopping power, I do not think a Jeffery .600 can be beaten. For lighter big game weapon I have found the .400 cordite by the same maker so useful that on my next trip I have decided to leave the .600 behind and take a pair of the former. The .256 Mannlicher Schonauer, with Jeffery telescopic sight, is still my favorite small bore rifle. With it I have killed animals of all sizes, from hippo to dik-dik. A shot and ball gun completes the battery I should advise.

It is noticeable in Powell-Cotton's accounts of actual shooting that the .600 was generally carried by a gun bearer and not always available when needed. A gun weighing 16 lbs. with a recoil of 100 foot pounds is not exactly a toy, nor an easy rifle for snap shooting especially by a hunter weighing 153 pounds. But this is not the only instance of a little man picking a big rifle.

Among other collectors of this period was the American Carl Akeley working for the Field Museum of Chicago and the American Museum of Natural History in New York. His weapons included a .475 Jeffery double barrel and a .30-06 Springfield although in the course of his several trips to Africa he used other rifles. Akeley in his African adventures was mauled by a leopard and almost crushed to death by an

DEER STALKING IN THE SCOTTISH HIGHLANDS.
From the Country Life Library of *Big Game Shooting*.

MAJOR W. D. M. BELL. AFRICAN HUNTER WITH A RECORD OF OVER 1000 ELEPHANTS. OFFICER IN THE R.A.F. IN WORLD WAR I.

From Barclay's *Big Game Shooting Records.*

MAJ. C. H. STIGAND OF THE KING'S AFRICAN RIFLES. BIG GAME HUNTER, EXPLORER, ADMINISTRATOR AND AUTHOR.

From D. D. Lyell's *African Adventure.*

JEFFERY .256 RUMANIAN MANNLICHER RIFLE, SIMILAR TO RIFLES USED BY
LITTLEDALE, LODER, PEASE, RADCLIFFE AND OTHERS.

7MM or 8MM MAUSER WITH 24-INCH BARREL.

From Mauser catalogue.

BULL ELEPHANT SHOT BY GEORGE GARDEN.

From D. D. Lyell's *African Adventure.*

CHAMOIS IN ITS NATIVE HAUNTS.

From the Badminton Library of *Big Game Shooting*.

MARTIN RYAN, PROFESSIONAL
IVORY HUNTER OF SOUTH EAST
AND CENTRAL AFRICA.

From D. D. Lyell's *African Adventure.*

"MY FAVORITE SHOOTING POSITION" MAJOR P.H.G. POWELL-
COTTON, BIG GAME HUNTER AND EXPLORER IN INDIA, ABYS-
SINIA AND CENTRAL AFRICA. ONE OF THE VERY FEW PICTURES
OF A RIFLE TELESCOPE SIGHT USED IN BIG GAME HUNTING.

From *A Sporting Trip through Abyssinia.*

ELEPHANT SHOT AT BANGALLA.

From James Sutherland's *The Adventures of an Elephant Hunter.*

FOUR ELEPHANTS TOGETHER.

From James Sutherland's *The Adventures of an Elephant Hunter.*

elephant only at last to die of fever and be buried on Mt. Mikeno in the Belgian Congo. Another collector of note in this same region of the Congo and more particularly along the Ituri River was a Dr. Cuthbert Christy sent there in 1898 to investigate measures to contend against sleeping sickness. His comments on rifles while hunting with the pygmies for okapi and other animals for the Belgian National Museum as told in his book *Big Game and Pygmies* are so interesting that they are quoted somewhat fully below:

Much depends it seems to me, upon the rifle and its sighting. With a heavy rifle I always found it easier than with a light one. That which I used was a double .500 cordite elephant gun with short barrels. It weighed over 12 pounds, and was sighted almost like a shot gun, with low foresight. The backsight consisted of the smallest flaps, scarcely raised above the rib level, with a wide shallow V. I got so used to this weapon that I could throw it up to my shoulder and make good shooting standing in the canoe. I could fire almost as quickly with it as I could with a shot-gun.

. . . On my more recent expeditions my second and third rifles have been the .276 Mauser and the little .22, the latter bored for long cartridges. In addition to these rifles I have generally taken a 12 bore shotgun and a small double .410 collecting gun or two of each if on a collecting expedition.

It is difficult to say exactly what proportion of hard-nosed ammunition to soft should be taken on any given expedition. Conditions and circumstances are not always the same. In an elephant country I have usually taken about 100 hard-nosed to 300 soft for my elephant gun. The former are practically only used for elephants, the latter for buffalo and other large game. At least that was invariably my practice. It seems to me asking for trouble to use hard-nosed bullets for buffalo. A soft nosed bullet will flatten or mushroom even without touching bone and the shock is severe, to say nothing of the larger internal wound. On the other hand, the hard-nosed bullet from a high-power rifle, if it happens to touch no bone, will go clean through a buffalo at a hundred yards . . .

When hunting with the Pygmies a second rifle cannot be taken into the forest. The little men could not and would not undertake to carry it. They are far too superstitious and afraid of a gun. One is obliged, therefore, to take the heavy rifle and carry it oneself. It must be relied upon for all game great or small. At any moment the "Lord of the Forest" may contest the way, or if not, he may be the possessor of tusks worth obtaining. Often during the day one has occasion to regret not having a small-bore and less noisy rifle, and not being able to hunt other animals when after elephant or okapi. But to carry a second weapon necessitates taking a gun bearer or second man, which means more noise and less sport . . .

In forest work a double .400 would be preferable to any heavier weapon, for the strain of carrying the latter is killing. Progression through the underwood in a doubled-up attitude holding the rifle with both hands is excessively fatiguing. It may be carried at arm's length, but it must be on "safety" for fear of accident, the little Pygmy Tracker being generally directly ahead. It cannot be slung to the shoulder, the easiest way of carrying it, because of the crouching attitude . . .

In choosing a rifle for forest work one must decide upon an all-round weapon. Bolt action repeating rifles are too noisy. They cannot be reloaded without vigorous action and considerable noise, of a sort absolutely unlike any other to be heard in the forest. Its direction is at once picked up by the sensitive ears of any animal standing near. I recollect finding myself in dense forest within twenty yards of eight or ten elephants all facing me and listening intently to my coming. From their attitude they had probably been listening for some minutes, wondering which of their forest acquaintances was approaching. As I hurriedly surveyed their position, and tried to take in details of their ivory, I moved off the safety catch of my double .500. The very instant I did so the foremost bulls, recognizing the metallic sound as nothing belonging to the forest, began to turn, giving the danger signal, and in a few seconds the herd was in full retreat. If animals can pick up so small a noise as a click of a safety-catch and recognize it as unusual, something to be feared, it is easy to realize how certain the rattle of a repeating rifle bolt will advertise the presence and position of the hunter to everything in hearing. Moreover, in absolutely still surroundings the action necessary to work the bolt is even more of a give-away than the noise of the safety-catch.

The rifle chosen should be a double-barreled non-ejector. With dangerous game it is, of course, far safer to be able to fire two shots on the instant, than to have five or more, only one of which can be fired without pumping the bolt and taking fresh aim. This especially so in the forest. Though not necessarily firing at dangerous game, one is often so near the animal, or the glimpse one gets of it may sometimes be so momentary, that only with a double-barreled rifle could a second shot be placed if it were required. The rifle must be the lightest one effective with elephants and it should be built and sighted as closely as possible on the lines of the double shot-gun, with front sight low on the rib, and the back sight on a wide V on the lowest possible of sunk flaps. Sighting for more than 100 yards is not necessary.

The barrels should be short, and care should be taken that the stock is not too long. The stock of my double .500 with its rubber heel-pad was made a half inch longer than that of my shotgun, with the idea that it would help to lessen recoil. Whether the extra length helped to do this or not I cannot say, but when shooting hurriedly it caused me occasionally to fire the left barrel first, and more than once, not knowing I had done this, I subsequently placed myself in a dangerous position by pulling the trigger of the empty barrel.

An important point is to insist that the gunmaker, whatever the type of foresight may be, and whatever its material, shall make the back of it for forest shooting on the slant away from the eye, even as much as nearly 45 degrees. If the back of the foresight, that is, its face, is vertical and one is looking towards the dark shade, the sight may be quite invisible in the dim light of the forest. If its face is at the correct slant it reflects what little light there may be from above directly to the eyes of the person aiming.

Kalman Kittenberger, collecting animals and specimens in German East Africa, Kenya and Uganda, between 1902 and 1927 for the Hungarian Zoo and Hungarian Natural History Museum had many interesting encounters with big game and is generous with his comments on the rifles he used. The following is from his book *Big Game Hunting in East Africa*:

I think I have mentioned already that a lion is not very tough and that a modern high-velocity small-bore rifle is quite sufficiently powerful. Percival advises a large-bore rifle for a sportsman on foot and a lighter one for the mounted hunter. I recommend the small-bore because on account of its light weight one can carry it himself. One should always carry one's weapon; those who do not, will often repent and I have missed many a good chance through my laziness. The gunbearer is usually not near enough and by the time he comes up to you the animal sighted for a movement will have gone. However hard it may seem to the parched and weary hunter in the extreme heat, he must have sufficient energy to carry his rifle himself.

In regard to ammunition, the soft nosed bullet is best for a small bore, while more readily expanding bullets should be used in a large-bore rifle. Many, for example, Percival and Bell, advise a solid bullet for use in a small-bore . . .

Here I must mention that this second bullet, although it was a solid one, did not go through the lioness, but stopped right under her skin or the other side. The steel jacket was split and the lead expanded and flattened. This was neither a good advertisement for the reliability of Austrian Mannlicher-Schonauer cartridges, nor very reassuring in regard to my anticipated elephant shooting, as only solid bullets should be used on elephants.

In regard to rifles and ammunition for elephants Kittenberger was still a small bore enthusiast although equipped with a heavy rifle for emergencies:

Any modern magazine rifle of great penetration will be good enough for elephant, but soft nosed or expanding bullets should naturally never be used, as they will be quite ineffective. The pointed bullets of the latest high-velocity rifles are not advisable either, because they are badly balanced and will often turn over in the body and so fail to reach the vital spots, especially in the case of a head shot.

It is hard to give advice as to the calibre which should be used. A deadly head-shot can be given with a small bore, and for head-shots such a rifle is preferable; but for shoulder-shots which mean the heart or lungs, a large bore rifle is better. My own personal opinion is that a small-bore rifle is what I want, but a beginner should take a large-bore double . . .

The smaller bore rifles are much handier, because first of all, a well-aimed, steady shot can be taken, and secondly, because the penetration is greater—two essentials for elephant hunting. The vital shots on an elephant are few and small. The head-shot is the best and least cruel, but it wants much practice. The elephant's brain is very small in comparison with his large skull, so the beginner will do better to try for the heart-shot.

But for buffalo Kittenberger chooses the big bore:

My experience is that a soft-nosed bullet from a big-bore, or a solid one from a small-bore are advisable. Which rifle to use is a question of individual preference. Personally I found that in thick grass or dense bush a double-barrelled big-bore was better than a small-bore magazine.

Kittenberger's recommendations for a battery for African shooting were as follows:

I would certainly take a very accurate, high velocity magazine rifle. This could be either a 6.7 Mannlicher-Schonauer or a 7 mm. Mauser.

But under no circumstances would I use Austrian ammunition for the Mannlicher-Schonauer. On my last Uganda excursion, as mentioned in a previous chapter, I was not satisfied with it. This, by the way, is not only my opinion. W. D. M. Bell, the famous elephant hunter, discarded the Mannlicher-Schonauer because of the Austrian ammunition and took to the 7 mm. Mauser.

Rifles regulated and sighted for the 'S' cartridges are no good for big African game such as the elephant and rhino, and I do not consider them suitable for African hunting.

It is advisable to take as well a big-bore double-barreled cordite rifle. The most common bore is now the .500/.465 which is especially convenient, as you can get ammunition for it in Africa. This large-bore double-barreled rifle is especially useful in dense forest or elephant grass.

The old-fashioned big-bore Paradox guns (4-, 8-, and 10-bore) are hardly ever used now. On our last trip amongst the sportsmen traveling on our ship there was only one who had a 10-bore Paradox, and it is very likely he never used it at all. In the days of high-velocity rifles these heavy pieces of artillery belong to the past, not only because the effect of the high-velocity small-bore rifle is so much greater, but because of their greater accuracy.

In case I would not be able to secure a double-barrelled cordite Express (these modern elephant rifles are exceedingly expensive) a 9.3 mm. Mauser or a 9.5 mm. Mannlicher-Schonauer would do very well instead. The latter only in the event—as with the 6.7 mm. Mannlicher-Schonauer —of D. W. M. K. or cordite ammunition being obtainable for it.

The designation 'S' cartridges refers to spitzer bullets and the 'D. W. M. K.' is Deutsche Waffen und Munitions Fabriken—Karlsruhe. One of the last of the East African hunters, hunting in this period, but not so well known was Frank Melland who has this to say about rifles:

On this occasion I was using an unsatisfactory falling-block .400 which I had before I went to Rigby, and it jammed after the first shot, a habit it had. So, I had to seize a .303 which I had just bought for one pound as a standby because of the bad behavior of my .400. It was very old and the barrel was badly worn; it was not gas tight and burned my cheek each time I fired it. The three elephants swung around to the shot, put their ears out, stretched out their trunks, trumpeted, and came for me in a V-shaped formation, the wounded one leading. I gave him a shot in the chest which tore through his heart and turned him. He went eighty yards and fell, but the other two meanwhile were coming on unchecked. I gave another an identical chest shot at about twelve yards with the same effect—it was the only vulnerable spot available, and my luck was holding. The third was then on to me. I fired again and hit him somewhere in the massive front—it was too close to say where. Mwana Kaunda let fly with his own muzzle-loader, Chuma with an old Snider he took from an Askari, and Kashimoto fired my shotgun. That volley at any rate served its purpose; it turned him within a trunk's length. As he went off, with exultation resulting from the successful stand, I gave him a raking shot behind in the ribs, a slanting shot which I thought would find his lungs, but, though we spoored him a little way that evening and many miles the next day, we never found him.

I have already mentioned the weight of the tusks (119 and 110 pounds). Not only were Shikulu's (grandfather) the best I ever got anywhere but I think I may be pardoned for adding that they were (and are) the best ever got in Northern Rhodesia, and Selous told me that as far as he knew they were a record for any elephant ever shot by a white man south of Tanganyika.

Later when hunting in East Africa, Melland, used a double .450 Rigby and then two .350 Rigby double rifles to save trouble with duplicating ammunition with a large bore and small bore, and because as he says, "I found that the .350 besides being unrivalled for smaller game would do all that the .450 would do with the bigger."

The small bore was a little slower to make progress in India. Of course, Littledale had used it for his trips into the Himalayas and Central Asia for sheep, but it was still considered unsafe for tiger and the shooting of elephant was largely controlled because of their domestic value. General R. G. Burton, of the British Army, and General A. E. Wardrop, of the Indian Police, refer in their books mostly to tiger shooting for which Burton used a .500 double-barreled Holland and made no mention of any other rifle, and Wardrop used for tiger and bison a double .470 cordite Express made by James Tolley and Sons, of Birmingham, and a .318 Westley Richards built on the Mauser action for sambur and black buck. Two other Indian sportsmen, Captain Glossop and E. P. Stebbing, used medium bore rifles, Glossop a .400 single shot Holland hunting bear and other Himalayan game in North India, and Stebbing who hunted in the plains country with a .500 black powder express. The latter has this to say of the small bore:

Perhaps the most dangerous weapon to use against a leopard is one of the small bore cordite rifles, dangerous to the owner I mean, not to the

animal. More so-called tiger and leopard accidents have probably happened in recent times from the use of the small bore rifles on dangerous
game than from any other cause. The small bore has no power to "stop"
a charge of a tiger, leopard or bear, and though the animal may be mortally wounded, he will get home and maul you before he dies if you are
pinning your faith to one of these weapons and are out on foot.

As Stebbing was a Forest Officer and did most of his early hunting in
jungle country he was speaking of the rifle needed for dangerous game
at close quarters. Later he used a .303 Lee Metford for Himalayan game.
Another Indian small-bore sportsman of this period was Major R. L.
Kennion, who used a .256 Mannlicher on markhor and ibex in the Himalayas and a .280 Ross on Persian ibex and gazelle. In his book *By
Mountain, Lake and Plain* he mentions using this latter rifle on tiger,
"not, óf course, a weapon one would select for tiger shooting, but still
no toy."

The only true convert to the small-bore for Indian shooting in this
period was H. Z. Darrah and his comments are interesting. However
it must be understood that he was speaking of purely mountain shooting
and not jungle work. Under such conditions range, accuracy and light
weight are at a premium. His comments as contained in the book *Sport
in the Highlands of Kashmir* follow:

The weapon which I think is best suited to shooting in Kashmir is a
sporting .303 Lee-Metford carbine, sighted to 500 yards, and provided
with the usual magazine for ten cartridges. I consider this weapon, for
Kashmir shooting, superior to any express. There is nothing an express
will do which the carbine will not do, and many things that can be done
by the carbine which would be impossible with the express. The carbine,
with a sporting bullet, will hit as hard as any express, has a flatter trajectory, and is accurate at far longer ranges. In eight months shooting I
only lost two animals which had been hit with the Lee-Metford. One
was a uryal, wounded on the leg, and the other the Ovis Ammon,
scratched by a splinter of a bullet. More than one animal fell to a single
shot, and the rifle was found enough for a full grown bull yak. The
advantages of the flat trajectory cannot be overrated in hill shooting, where
judging distance is such a serious difficulty. It is hard enough to estimate
correctly a distance on the flat, but to do it with a ravine between the
shooter and his game requires long practice. The advantage, therefore,
of a weapon with which an error of a hundred yards is comparatively un-
important is very great indeed.

But it is in its accuracy at long ranges that the carbine is most markedly superior to the express. The hollow bullet cannot be depended on beyond 200 yards, and even at that range, the shooting of most express rifles is erratic. But the Lee-Metford is almost as true at 500 yards, as at 200. No animal standing inside of 500 yards from the rifle is really safe, and as yet few animals, if any, are aware of the fact. An ibex will run off to 300 yards or so, and then turn and calmly watch his pursuer. He would be practically safe from an express, but is in almost as much danger there from the Lee-Metford as if he had been only 200 yards off. My shikaris thought I was throwing away cartridges, when they saw me firing at over 200 yards. It was not until they saw the dust fly all around the animal aimed at, and occasionally saw him come down, that they began to believe in the accuracy of the little rifle. This is why I think the carbine selected should be sighted to 500 yards. All sporting carbines used to be sighted to this range, but recently those brought to India have been only sighted to 300. This is not, I think, sufficient. The weapon is quite accurate enough for the longer range, and a sportsman is, I think, badly handicapped if he has no sight for anything beyond 300 yards.

As minor advantages I may mention the slight noise made by the report, the absence of smoke, the absence of recoil, and the lightness of the cartridges. Until I showed myself, most of the game I fired at did not know where the shot came from. The three antelope killed on the 30th of August would probably never have been bagged if I had been using an express, as the shots fired at the first one I saw that day, would in that case have cleared them out of the country. The lightness of the cartridges is not a matter of much moment; still it is a point distinctly in favor of the .303. Perhaps also the difference in the original cost might be mentioned. A first class express by a good maker will cost 60 guineas. The best Lee-Metford carbine in the market can be bought for about a fifth of this sum.

All the gunmakers now sell double-barrelled weapons of .303 bore. I do not think these are as good as the carbine with the magazine. It is true that the second barrel enables a second shot to be put in much quicker than can be done when the rifle has to be taken from the shoulder, to allow another cartridge to be fed up from the magazine. But it is very rarely that this extra speed is of any advantage. I remember one occasion, and one only, while I was out, when I should have been glad to have had a second barrel. On all other occasions I found that the magazine supplied me quite fast enough with a second cartridge. And it did more. It supplied me with nine others as fast as it had given me a second. Consequently all subsequent loading, after the first two shots had been fired, was done much faster with the carbine than would have been possible with a double barrel. But there is another point. It must be very difficult to aline two barrels, so that they shall both throw accurately to 500 yards. I have never tried a double barrelled .303 at this distance, and do not know, consequently, how it behaves, but I cannot help thinking that a single rifle like the carbine, must be more accurate at this long range than any double could be . . .

Closely connected with the question of the rifle to use is that of the bullet. I used Jeffrey's split bullets in mine, and found them to work well. But I have heard men say, and it is, I should think, very probable, that they are not as accurate at long ranges as the full-sized uncut bullet, and that in a rifle sighted with the latter they go high. I never have had time to test my rifle on a range, but I know that with the Jeffrey bullet and its present sighting, it shoots very high indeed. This objection would probably not apply if the Tweedie or Dumdum expanding bullets were used, as they must be of the same weight as the old service bullet, and if I were going again, I should, I think, try some cartridges with these expanding bullets. But I would not again use the unslit truncated bullet— that is, the bullet with the nose only cut off. I had a few of these, and believe that is was owing to them that I nearly lost an ibex, and did for a time lose the first uryal I hit. I do not think they expand or break up in passing through, and if my surmise is correct they are quite useless. The Jeffrey bullet is truncated also, but the slits down the sides generally ensures its breaking up on impact, and though the bullet goes through in the majority of cases, the wound it makes is terrible.

The .303 Lee-Metford was later prohibited in India except by special permission. This may account also for the fact that Darrah's sporting carbine was sighted only to 300 yards. Probably the game soon got wise to the increased range of the small bore rifle.

For hunting in Malaya, T. R. Hubback used a double barreled .500 by Evans, and being a heavy bore advocate took a double .400 Evans and a double .375 by Cogswell and Harrison to Alaska in 1918 for a successful hunt after moose, sheep and bear but he had little comment on their performance.

In America the lever action, descendant of the Spencer, Sharps, Ballard, and Stevens, was so firmly intrenched in popular favor that, when the small bore entered with the .30-30 Winchester and .30-40 Krag army cartridge in 1892, or the .303 Savage in 1895, these rifles whether single shot or magazine for sporting use were on the same lever-action principle. The above cartridges were very popular with American hunters: Roosevelt, Wright, Burnham, Caswell, Riggal, and Lee mention using the

.30-30; White, Whelen, Roberts, Robinson, House, McGuire, Kidder, Kermit Roosevelt and McCracken the .30-40; and the .303 Savage was used at one time by Hornaday, Caldwell and Lee. The .303 Mannlicher used in Mexico before 1900 by Charles Sheldon was undoubtedly the British Army cartridge. However, for all of his later hunting Sheldon used a Jeffery .256 Mannlicher shooting the 160 grain bullet from a 22.5 inch barrel at about 2,300 foot-seconds velocity. In his very interesting three books on Alaskan hunting, Sheldon seldom mentions the rifle. Once during the Winter of 1907 while hunting white sheep in subzero weather he had the oil on the bolt freeze so that the rifle would not fire. When boiled to remove the oil, the bolt still refused to work either, so that finally he applied a coating of vaseline and had no further trouble.

In reply to a letter from D. D. Lyell, Sheldon had the following to say about the Mannlicher:

It seems to me perfectly clear that the .256 with the right bullet at a muzzle velocity of 2,300 feet is completely satisfactory for all game on this continent, including moose, caribou, and the large bears, many of which I have killed during years of hunting them. My experience to me is a demonstration that with .256 it is only a question of directing the bullet at a vital or disabling spot.

Three of the widest traveled hunters of this period were E. J. House, H. K. H. Prichard, and John G. Millais. For North American game from sheep and goat to moose and walrus, House used a .30-40 Model 95 Winchester and a 9mm Mauser. In Africa where he secured all game but lion he used the 9mm Mauser, plus a .450 double cordite Express. Prichard after a trip to Argentina and Chile, in which he used a 7mm Mauser with indifferent success, made four trips to Newfoundland, Labrador, and Quebec for moose and caribou. His rifles on these later trips were a .350 Rigby Mauser in Labrador and a .256 Mannlicher both of which apparently gave perfect service since he seldom comments on them and they seemed to perform with deadly accuracy. The Mannlicher was his only weapon in Newfoundland. Prichard's most famous work was his book on the first World War entitled, *Sniping in France,* which is about the school he ran for snipers in the British Army. His account of the circumvention and demise of Willibald, the German sniper who had killed many English soldiers with his scope sighted rifle, is a rifleman's classic.

John G. Millais, author, artist, sportsman, and naturalist, probably one of the greatest authorities on aquatic game of the British Isles, hunted big game on three continents and was personally acquainted with more big-game hunters than probably any other one man. His observations on rifles are, therefore, particularly fitting at the close of this early small-bore period. The following is from his *Life of Frederick Courtenay Selous*:

All of us who are big-game hunters, however, know how greatly the average of hits had advanced since the introduction of the small-bore, high-velocity rifle. In 1895 came the British .303, the German .275 Mauser, and the Roumanian .256 Mannlicher, and these weapons possess such accuracy and flatness of trajectory that a poor shot becomes a moderate one, a good shot a first-class one, and a first-class performer something remarkable. Since 1900 some firms, notably John Rigby, have utilized the best points of these smaller weapons to make them successful, on the largest and most dangerous game in the hands of experienced men, and have invented weapons of tremendous hitting power with magazine rapidity of fire.

Millais' statement of the improvement in marksmanship possible with the accuracy and flat trajectory of the small bore makes no mention of the contribution made by the reduction in rifle weight and recoil.

There are forty-nine men listed in this period who used and mentioned 170 rifles of fifty-six different cartridges or calibers. There were eighteen large bores from 8 to 12 gauge, fifty-three medium bores from .40 to .600 caliber, and ninety-nine small bores from .22 to .375 caliber (the .22 caliber Savage rifles were really of the next period). The most popular small bore was the .256 Mannlicher, followed by the .303 Lee Metford and the 7mm Mauser. In the medium bores the double .450 is first, followed by the double .500 and .400. Eleven big-game hunters used 8, 10 and 12 bore Paradox ball and shot guns made by Holland and others, for reserve guns on dangerous game.

APPENDIX C

PART III—1893-1905—The Small Bores

NAME	WHEN	WHERE
64 Sir Alfred Pease	1892-1895	North Africa
"	1896-1924	East Africa
65 Col. Townsend Whelen	1892-1910	North America
"	1911-1914	Panama
"	1915-1946	N. America
66 Maj. R. L. Kennion	1893-1905	India
"	1906-1910	Persia
67 John G. Millais	1893-1894	South Africa
"	1906-1909	Newfoundland-Alaska
"	1913-1914	East Africa
"	1916-1917	Norway
"	1920-1922	Scotland
"	1922-1924	East Africa
68 E. P. Stebbing	1894-1914	North India
69 P. H. G. Powell-Cotton	1895-1898	Himalayas
"	1899-1901	Abyssinia
"	1902-1904	Central Africa
70 Denis D. Lyell	1895-1896	India
"	1897-1903	South Africa
"	1903-1920	East Africa
71 Capt. B. R. M. Glossop	1895-1897	India
"	1897-1905	Somaliland
72 Gen. R. G. Burton	1895-1933	India
73 Maj. Gen. A. E. Wardrop	1895-1923	India
74 H. Z. Darrah	1896-1897	Himalayas

APPENDIX C

PART III—1893-1905—The Small Bores

ANIMALS HUNTED	RIFLES USED
64 Moufflon, Boar, Gazelle	10 bore Paradox, .256 Mannlicher*
Elephant, Lion, Rhino, Buffalo, Antelope	10 bore Paradox, .350 Rigby, .333 Jeffery, .404 Jeffery, .256 Mannlicher*
65 Moose, Elk, Bear, Sheep, Deer	.40-72 Win., .30-40 SS Winchester*
Deer	.30-06 Springfield
Moose, Caribou, Elk, Bear, Sheep, Goat	.35 Whelen, .30-06 Springfield, .270 Winch.*
66 Tiger, Markhor, Sheep, Ibex, Sambur	303 Lee M, .256 Mannlicher*
Ibex, Sheep, Gazelle, Deer	.280 Ross*, .256 Mannl., .303 Lee M.
67 Antelope	.256 Mannlicher*
Moose, Caribou, Elk, Sheep, Goat, Bear	.256 Mannlicher*
Lion, Antelope	.256 Mannlicher*
Elk, Reindeer	.256 Mannlicher*
Deer	.256 Mannlicher*
Ibex, Kudu, Eland	.256 Mannlicher*
68 Tiger, Bison, Bear, Sambur, Markhor	10 bore Paradox, .500 DB Holland*, .303 Lee Metford
69 Markhor, Ibex, Sheep, Bear	.400 DB Jeffery, .256 Mannlicher*
Ibex, Antelope, Elephant	8 and 12 bore Paradox, .400 DB Jeffery*, .256 Mannlicher* *
Elephant, Lion, Rhino, Buffalo, Antelope	12 bore Paradox, .600 DB Jeffrey, .400 DB Jeffery*, .256 Mannlicher*
70 Sambur	10 bore DB Purdey, .450 SS Henry, .303 Lee M., .303 SS Fraser*
Elephant, Lion, Antelope	.404 Jeffery, .303 SS Fraser, 7.9 Rigby*, .318 Westley R.
Elephant, Lion, Rhino, Buffalo, Antelope	.404 Jeffery, 7.9 Rigby, 7 Rigby, .256 Mannlicher*
71 Bear, Sambur, Goral, Thar, Serow	12 bore DB Paradox, .400 SS Holland*
Lion, Antelope	12 bore DB, .500 DB Express*
72 Tiger, Bear, Panther	.500 DB Holland*
73 Elephant, Tiger, Bear, Bison, Sambur	8 bore Paradox, .470 DB Tolley*, .400 DB .318 Westley
74 Bear, Sambur, Markhor, Ibex, Sheep	12 bore Paradox, .450 DB Rigby, .303 Lee Metford*

* The asterisk indicates the favorite rifle.

1893-1905—The Small Bores

NAME	WHEN	WHERE
75 R. C. F. Maugham	1896-1906	Port E. Africa
"	1907-1919	Central Africa
76 James Sutherland	1896-1932	Central Africa
77 Norman B. Smith	1896-1910	East Africa
"	1911-1912	Sudan
78 Carl E. Akeley	1896-1906	East Africa
"	1912-1926	Central Africa
79 Archibald Rutledge	1896-1946	N. America
80 Marcus Daly	1897-1936	Africa
81 Charles Sheldon	1897-1902	Mexico
"	1904-1909	Alaska-Yukon
"	1916-1921	Mexico-U. S.
82 Col. John Caswell	1897-1909	N. America
"	1910-1912	East Africa
83 Lt. Col. J. H. Patterson	1898-1908	East Africa
84 W. D. M Bell	1898-1921	Central Africa
85 Paul Niedieck	1898-1899	India-Ceylon
"	1900-1901	N. America
"	1902	Sudan
"	1903	Alaska-Canada
86 T R. Hubback	1898-1917	Malaya
"	1918-1921	Alaska
87 Dr. Cuthbert Christy	1898-1924	Central Africa
88 Edward J. House	1898-1899	Greenland
"	1900-1905	Canada-Newfoundland
"	1906-1907	East Africa
"	1907-1908	N. America
89 John A. McGuire	1898-1916	U. S.-Canada
"	1917-1918	Alaska

ANIMALS HUNTED	RIFLES USED
75 Elephant, Lion, Rhino, Buffalo, Antelope	8 bore DB, 10 bore Paradox, .500 DB, .303 DB Holland*
Elephant, Lion, Rhino, Buffalo, Antelope	.450 DB Holland, .375 DB Holland*, .303 DB Holland
76 Elephant, Lion, Rhino, Buffalo, Antelope	.577 DB Westley*, 10.75 Mauser, .303 Lee M., .318 Westley
77 Elephant, Lion, Rhino, Buffalo, Antelope	10 bore DB, 10 bore Paradox, .475 DB Jeffery*, .500 DB, .400 DB
Lion, Antelope	.475 DB Jeffery*, .303 Lee M., .256 Mannl.
78 Elephant, Lion, Rhino, Buffalo, Antelope	.470 DB*, 9mm Mannl, .256 Mannl.
Elephant, Lion, Leopard, Gorilla	.475 DB Jeffery*, 7.9mm Mauser, .30-06 Spr., .275 Hoffman
79 Deer, Bear, Boar	12 ga. DB Parker*, .250-300 Savage
80 Elephant, Lion, Rhino, Buffalo	.450 Martini, .416 Rigby, 10.75 Mauser*
81 Sheep, Deer, Bear	.303 Mannl., .256 Mannlicher*
Moose, Caribou, Sheep, Bear	.256 Jeffery Mannlicher*
Sheep	.256 Jeffery Mannlicher*
82 Moose, Bear, Deer	.30-30 Win., .303 Win., .375 Holland*
Elephant, Lion, Rhino, Antelope	.465 DB Purdey, 375 DB Holland*, 30-06 Springfield
83 Lion, Elephant, Rhino, Antelope	.450 DB Exp., .303 Lee Mtford
84 Elephant, Lion, Rhino, Buffalo, Antelope	.400 DB, .318 Jeffery Mauser, .275 Rigby Mauser*
85 Elephant, Tiger, Buffalo, Bear, Sambur	10 bore Paradox, 11mm DB*, .500 DB Exp.
Caribou, Moose, Elk, Deer	.500 DB Express*, 11mm DB
Elephant, Lion, Rhino, Buffalo, Antelope	10 bore Paradox, 9mm Mauser*, .375 DB
Moose, Caribou, Bear, Sheep	.375 DB Cordite Exp.*
86 Elephant, Tiger, Seladang	8 bore DB Manton, .500 DB Evans*
Moose, Bear, Caribou, Sheep	.450 SS Bland, .375 DB Cogswell & Harrison, .400 DB Evans*
87 Elephant, Buffalo, Okapi, Bougo	12 bore DB, .500 DB Exp.*, .303 Lee M., 7mm Mauser
88 Walrus, Caribou	.30-40 Winchester*
Moose, Caribou, Elk, Sheep, Goat, Bear	.30-40 Winchester, 9mm Mauser*
Elephant, Rhino, Antelope	.450 DB Exp., 9mm Mauser*
Bear, Elk	9mm Mauser*
89 Bear, Cougar, Elk, Sheep, Deer	.30-40 Winchester, .30-60 Winchester*
Moose, Caribou, Sheep	.30-06 Winchester*

* The asterisk indicates the favorite rifle.

1893-1905—The Small Bores

NAME	WHEN	WHERE
90　Malcolm S. Mackay	1899-1925	United States
"	1925-1927	Alaska
91　Horace Kephart	1899-1927	United States
92　Rev. Harry Caldwell	1899-1918	South China
"	1919-1920	Mongolia
93　Maj. C. H. Stigand	1899-1902	Somaliland
"	1903-1919	Central Africa
94　James H. Kidder	1900-1901	Alaska
95　Maj. Charles Askins	1900-1917	United States
"	1920-1940	United States
96　A. Blayney Percival	1900-1925	East Africa
97　Hesketh K. H. Prichard	1900-1901	S. America
"	1903-1907	Newfoundland-Canada
"	1908-1909	Sardinia
"	1909-1910	Labrador
98　Col. J. Stevenson Hamilton	1900-1926	East Africa
99　F. H. Riggall	1902-1930	Br. Columbia
100　Capt. H. A. Wilson	1902-1913	East Africa
101　Lieut. A. W. Hodson	1902-1912	South Africa
102　Kalman Kittenberger	1902-1912	East Africa
"	1925-1929	Central Africa
103　Charles Cottar	1902-1940	East Africa

1893-1905—The Small Bores

ANIMALS HUNTED	RIFLES USED
90 Elk, Sheep, Bear, Deer	50-110 Win., .45-90 Win.*, .33 Win.
Moose, Bear, Sheep	.405 Win.*, .30-06 Springfield
91 Deer, Bear	.30-40 SS Win.,* .30-40 Rem. Lee
92 Tiger, Serow, Takin, Boar	.303 Savage, .22 HP Savage*
Elk, Sheep	.250-3000 Savage*
93 Lion, Ibex, Addax, Kudu, Oryx	.450 DB, .256 Mannlicher*
Elephant, Lion, Rhino, Buffalo, Antelope	450 DB, .318 Jeffery, .256 Mannlicher*
94 Bear, Moose, Sheep, Caribou	.50-110 Winchester, .30-40 Winchester*
95 Bear, Elk, Deer	.45-90 W, .30-06 Spr., .22 HP, .250 Sav., .256 Newton*
Bear, Elk, Deer	7 mm Mauser, .276 Hoffman,* 35 Rem-Auto., .270 Winchester*
96 Lion, Elephant, Rhino, Antelope	.450 DB Rigby, 360 DB, .256 Mannlicher*
97 Guanaco, Wild Cattle, Deer	7 mm Mauser
Caribou Moose	.256 Mannlicher*
Moufflon	.256 Mannlicher*
Caribou	.256 Mannl., .350 Rigby Mauser*
98 Lion, Elephant, Antelope	.577 DB, .416 Rigby, .350 Rigby Mauser,* .303 Lee Metford
99 Bear, Deer, Goat, Sheep	.30-30 Win., .250 Savage, 7 mm Mauser*
100 Elephant, Lion, Rhino, Buffalo, Antelope	.450 DB Lang, .256 Jeffery Mannlicher*
101 Lion, Antelope	.450 SS Gibbs*, .303 Lee Metford
102 Elephant, Lion, Rhino, Buffalo, Antelope	.465 DB Holland, 8 mm Mannl.,* 7 mm Mauser, .256 Mannlicher
Elephant, Lion, Rhino, Buffalo, Antelope	.465 DB Holland, 8 mm Mannl., 9 mm Mannlicher*
103 Elephant, Lion, Rhino, Buffalo, Antelope	.470 DB Rigby, .405 Win.,* .35 Newton,* .250 Savage

* The asterisk indicates the favorite rifle.

1893-1905—The Small Bores

	NAME	WHEN	WHERE
104	C. E. R. Radcliffe	1903-1904	Alaska
105	Maj. Henry Darley	1903-1919	Abyssinia
106	Martin Ryan	1903-1917	East Africa
107	A. L. Barnshaw	1903-1907	Central Africa
108	W. S. Chadwick	1903-1928	South Africa
109	T. A. Barns	1903-1930	Central Africa
110	Frank Melland	1904-1930	Central Africa
111	Carl Rungius	1904-1906	Yukon
	"	1907-1946	United States
112	A. A. Dunbar Brander	1904-1923	India

1893-1905—The Small Bores

ANIMALS HUNTED	RIFLES USED
104 Moose, Bear	8 mm Mannl.*, .256 Mannlicher
105 Elephant, Lion, Rhino, Antelope	.450 DB Express*, .303 Lee Metford
106 Elephant, Lion, Rhino, Antelope	.416 Rigby Mauser, .375 M Holland, 7.9 mm Mauser*
107 Elephant, Lion, Rhino, Buffalo, Antelope	.303 Lee M, 7 mm Mauser, 7.9 mm Mauser,* 9 mm Mauser, .256 Mannlicher
108 Elephant, Lion, Rhino, Buffalo, Antelope	.450 DB, 9.3 Mauser*, .303 Lee Metford
109 Elephant, Lion, Rhino, Buffalo, Antelope	7.9 mm Mauser*
110 Elephant, Lion, Rhino, Buffalo	.450 DB Rigby, .350 DB Rigby*
111 Moose, Caribou, Sheep, Bear	.256 Mannlicher
Elk, Bear, Deer	.256 Mannlicher
112 Tiger, Elephant, Panther, Bison, Bear	12 bore DB, .577 DB

* The asterisk indicates the favorite rifle.

1893-1905—Summary of The Small Bores

LARGE BORES	USED BY	TOTAL
8 bore DB	75, 86	2
10 bore DB	70, 77	2
12 bore DB	71, 87, 112	3
8 bore Paradox	69, 73	2
10 bore Paradox	64, 68, 75, 77, 85	5
12 bore Paradox	69, 71, 74, 79	4
Total		18

MEDIUM BORES	USED BY	TOTAL
.600 DB	69	1
.577 DB	76, 98, 112	3
.500 DB	68, 71, 72, 75, 77, 85, 86, 87	8
.50-110W	90, 94	2
.475 DB	77, 78	2
.470 DB	73, 78, 103	3
.465 DB	82, 102	2
.450 DB	74, 75, 83, 88, 93, 96, 100, 105, 108, 110	10
.450 SS	70, 80, 86, 101	4
.45-90 M	90, 95	2
11mm DB	85	1
10.75mm M	76, 80	2
.416 M	98, 106	2
.405 Win.	90, 103	2
.404 M	64, 70	2
.400 DB	69, 73, 77, 84, 86	5
.400 SS	71	1
.40-72 Win.	65	1
Total		53

1893-1905—Summary of The Small Bores

SMALL BORES	USED BY	TOTAL
.375 DB	75, 85, 86	3
.375 M	82, 106	2
9.3mm M	108	1
.360 DB	96	1
9mm M	78, 85, 88, 102, 106	5
.350 M	64, 98, 97	3
.35 M	65, 103	2
350 DB	110	1
.35 Rem.	95	1
.333 M	64	1
.33 Win.	90	1
.318 M	70, 73, 76, 84, 93	5
8mm M	102, 104	2
7.9mm M	70, 106, 109	3
.303 M	66, 68, 70, 74, 76, 77, 81, 82, 83, 87, 98, 101, 105, 106, 108	15
.303 DB	75	1
.303 SS	70	1
.303 Sav.	92	1
.30-06 M	65, 78, 82, 89, 90, 95	6
.30-40 M	88, 89, 91, 94	4
.30-40 SS	65, 91	2
.30-30 M	82, 99	2
.280 M	66	1
.276 M	78, 95	2
7mm M	70, 84, 87, 95, 97, 99, 102	7
.270 M	65, 95	2
.256 Newton	95	1
.256 Mannl.	64, 66, 67, 69, 70, 77, 78, 81, 93, 96, 97, 100, 102, 104, 106, 111	16
.250 Sav.	79, 92, 95, 99, 103	5
.22 Sav.	92, 95	2
Total		99

SUMMARY

Large Bore	18
Medium Bore	53
Small Bore	99
Total	170

Hunters 49—Rifles per hunter 3.4

PART IV
HIGH VELOCITY
SMALL BORES
1906 TO 1946

CHAPTER 7

HIGH VELOCITY RIFLES

*H*AVING perfected the small-bore rifle as a type, through the adoption of the metal-cased bullet and smokeless powder, gunmakers were at the end of the type improvement of the rifle. This is evidenced by the fact that the rifles still in use today as sporting weapons are predominantly the same designs as were in use in the period from 1895 to 1903. With the exception of the semiautomatic, which in the 35 Remington has reached some degree of popularity for deer hunting in this country, no essential change has occurred in the rifle mechanisms since that date. The Mauser and Mannlicher bolt rifles, the Winchester and Savage lever action repeaters, the custom-made double rifles and falling block single shot rifles are, except for changes in heat treatment or finish, the same today as they were forty years ago. In fact some of the actions of forty to fifty years ago are at a premium today because of their strength and excellent design. Yet there is no question that rifle performance has improved and is continuing to improve. But the improvement has been one of detail and refinement of barrel and chamber design, bullets and powder, and in the development of other accessories.

These refinements of small-bore rifle design and performance have kept pace with a change in the characteristics of big game hunting. The day of the professional hunter, looking for ivory, meat or skins, terminated with the universal adoption of game laws. These men were forced to develop other professions as guides and outfitters, or if their means permitted and they still wished to follow big game hunting as a sport, they had to travel extensively. In their stead came a throng of occasional sportsmen whose knowledge of hunting and of the rifle as a hunting weapon was only rudimentary. With only a short vacation period to devote to hunting, lacking knowledge or experience in stalking, they wanted results in the way of trophies from often poorly directed, long range, snap shots. This change in hunting characteristics gave rise to all manner of untried fads in the way of rifles and ammunition, many of which enjoyed temporary popularity and then passed out. But the one factor which had originally assisted in bringing the small bore into popular favor was still relatively undeveloped. Since the advent of the rifle as a weapon, no one had gone much above 2,000 fet per second in velocity. True this was a feature in the performance of the early American rifle, but it had been lost in the reversion to heavy bores and the long conical bullet after 1800, so that the velocity of 2,000 feet per second developed by the smokeless powder small bore rifles introduced between 1885 and 1895 came almost as an innovation.

But it remained for two men to foster the final great development in rifle performance, although their other efforts toward the improvement of rifle design were ill-fated and led to their being discredited and now virtually forgotten. The characteristic performance of the metal-cased bullet in the small-bore smokeless-powder rifle had been increased velocity, improved accuracy and great penetration but with very little increase in stopping power unless a vital part were hit. To correct this, the soft-nosed bullet had been introduced to increase the area of impact in flesh and improve the stopping power. Even so, the small-bore still lacked effectiveness. Several American sportsmen including Colonel Whelen, Edward Crossman, and Stewart Edward White on his trips to Africa had experimented with the Springfield army rifle in custom-made sporter models, using the sharp-pointed "Spitzer" bullet adopted by the German army in 1905 and by our own Army in 1906, and had reported quite favorable results on game. Yet it was the .280 Ross cartridge, introduced by Sir Charles Ross in 1910, and the Savage .22 Hi Power of 1911 and the .250-3000 in 1914, both cartridges designed by Charles Newton, that really revolutionized small bore performance on big game.

At velocities of 2800 to 3100 feet per second, the lighter sharp pointed bullets of these rifles introduced a new element of shock as a part of bullet performance. It was found by innumerable experiments that, on thin skinned game, even if vital centers were missed through inexperience or inaccurate shooting, instantaneous kills might still result from shock-power. This greatly increased the ability of the casual hunter to kill game even though his hunting and shooting ability were far below that of the guide or professional hunter. It also introduced an element of great danger and one which is impossible to avoid. The lighter pointed bullet because of its shape was easily deflected by brush or bone, and against solid material it frequently disintegrated entirely, with little more effect on game than a charge of bird-shot. Confronted with such unpredictable results the manufacturers and hunters started all over again in their search for bullets which would be effective at high velocity. Some of these are mentioned later in the chapter on accessories but it is sufficient to say here that these faults have still to be overcome if the rifle of ultra high velocity is to be as effective as the earlier small bores.

The further development of accuracy and shock because of higher velocities created a tremendous increase in the interest and knowledge of rifle performance. Just as there are now scores of "wildcat" varmint cartridges, in the period just prior and subsequent to World War I, there was a deluge of "Supers," "Magnums," "Ultras," etc., very few of which had sufficient merit to become permanently established. But these new designs did obscure the value of the already tried and well established small bores of the past. As a consequence during the past thirty years only five real big game cartridges have been developed which are of lasting merit; the .375 Holland Magnum; the .300 Holland Magnum made in this country by Hoffman, Griffin and Howe, and Winchester; the .300 Savage, a shortened Springfield cartridge; the .270 Winchester, a Springfield cartridge of reduced bore; and the .257 Roberts which is a reduced 7mm Mauser. This does not include the English .240 Super cartridges or the .220 Winchester Swift, as these, although they develop under certain circumstances a maximum shock effect, at other times are almost completely ineffective on big game. It is hardly surprising that with so many minds and so many possibilities, the manufacturers have been able to work out so little of permanent value, either in the development of new cartridges or in the improvement of the old ones. Anyone who might have worked out some worthwhile improvement in the performance of the .30-30, .30-40, 7mm or Springfield was considered old fashioned, and the majority opinion favored the small bullet at ultra high velocity.

The following from the third edition of Major Burrard's *Notes on Sporting Rifles* published in 1932 illustrates this swing to high velocities and the impatience with small bore rifles which other greater hunters had found perfectly satisfactory:

The ordinary .256, .275 and .303 small bores (not magnums) used to be favourite rifles with many. I have tried them all against game and do not like them. All three lack killing power, and in this respect cannot be compared to the .280. One goral I shot with a .256 Mannlicher was hit three times before it could be caught and killed. All these three shots were placed just behind the shoulder in a group which I could cover with the palm of my hand. Any one of them must have proved fatal in the end, but all three were not sufficient to kill, although they all seemed perfectly placed. The bullets were soft nosed split.

The shock given to an animal when hit by a bullet travelling with an initial velocity of about 3000 feet per second is enormous, and seems to have a paralyzing effect. I do not think the reasons for this are quite understood. I believe there is something in it more than mere bullet energy. When a muzzle velocity 2500 foot seconds is exceeded the blow of the impact seems to have a different effect on the tissues struck to the effect obtained with a bullet travelling at a lower speed. It is this peculiar property of shock which makes the magnum small bore such a splendid killing weapon, provided it is not abused by being employed against very heavy dangerous game at close quarters. But even with a magnum small bore it is best to use as large a caliber as possible. The greater the diameter of the bullet the more the blow is spread over a larger area of tissue instantaneously, and the greater the resulting shock to the system. A long thin bullet gives better ballistics at extreme range than a shorter one of greater diameter but equal weight, but the latter shoots equally well over sporting distances—i.e., up to 300 yards—and gives a more deadly wound. If the animal makes off, the larger entrance hole to the wound makes a more reliable blood trail, which is important when bear shooting. Looking at the list of magnum small bores, the .375 Magnum will at once strike one on account of its large diametered bullet of good weight and a muzzle velocity of 2800 foot seconds. The result must be extremely flat trajectory and great killing power. The .404 when used with the 300 grain bullet should also prove a most suitable weapon, although it has not got quite such a flat trajectory as has the .375 magnum.

The .360 and .333 are both excellent weapons with heavy bullets and flat trajectories, while the .350 Magnum and .318 (with the 180 grain bullet) run them very close. The .375/.300 combines a good bullet weight with an extremely flat trajectory. Practical experience, however, has shown that the 150 grain bullet is an extraordinarily good killer, and since this bullet gives a flatter trajectory I would myself use this rifle with confidence against all Himalayan game. The .330 and .280's follow very close in bullet weight and have very flat trajectories. I must, however, admit that I prefer a bullet of at least 150 grains, and I would not in any circumstances recommend one of the .240 group for Himalayan shooting on account of their very light bullets. The .270 Winchester has too light a bullet and too high a pressure for my liking.

Burrard, in his dismissal of the .256, .275 and .303 calibers, is so greatly in disagreement with men such as Pease, Littledale, Loder, Lyell, Stigand, Powell-Cotton, Percival, Bell Sheldon, Stefansson and others that one is concerned with his judgment on other rifle matters. Sheldon, as stated in a previous chapter, considered the .256 ample for any American game and proved his statement on sheep, caribou, moose, grizzly and Alaskan brown bear. Pease and Percival used it successfully on lion with a heavier rifle to back it up. Littledale and Loder found the .256 a perfect weapon for chamois, ibex, and sheep, all animals as large or larger than goral. Burrard's Lancaster .280 was the Ross cartridge with 140 grain bullet loaded to 2900 foot seconds velocity by the English cartridge makers and was of about the same power as the .270 Winchester which he disapproves. The .375/.300 is the .300 Holland Magnum, or a .30 caliber bullet in the .375 magnum case necked down, a cartridge which has become highly popular in this country for long range target and hunting work but requires at least a 10 pound rifle for full accuracy and comfort from recoil.

The .280 Ross cartridge was far ahead of its time. With some of the later types of stronger jacketed bullets of greater weight up to 180 grains this cartridge could have become as famous as the .300 Magnum mentioned above. But the Ross action with its straight pull was defective and had little extractive power, and the Mauser action for it was developed after it had become discredited, too late to save a cartridge with some of the finest ballistic properties so far developed. There were many riflemen, however, who could see little advantage in the Ross hunting cartridge over other cartridges of the time and one of these was Capt. E. C. Crossman. The following is quoted from his *Book of the Springfield* in which he praises the .250-3000 Savage and compares it not unfavorably with the .280:

The chief bone of contention among modern hunters is as to whether high velocity is as effective as it is supposed to be by many hunters and some ammunition makers. The row arose about 1911 when the 22 Hi Power was put on the market by the Savage Company in its Model 1899 rifle, and the high speed little bullet developed the most amazing results with its 2800 feet per second and yet only 69 grains of weight.

The second prop for the high velocity claim was the .250-3000 also put out by the Savage Company for its Model 1899 lever action rifles. Two pilot rifles were sent to me in 1914 about the time the Great War broke. The lady and I took them into the Siskyous after the Germans had started their march for Paris and we came out five weeks later fully expecting to find Paris in the German hands and the war over. It was unthinkable that a lot of "Frog" soldiers with their funny red pants and long-tailed coats could stop those grey-clad hordes which had blown the Liege forts off the face of the earth with guns of size which no artillerist had dreamed could be moved on land.

We killed many deer with the rifles in various hands in the party and came out greatly admiring the new cartridge—an admiration which I still retain although I am fully cognizant of its weak spots. The chap with whom I hunted had been using for the three years prior a very heavy .280 Ross with 30 inch barrel and had killed much game with it. He brought it on his trip and we had a chance to compare the .250 with the deadly and certain work of this great copper tube bullet. There was little difference on deer except that the Ross blew up more deer. Both were dead promptly on being hit squarely almost anywhere, or else stopped in their tracks for the coup de grace.

However, as a result of the .280 Ross, the .250 Savage and the .300 Magnum, velocities have been definitely stepped up and powders developed to make these velocities possible in many of the older cartridges in spite of their smaller case capacities. The old 2000 foot small bores are a thing of the past and the task before the cartridge makers has been to develop bullets which will hold together at the higher velocities. During this period of high velocity development and aside from the five cartridges listed as permanent improvements there have been a host of calibers brought out which have had some small popularity but are either now discontinued or little in demand. In England these cartridges were in all calibers from .240 to .505, the Germans produced metric sizes of various calibers from 6mm to 11.3mm with cases of various lengths to meet any requirement, and in America the cartridges ran from the .22 Savage and Newton to the .400 Whelen. Many of these are so nearly alike in caliber and performance that it seems unfortunate that there could not have been some simplification and standardization such as the Germans started at one time in their 6, 6.5, 7, 8 and 9 by 57 millimeter brass cartridge cases, all of which would run through the same magazine and bolt action.

And now to review the rifles developed in this period to meet the demands of the new type of sportsmen and solve their attempts to obtain the all round one shot special. Convinced of the continued popularity of the magazine rifle the English gunmakers produced these, as stated, in all calibers from .240 to .505 only two of which have reached any degree of popularity, the .375 and .300 Holland Magnums, the Germans produced a whole series of metric sizes from 6.5 to 11 millimeters, of which two became popular, the 9.3 and 10.75mm Mausers, and the Americans brought out cartridges from .22 to .400 caliber of which four appear in our listing, the .250 Savage, the .270 Winchester, the .280 Ross and the .35 Whelen. Other miscellaneous calibers are still in use and have their supporters, but none have been of enough popularity to receive continued mention in the accounts of big game hunting. Most of these have been included in addition to the ones noted above in the following list of cartridges and performances:

RIFLES OF THE HIGH VELOCITY PERIOD

English
.300 Caliber and Over

Rifle	Caliber	Bullet	Velocity	Energy
Gibbs	.505	525	2300	6170
Westley	.425	410	2350	5020
Rigby	.416	410	2350	5020
Gibbs	.404	400	2125	4010
Holland	.375	270	2650	4200
Rigby	.350	225	2600	3400
Jeffery	.333	180	2500	3470

Under .300 Caliber

Rifle	Caliber	Bullet	Velocity	Energy
Rigby	.275	140	2825	2480
Rigby	.275	160	2700	2590
B. S. A.	.260	110	3100	2350
Gibbs	.256	135	2800	2348
Purdey	.246	100	2950	1940
Vickers	.242	100	3000	2000
Holland	.240	100	2950	1940

American
.300 Caliber and Over

Rifle	Caliber	Bullet	Velocity	Energy
Whelen	.400	350	2250	3940
Newton	.35	250	2975	4925
Whelen	.35	250	2450	3330
Winchester	.348	200	2535	2860
Springfield	.30	150	3000	3045
Newton	.30	172	3000	3440
Savage	.30	150	2660	2360

Under .300 Caliber

Rifle	Caliber	Bullet	Velocity	Energy
Ross	.280	145	3100	3090
Dubiel	.280	180	2800	3135
Hoffman	.276	160	2800	2790
G. & H.	7mm	139	3000	2780
Winchester	.270	130	3120	2810
Newton	.256	123	3103	2632
Roberts	.257	117	2630	1800
Savage	.250	87	3000	1740
Savage	.22	70	2800	1220
Winchester	.220	48	4140	1830

German
.300 Caliber and Over

Rifle	Caliber	Bullet	Velocity	Energy
Mauser	11.2 x 60	332	2450	4420
Mauser	10.75 x 73	400	2300	4700
Mauser	10.75 x 68	347	2300	4070
Mauser	9.3 x 70	300	2800	5200
Mauser	9.3 x 62	255	2700	4100
Mauser	9.3 x 62	285	2346	3486
Mannlicher	9 x 56	205	2225	2350
Mauser	8 x 60	186	2900	3450

Under .300 Caliber

Rifle	Caliber	Bullet	Velocity	Energy
Halger	.280	180	3000	3600
Halger	.280	143	3450	3780
Halger	.280	100	3800	3210
Hoffman	7 x 73	170	3350	4020
Mauser	7 x 64	173	2775	2940
Mauser	6.5 x 61	155	2750	2600
Mauser	6.5 x 54	136	2675	2160
Mannlicher	6.5 x 54	127	2690	2040
Mauser	6 x 58	123	2675	1950

LOOK OUT!

From the *American Rifleman*, taken by A. R. Siedentopf.

CHARLES SHELDON. AIR-BRAKE MANUFACTURER, BIG GAME HUNTER, NATURALIST, AUTHOR AND COLLECTOR.

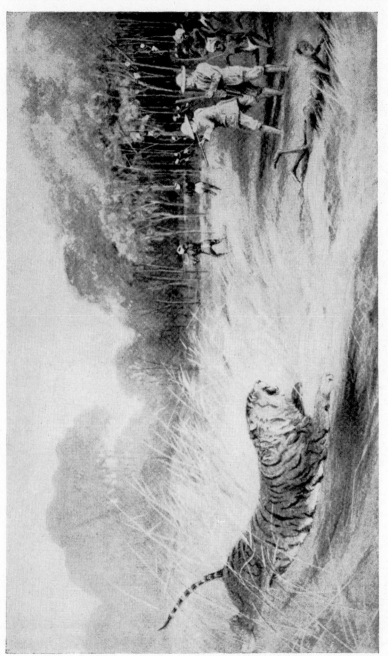

A CHARGING TIGER.

From the Badminton Library of *Big Game Shooting.*

TIGER HUNTING IN MYSORE, INDIA.

CHAPTER 8

HIGH VELOCITY ON BIG GAME

WE have seen how the success of the small-bore on big game and its easy adaptation from mass-produced military arms opened a new era for the rifleman-hunter. Luckily, and not quite too late came also a consciousness that game must be conserved. The number and effectiveness of hunters and their weapons was becoming too destructive. These game conservation laws put an end to the market hunter and left the hunting of big game a part-time sport for the many. The increasing scarcity of game and the restricted hunting season brought into use guides and the setting up of camps and game preserves. More than this, it brought to big-game hunting each year men who had had very little shooting the rest of the year and who found the small bores not quite as effective as the experts had led them to believe. This and the willingness of the manufacturers to increase sales and at the same time satisfy the popular demands resulted, as already remarked, in many new cartridges and rifle models. When these new cartridges were simply an increase in the shell capacity for the same caliber they became "Magnums." Others of new form or caliber were termed variously "Supers," "High Velocity," "Hi Power," "Nitro Express," etc. But the object behind these changes, in every case, was the same, to give the one-shot sportsman the killing power of the expert game shot. And the result was not always fortunate.

The first of these new rifles was the .280 Ross, already mentioned, brought out by the Ross Rifle Co. of Quebec, Canada in 1910. Because of the unfortunate death of Mr. George Grey who, when hunting with Sir Alfred Pease in East Africa, failed to stop a charging lion with the 145 grain bullet and was badly mauled on that account, and also because the straight pull action was found defective by the Canadian Army in the mud of Flanders in 1914-15 this otherwise excellent rifle and its remarkable .280 cartridges have passed virtually into oblivion.

That Sir Charles Ross was no novice with the rifle is evident from the following quoted from a letter received from him some time before his

death, written from his home at Passagrille, Florida, to which he had retired from work as a consulting engineer in Washington, D. C.:

I started off at the age of 10 with a single-barrel muzzle-loading rifle—
bore about 14 gauge, sights for 50, 75 and 100 yards. You loaded the
thing at the house, rammed the charge home, primed the nipple, put on
a cap and put the hammer down on a wad. You wrapped it up in oil-
cloth and set out. If you were able to crawl within 60 yards or so of the
stag, you hoped to God that the rifle would not miss fire or the stag jump
at the flash. If all went well in due course there was a resounding thump.
My father bought a pair of breech-loading Snider rifles of the pin-fire
variety, bore .577 caliber. Next came along Martini-Henry .450 caliber
which Alexander Henry of Edinburgh promptly converted into an Express
rifle by the simple means of cutting the lead off from the bullet and increasing the powder charge.
Then I came along with bottle-shaped cartridges and a bullet of .360
caliber. The rifle was double barreled and made up by Alexander Henry
of Edinburgh. All of the above were black powder rifles and covered
the period from 1882 to 1893. Somewhere about this time the advent
of the true small bore occurred, which I think was contemporaneous with
the discovery of smokeless powder. I think the British .303 was a copy
inspired by Continental practice in rifle making, of which I secured and
used a Roumanian .256 Mannlicher.
About 1905, by which time I had gone into the rifle business, the Germans or myself discovered the startling fact that the bullet went through
the air a good deal more easily with a sharp nose than with a blunt nose. I
think the discovery was probably simultaneous, but the Germans got the
credit for the Spitzer or sharp pointed bullet by being smart enough to
publish first. What has only been discovered recently, within the last
10 or 20 years, is that the sharp pointed bullet takes effect where the
speed of the bullet exceeds the speed of sound. If you think of a bullet
as pear shaped, you get the least resistance by shooting the sharp end first.
When you dropped the velocity of the bullet to the speed of sound, the
blunt nose gives you the least resistance. You will note that the longitudinal section of the pear shaped bullet has a very close resemblance to
the aeroplane wing.

In regard to the fine points of the Ross rifle and .280 cartridge, the
following is quoted from *The Book of the Springfield* by Capt. E. C.
Crossman:

Sir Charles Ross with his .280 match rifles upset all accuracy standards
for match and service rifles at Bisley from 1908 to the Great War, the

.303 Canadian service Ross winning steadily in the hands of the crack Canadian riflemen against the teams from the home country and other colonies, while the .280 match rifles cleaned the boards in the long range matches. Some of this superiority for the .280 was due to the huge case, the high sectional density of the bullet combined with its high velocity. This, however, applied chiefly to the windjamming ability. Accuracy— the ability to group in a small angle—is different again. Much of it was due to the careful experimental work of the Ross outfit as to getting out the best barrel form.

Ross wrote to me at one time that: "The distribution of metal makes a great difference and in the most surprising places; I knew of a case in a Ross match barrel where the removal of $\frac{1}{4}$ oz. from the straight part of the barrel just forward of the receiver completely destroyed its accuracy. It is a question of barrel vibration. You want to think of the barrel as flapping up and down and then jockey the length or distribution so as to compensate the unavoidable variations of the velocities.

Other cartridges of the type which have been more or less popular were the 22 Hi Power Savage, the .256 Gibbs Magnum, the .275 Holland Magnum later copied in this country by Hoffman and Dubiel, the .250-3000 Savage, and the .256 Newton. The performance of some of these has already been referred to and more will appear in this chapter, but the period is generally one of mixed preferences, and lacks the evidence of consistent and continuous use of a few calibers which characterized the early small bores. Almost any of these rifles in capable hands, and within limitations were effective big game weapons. But in the hands of an untrained hunter, they were frequently little better than suicidal. It is on that account that guides and expert game shots have argued for heavier bores for the one-shot sportsman.

Lt. Col. C. H. Stockley, commenting on the .280 Ross in his book *Stalking in the Himalayas and Northern India,* said:

As the "magnum" rifles came in I took to a .280 Ross, the muzzle velocity being 2,900 feet per second, and was very successful with it until an accidental meeting with a tiger in Siam, which tried to take my dog off the path in front of me. I fired two soft-nosed bullets at twenty-three and five yards, the first penetrating about five inches into the chest, the second about three and one-half inches at the back of the shoulder blade. The bullets smashed into minute fragments, and while the first did break up the big blood vessels which lie just behind the breast bone, the second merely made a bad surface wound, though it knocked the tiger down by force of impact. He carried on past me into thick cover and died 100 yards away. It was particularly noticeable that the penetration was much less with the bullet fired at the closer range.

In contrast to this, I fired a .318 bullet at a Kashmir stag standing facing me at seventy yards. It went through the center of his chest, and I picked it out, nicely mushroomed, from under the skin of his right hip. A Kashmir stag has as big a body as a tiger.

Stockley thought that the expanding bullets with velocities over 2,600 feet per second were likely to prove extremely dangerous by flying to pieces at ranges under 100 yards. Major Gerald Burrard used a heavy .280 single-shot Lancaster for Himalayan game and Capt. W. T. Short-hose used a .280 Lancaster Mauser in Africa. Both used the usual 140 grain copper tube bullet. Burrard considered this bullet excellent for Himalayan shooting where ranges were usually 300 yards or over. He was strong for a heavy, fairly long-barrelled rifle, with a bearer to carry it for him. None of these men had any experience with the 180 grain bullet which should have been a much better performer on game. Capt. Shorthose who had used a .470 double Lancaster, a .318 Westley-Richards and a .280 Lancaster Mauser interchangeably between 1910 and 1919 on elephant with indifferent success, discarded them all and ordered a double .577 from Lancaster after being caught and severely injured by an elephant that he had hit twice with the .318 and then failed to stop with the .470 when charging.

And now for experiences with the smallest big-game rifle listed, the .22 Hi-power Savage. The Reverend Harry Caldwell, author of *Blue Tiger,* a book of his hunting experiences in China, used a .303 Savage until the .22 came out. With this latter rifle he hunted tiger in South China. It is his picture which appeared in the Savage catalogues of about 1920, standing with the .22 Savage rifle behind a tiger laid out on wooden trestles. His account of the killing of this maneater follows:

I saw the time had come to fire. Further delay might prove a serious matter. I was armed with the then most talked of gun on the American market, a .22 Hi-power Savage rifle. The theorist had pronounced this ball too light to prove effective in big-game shooting, while on the other side guides in the Rockies had reported it as being effective on both bear and big-horn sheep. The discussion I had read pro and con in the sporting magazines concerning this gun confronted me as I was brought to a place of severe test, but I dared not reflect long over these things. I fired with great deliberation, covering as best I could my sights in the gloom, and striking the animal squarely back of the ribs. It was far too dark to pick any vital spot.   The big cat lunged into the air coming down dead. The ball entered the stomach cavity, doing terrible execution.   Had the animal swallowed an explosive bomb, the results could not have been more disastrous.   No animal could sustain such a shock and live to do much damage.

Later when Caldwell hunted wapiti and big-horn sheep with Roy Chapman Andrews in North China in 1919, he used a .250-3000 Savage with which he bagged a world's record head of the Ovis Comosa with horns of sixty-two inches.   The three shots at the large ram were made at long range but could be covered by one hand.   Of the effect of the 87 grain bullet on a large wapiti bull Caldwell says:

My first shot had completely shattered the left shoulder, part of the ball ripping great holes through the lungs, while the metal jacket passed through the right shoulder blade and was found just under the skin on the off side.   It was a demonstration of the terrific shocking power of the .250-3000 cartridge.

In a recent letter to me from his present home in this country, Dr. Caldwell said he was forced to leave everything when he last came out of China, but promised to publish at some later time an even more thrilling account of his further hunting adventures in that country.   In the interim between his work in China, he has kept up his rifle practice by hunting wild boars in the Great Smokies and the brown bear in Alaska. Of this latter he says:

I knocked over an Alaskan brown bear with a single body shot with a .300 Savage.   The sourdoughs and Indians at the cannery from whence we launched our first hunt pleaded with me not to even attempt to kill one of those huge bears with such a gun.   The Indians declared my wife would become a widow and my children would be left fatherless if I enraged one of those fierce brutes.   Well, I sure put the big boy down to stay with a single shot.   Later on I did exactly what Roy Chapman Andrews did, and returned to the .250-3000 as the more powerful gun of the two.

Further commendation of both these Savage rifles is given by F. H. Riggal in a communication to *The American Rifleman* several years ago:

The two big seventeen-inch rams killed last fall were shot one with an 8 mm. Mauser using 236 grain soft-pointed bullets, and the other with a .250-3000; and the .250-3000 did much the better job; although its ram was over 200 yards away and the 8 mm.'s not over twenty-five feet. The ram shot by the 8 mm. lived five minutes after a chest shot and the one killed by the .250-3000 was stone dead inside of five seconds; although struck in the lungs only and heart not touched. From these and many other experiences, I have a very high opinion of the .250 Savage and believe that far more game is lost or merely wounded through flinching than from inadequate power in the rifles used, and owing to its light recoil the .250 or .256 will get game for men for whom the .30M, .35 W.C.F., .450 W.C.F., et cetera will simply be impossible. I had a similar experience with a .22 H.P. and a small ram. I had that morning already killed a big ram at 120 yards with the .22, shooting him through the spine at the base of the neck, one-third down from the withers (the bullet shattered the spine and passed out in front of the shoulder on the far side).

But not all the users of the .250 were so enthusiastic. Charles Cottar had excellent luck with it on smaller antelope in East Africa, but it failed on crocodile and the larger antelope. After experimenting on a charging rhino which was downed with four shots between twenty-five yards and eight yards, with two of the bullets flattening on the beast's skull, he reported as follows in *Outdoor Life* magazine for June 1916:

Allow me to say that I will never try such an experiment again—and will never forget this one. Behind me the steady click of the camera and in front 4,000 pounds of infuriation with a horn on its bow, headed straight on, with only an 87 grain missile to stop it. It isn't a pleasant thought, even yet.

His final comment on the .250 Savage seems to place it in its proper class, even though given thirty years ago in a foreign land:

The flatness of trajectory and swift-flying missile renders the .250 one of the best guns possible for game up to the size of white-tail deer and black bear, when in competent hands, and with proper ammunition, a good weapon for all American game, when in the hands of a hunter; but, too small, with any ammunition, when in the hands of individuals who shoot only occasionally. These fellows should use a weapon that will tear a leg off at the hip, or disembowel an animal if the skin on the abdomen is touched. The .250 will not do it. It has its limitations and is a beauty and a killer in its limits. Don't expect it to rank with the Ross, the Springfield, the big Winchesters or the Mausers. On the other hand, for accuracy, flatness of trajectory, slightness of recoil and lightness in weight, it has them all skinned a country block.

It's not surprising that many hunters with such experiences gave up the extreme convenience of the small bore, even when speeded up, and specialized on heavier rifles. Of this category are Major G. P. Evans, hunting in Burma; Col. A. E. Stewart for tiger in India; Wilfred Robertson and D. E. Blunt in Africa, the Roosevelts on their hunt in Central Asia, and Doctor Sutton in Africa and Indo-China. Their reasons are well stated by Major Evans:

As to rifles, the writer believes implicitly in a D.B. .450-400 high-velocity rifle taking the equivalent of 60 grains of cordite in axite, and a 400 grain bullet. With this rifle elephants, bison, and tsine have been shot in the densest cover and in the open alike. It has now been in use several years and during that time it has not lost its owner a single beast shot at. Generally one, or at most two, bullets have been sufficient to account for the biggest animals; but I have had occasionally to give a beast as many as half a dozen shots before securing him. This, however, has been under exceptional circumstances when either the denseness of the jungle or the failing light has prevented an accurate aim being taken.

Major Evans account of how he came to pick out his favorite .400 caliber express is interesting as showing some of the difficulties encountered with custom gun makers:

While in England I went to one or two of the leading rifle makers, but was confronted with the difficulty with regard to cartridges which had caused me so much bother and expense with the 10 bore. The makers declined to supply rifles to take Kynoch's or Eley's cases. The reason alleged was that the importance of a rifle cartridge being absolutely reliable was so great that the rifle makers did not care to risk cartridges turned out by others. This objection has always seemed to me to be puerile. Cartridge manufacturers like Eley and Kynoch do not supply bad cartridges, and a misfire from one of their cartridges is not more likely to occur than from a cartridge supplied by the maker of the rifle. The real reason was not far to seek. However, I had suffered such inconvenience in Burma from having to get my cartridges sent out direct from England, and had been put to such expense in the matter of freight, duty and finally, carriage to my destination, not to mention the fact that the actual price of special cartridges was considerably higher than the price of those turned out by cartridge manufacturers, that I decided to go for my rifle where I could get one taking Eley's or Kynoch's cases. I therefore went to the Army and Navy Stores in Victoria Street, and have never regretted having done so. I had no experience of high velocity rifles, but decided on a .450 bore, as I thought a .400 would prove too light a weapon for efficient use on heavy game.

Having appointed a day for the trial of a couple of rifles at the Society's range at Nunhead, I went down there shortly before returning to Burma. To my dismay the .450 rifles were not forth coming, but the Society's employe had brought with him a couple of .450-400 rifles instead. He explained that, owing to the new rule prohibiting the importation into India of .450 rifles the Society was unable to supply one. The regulation had only just been published. Fortunately for myself the specialist in the gun department had neglected to send down a couple of .500 rifles for trial in addition to the .400, or I would almost certainly have plumped for one of these, and so have unnecessarily overweighted myself. Here was a dilemma! I could only spare one more day at Nunhead to try the rifle again, when a particular form of backsight I had designed was fitted. And I had little faith in the .400 bore. However, here I was, and here were the rifles, I might just as well try them, now that I had troubled to come down. I did so, and was so pleased with their accuracy and penetration that I selected the one which had given the best results, and ordered the backsight to be fitted, and the stock cut to my measurements. For good or ill I was now pledged to the .400. I tried it again with the new backsight, and it made wonderful shooting, so that, as far as accuracy went, I had a rifle I could rely on. On getting out to Burma the first thing I tackled with it was a bull bison. The bullet a solid nickel, struck the animal in the chest and was cut out close to the tail. The bull galloped for a hundred yards and fell over dead. The next time I used it was also against bison, in very thick cover in August. I got up to within six yards of the beast before I could see him at all. A soft nosed bullet behind the shoulder, as he stood broadside on, bowled him over, and I gave him two more shots merely to prevent him getting on his legs in the dense stuff in which he was. The bull was really killed by the first shot . . .

Space does not avail to relate the subsequent performances of this insignificant-looking little rifle, but it will suffice to say that it has accounted for close on eighty head of game, both in India and Burma, from goral to elephants, and has never yet failed me. It has killed among other game some thirty thick-skinned animals; so that it has been thoroughly tested. I have missed with it occasionally, of course, when firing long shots at goral or barking deer; but the fault has lain with me not with the rifle. The cartridges (Kynoch's) can be supplied either with cordite or axite powder. Personally, I prefer the last. Axite is practically unaffected by tropical temperature, does not corrode the barrels as cordite does, and is just as powerful. The rifle is more easily cleaned than when cordite is used, and there is not the same necessity for wiping out the barrels immediately after use. The cartridges are obtainable from the Army and Navy Stores, Calcutta, or from any of the gun-makers in the large Presidency towns of India, or from Rangoon. Provided that one is careful to purchase only cartridges newly arrived from England, there is no fear of their proving unsatisfactory, either as regards misfires or deficiency in penetration. The writer has used cartridges which have been opened for two years and has never had a misfire or found them lacking either in penetration or accuracy.

Dr. Sutton was not quite so extreme, believing in a medium small bore supported by a bonebreaking stopper for dangerous game at close range. His comments, based on a long hunting experience including trips to Africa, Asia and the Arctic, come close to defining the all-round rifle. This is from his book *An African Holiday*:

With the majority of sportsmen, the gun question is one of great moment. In America, we feel the Springfield is the sporting weapon par excellence. It is light, powerful, easily handled, and has a very low trajectory, and great striking power. For animals of moderate vitality, as bear, moose, and elk, it fills the bill to perfection. But in the hands of the average man, it carries too light a bullet for African game. If one could hit a vital spot every time, well and good, but how many of us can invariably do this? I have seen a Grant's gazelle, a dainty little animal weighing not more than one hundred pounds, staggering along with no less than six thirty caliber bullet holes through its neck, shoulders, abdomen, and leg! It was not the fault of the cartridges, for we tried three different standard makes, and all mushroomed perfectly. With zebra it was the same story. The 180 grain projectiles appeared to do much more damage than those of lesser weight, but all were too light, and possessed insufficient shocking power.

The first bullet that strikes the animal is the important one. After that a beast can be fairly riddled, and will still crawl miserably along.

Judging from my own observations on the results secured by eight different men with whom I hunted at various times, I think that a bullet weighing at least two hundred and twenty, or better, two hundred and fifty grains, is best. In a modern rifle, a projectile of this weight gives a terrific punch and possesses great killing power. I am thoroughly conversant with the thousand and one library arguments in favor of the small bore high velocity rifle, and I have owned and hunted with a number of them, from the .22 Hi-power to the .280 Ross. But I am now speaking of practical game killers for African game.

The .35 Whelen cartridge should prove very effective for this work. It is a highly scientific combination, and appeals to me very much. The .300 Savage also is good, and a great favorite with the Cottars. The .35 caliber Winchester is much used in America, but is one of the most wretchedly balanced guns in the world, and for this reason few English-men will use it. At the principal gun store in Nairobi, I have seen the proprietor actually offer a model '95 Winchester, as a sort of premium, to a customer who was willing to purchase a few hundred cartridges. For those who prefer a bolt action rifle, I would suggest a .318 Westley-Richards, or Gibbs, or an 8mm Mauser. The 9mm Mannlicher-Schoen-auer is a popular all-round weapon on the frontier. It was first recom-mended to me by my friend, Dr. Stefansson, the Arctic explorer, and the pre-war weapons undoubtedly were most admirable pieces of workmanship. Unfortunately, the quality of some of those of post-war manufacture is open to suspicion, and lack of confidence in a sporting weapon is a fatal defect.

Of the various heavy rifles, there is little choice. Formerly those of .450 caliber were most popular, but owing to the fact that the cartridges are interchangeable with those of the old Martini, and the ever present danger of native uprisings, rifles and ammunition of this size cannot be imported into India or into Uganda. This has had a serious effect on the second-hand value of the big rifles. Few men care to pay one hundred pounds or more for a gun that cannot readily be resold. In order to comply with this regulation, British manufacturers are now making guns of various other calibres, varying from .465 to .600. The majority are double-barreled ejectors, weighing from nine to sixteen pounds. The muzzle energy is from 4000 to 8000 pounds, and the weapons are sur-prisingly accurate. The standard price in London, for an A Grade gun is about $650.00. Most of the heavy game was killed with a .465 Hol-land and Holland, a duplicate of the one used by Colonel Roosevelt, in 1909, and it proved a most excellent and dependable arm. Despite the large charge of powder, the recoil is negligible. Our other big gun, a .577 Westley-Richards, was too heavy for quick work and snap shooting, but it was a very powerful and trustworthy weapon, and one which could be relied upon in any emergency. Few animals can withstand the impact of a seven hundred and fifty grain bullet, backed by one hundred and ten grains of cordite, and more than one shot seldom is required.

Used double rifles in gun crank condition, can be purchased very cheaply in Nairobi, and by doing this the payment of the 30 percent import tax can be avoided. Cartridges of all calibres also are obtainable, and at prices almost identical with our retail prices at home.

Wilfred Robertson, who has contributed many articles to *The American Rifleman,* is another advocate of the medium bore double .400 for use on African game as will be shown by the following, quoted from *The American Rifleman* of September, 1930:

The finest rifle I have ever used was a .450-400 bore, double-barreled ejector Express rifle by Jeffery of London. This rifle was absolutely accurate, flat in its trajectory, and possessed wonderful killing power. With this bore I have shot all sizes of African game, from elephant downwards. It fires a 400 grain bullet driven by a charge of 55 to 60 grains of Cordite. The recoil is but small provided the rifle is held properly and allowed to swing with the shot. Of course, those who hold a rifle of this bore and charge loosely or stand rigid to the recoil must expect to be bumped by the recoil.

Commander David E. Blunt, a retired British naval officer in charge of game control in Tanganyika Territory, East Africa, preferred a magazine rifle to the double barrel, but it had to be of fairly large bore as the following quoted from his book *Elephant,* published in 1938, will indicate:

The .416 Rigby magazine I have always used has the same muzzle energy as a double-barrel .470, but the bullet has greater penetration and the weapon is, in my opinion, the most perfectly balanced rifle in every way for elephant. The double .600 has too heavy a bullet for the charge of Cordite. For other game I recommend the .318 Westley-Richards and nothing smaller. If two rifles are taken out after elephant, then they should be of identical make, bore, and action. I do not consider that a man has to be a very good shot to be an elephant hunter. As with all game, the thrill is in the close approach rather than in the killing. If a sportsman has made a successful stalk after a buck, and wants the horns for a trophy, then the animal should be put to death in the most humane way; and there is no doubt that with the average shot the big-bore rifle is the most humane weapon, for, if a vital spot is missed, the quarry will not go far and will most certainly be put out of its pain quickly.

Col. A. E. Stewart in his vade mecum for tiger shooting, *Tiger,* argues for nothing less than a double .475 Cordite Express. Kermit and Theodore Roosevelt took .30-'06 Springfields and .375 Hoffman magazine rifles on their trip to Central Asia.   Dr. James L. Clark has collected and set up groups of mammals for the American Museum of Natural History from North America, Africa and Asia.   His first experience in Africa was in protecting A. Radcliffe Dugmore when photographing wild game. The finest picture ever taken of a charging rhino was of a rhino bull that was stopped eleven yards from the camera by the second barrel of his .470 double rifle.   With this rifle he had a 7.9 Mauser as a reserve.   On his trip with Morden to Central Asia they were armed with Springfields. When he went to Indo-China for gaur, buffalo, etc., he took a .465 Holland in addition to the .470 Evans with a .318 Rigby and a Springfield in reserve.

While Steward Edward White was listed in an earlier period this is an excellent place to include his comments on the small bore and medium bore in Africa as recounted in his book *The Rediscovered Country* published in 1915:

I shot again the new Springfield rifle, using the spitzer pointed bullet of 165 grains and 172 grains weight.   Some of these had been exposed to tropical conditions for three years, but I could see no deterioration. Their performance was uniform and very deadly.   The same could not be said of the 150 grain service bullet, forty rounds of which I used as a trial.   Their action was too erratic, as a certain proportion of them showed a tendency to dive outrageously.   In my opinion the 172 grain U.M.C. bullet is an ideal hunting cartridge; as was also the Winchester 165 grain. The latter unfortunately is no longer manufactured.   An analysis of the work done by this weapon results as follows:

Shots fired	260	Animals shot at ...	161
Hits	199	Animals missed ...	26
Misses	61	Animals killed	135

Of the above 135 animals killed with this rifle, 98 went down to one shot each.   The longest range was 421 yards; the average for antelope, 196 yards.   These measurements were all paced.

For the second gun I used, as before, the .405 Winchester.   It is light, handy, and delivers a very hard blow at close ranges.   Beyond 150 yards, however, it loses velocity too fast to make it of the first use.   It is a good brush gun, and has always done me well with lions.   Its record was:

Shots fired	33	Animals shot at ...	14
Hits	29	Animals killed	14
Misses	4		

In the case of the four lions I was forced to take on at once, I used alternately the Springfield and the Winchester. One of these was a bolt action, the other a lever action arm. According to those who argue most vigorously on either side of the rather bitter controversy, this alternating of weapons should have confused me, or at least caused me to take thought. As a matter of fact, it did nothing of the kind. I used either with equal facility and with equal unconsciousness. My firm belief is that neither action has the slightest advantage over the other in practical work.

My third reserve weapon was the Holland and Holland .465 cordite. This was useful only on the heaviest game. Except for buffalo, rhinoceros, and perhaps elephants, I could very well get on without it.

White's experience with the Winchester .405, and the experience of the Roosevelts, Cottar, Bronson and Burbridge with the same rifle, label it as a pretty reliable, close range weapon and none of them complain of jamming such as occasionally happened to the 1895 Winchester made for the .30-40 U. S. cartridge and occasionally to other models of lever action magazine rifles. This fault commented on by Dr. Sutton may have been due to the rimmed cartridge being caught in the magazine or the rifle being operated out of the vertical plane. According to Arthur Young, who with Sexton Pope tried lion hunting with bow and arrow but gave it up as a bad job, Leslie Simpson killed 40 lions with a .30-06, 1895 Winchester and 220 grain bullets. Young using the same rifle killed an additional 25 lions. At the time they were hunting, in 1925, Simpson was using just two rifles a .577 double barrel and the .30-06 Winchester which was his favorite. His comments on the .30-06 as an all-round rifle will be found in the next chapter. Before the .30-06 he had used the .416 Rigby and the .318 Westley-Richards.

The .318 Rigby and .318 Westley Richards were an outgrowth of the 7.9mm Mauser, which, though widely used as a hunting rifle had received very little notice except for being the German Army rifle. Lyell rated it a better killer than the .256, .275, or .303. It was also used by Martin Ryan and T. A. Barns in Africa for all types of game including elephant. But its most enthusiastic user was Maj. H. C. Maydon, editor of the Lonsdale Library volume *Big Game Shooting in Africa,* and author of several very interesting books on big-game hunting in India and Africa. In one of these he has this to say about rifles in general and the 7.9mm Mauser in particular:

By an 'all-round' rifle I mean a medium magazine rifle. Not so small bored that it won't kill clean, nor so big that it will lure you to false security. I have tried many varieties and my own preference is a 7.9 Mauser (about .311 English). I like a .303 too, but there is likely to be trouble importing ammunition through some customs. I have seldom owned any magazine rifle that was not secondhand, and I have never paid more than £10 for one. When you are abroad and can own several rifles without feeling that you are 'suspect' as we feel at home, you will, sooner or later, begin acquiring rifles as some men do polo ponies and, the less lucky, golf clubs. There is a certain feel about a nice rifle; you love to handle it. I fancy it is the cartridge-maker who lets you down at last. They won't be happy with a good thing and must be forever tinkering (like cars again) until a year comes when your rifle won't shoot as it used to do and it must go. But I am still using my old 7.9 Mauser, now close on twenty years and I'm still using nothing but wartime German service ammunition. The old Boche knew something about rifles. Choose a carbine or short rifle since it is easier to carry slung in thick bush and you will not need long shots. Try to get a rifle with a flat trajectory up to 200 yards and tear off all other sighting leaves. They only put you off or get pushed up by accident at the wrong moment, or persuade you that you can kill further than you ought. The best range is the nearest possible, with 200 yards as your limit. Never further than 200 yards? Well, almost never. When you must break that golden rule, take a full sight and pin your faith on Nimrod. He'll play up if you are playing fair . . . . Shoot as much ordinary game as you can with the magazine rifle until you have learnt something of stalking, of judging distances, of native guides, of fatal shots, and, above all, of your own self-confidence, Then, and only then, collect your heavy rifle and go 'for the heavy game.

So that the reader will not think from the above that the use of bores smaller than the 7.9mm or .30 caliber has become passé in African hunting after Neumann, Pease, Percival, Stigand and Bell, the following is quoted from articles contributed to the *American Rifleman* in 1928 to 1932 by Vasco Da Gama, a Portuguese nobleman who spent two years hunting and collecting in French Equatorial Africa between 1925 and 1928:

The 7mm or .276 is a cartridge having much higher characteristics (than the Mannlicher) due to the heavier weight of the bullet—173 grains, which with 37.8 grains of powder, is given a muzzle velocity of 2362 f. s. and an energy of 2140 ft. lbs. This I have used on almost all kinds of game in Africa. The form of the bullet appeals to me extremely, as the ratio of diameter to length is arranged in such a successful fashion as to prevent both deflection and loss of shape, which naturally means loss of accuracy, if the bullet goes through heavy bones. This ammunition can be used not only in standard-make Mauser rifles but also in the very remarkable little weapon made by Messrs. John Rigby of London, weighing but 6½ pounds, with a short barrel, and being 100 percent accurate and effective at 200 and 250 yards. Although this rifle looks like a toy, such masters of elephant hunting as W. D. Bell, Neumann and others used it to the exclusion of every other during most of their hunts through the wilds of Africa. Such a rifle, particularly if made in England, is admirably well-balanced. It can be carried all the time without any physical fatigue. The shortness of the cartridge case makes it very easy to operate the bolt while the gun is still at the shoulder, doing away with the loss of time and aim which is incurred if the weapon is taken down from the shoulder to operate the repeat action. A little practice will permit you to fire the five cartridges contained in the magazine and chamber with the same rapidity as that of an automatic pistol. . .

For anyone wanting an all-round rifle for any game at all at tolerably short range, the 7mm Mauser ammunition used, preferably, in a London-made gun, will prove very successful; although on animals like antelopes, on whose moderate weight the shock of a heavier bullet might register, perhaps a bigger bullet could be advised.

Da Gama killed 42 elephants in his two year trip and tried out several of the English double barrel expresses, of two of which, the .577 and .600 he had this to say:

The former of these two rifles fires a bullet weighing 750 grains, with 90 grains of powder, delivering a blow of 5483 pounds; while the .500 firing a bullet of 900 grains with 100 grains of powder, delivers a blow of 6800 ft. lbs. The terrific recoil of these two weapons does away with the main advantage of expresses, viz., the possibility of firing almost instantaneously the second shot. These rifles weigh between 14 and 16 pounds. They are, consequently, very difficult to manipulate and carry, and the noise developed by the terrific amount of powder which they fire warns the game in a radius of many miles of the presence of the hunter, and from that aspect alone they are not to be recommended.

But perhaps we should have some idea of what should be considered the best calibers of rifles for hunting our commonest form of big game, in this country, the Virginia deer.   A. H. Carhart uses a .25-35, Newsom and Lee found the .256 Mannlicher and .250 Savage excellent.   C. E. Hagie makes an excellent summary of the rifles needed in his recent book *How to Hunt North American Big Game.*

For short range shooting in brushy country the .30-30 Winchester and .30 Remington which are ballistically identical, are hard to beat in spite of the fact that the load is more than fifty years old.   The .30-40 is more powerful than necessary, but is an excellent brush cartridge.   Both the .25-35 Winchester and the .25 Remington are adequate for white-tails, and the .250-3000 Savage is about as near the last word in deer rifles as will ever be built.

The 87 grain hollow-point bullet in the .250-3000 Savage is not surpassed by any cartridge in use today for killing qualities on such game as deer; but it is almost useless in thick brush since it will go to pieces on impact with twigs.   But the 100 grain Winchester Silvertip bullet in this cartridge will do a very satisfactory job in brushy country, because it holds together exceptionally well.

One of the foremost American authorities on rifles is Colonel Townsend Whelen, who has hunted all species of American game from Panama to Alaska.   During some fifty years of hunting, the Colonel has used many rifles, but will probably admit that his favorites have been the .30-40 U. S. which he used in a Winchester single shot, the .30-06 Springfield which he used in a remodeled Springfield and the .270 Model 70 Winchester.   A review of his many articles and books would indicate that he used the .30-06 longer and killed more game with it than any other rifle, although a recent series of articles written after his strenuous hunting trip to British Colombia late in 1946 devotes considerable space to the .270 which he has used since 1930.   Consequently, although he now considers the .270 sufficient for any American game, in my tabulation of favorite rifles in a later chapter, the .30-06 is set opposite his name, as I believe he would consider it the best all-purpose rifle for this continent.

All this goes to show the great diversity of opinion on rifles suitable for big game hunting.   Each hunter in turn, from the man who carried the 4 bore muzzle loader, to the hunter with a .270 Winchester or a .300 Holland Magnum, has thought for the time being that he had the only proper weapon.   And, each of them has found sooner or later that under some circumstances his chosen rifle would not perform as expected.

IBEX IN THE HIMALAYAS.

From the Badminton Library of *Big Game Shooting*.

OORIAL IN THE HIMALAYAS.

From the Badminton Library of *Big Game Shooting.*

TYPICAL HIMALAYAN HUNTING COUNTRY.

From Joseph C. Grew's *Sport and Travel in the Far East.*

HUNTING IN NEWFOUNDLAND.

From the Country Life Library of *Big Game Shooting.*

APPENDIX D

PART IV—1906-1946—The High-Velocity Small Bores

	NAME	WHEN	WHERE
113	Lt. Col. C. H. Stockley	1905-1933	India
114	S. Eardley Wilmot	1905-1930	India
115	Frantz Rosenberg	1906-1907	East Africa
	"	1908-1909	Central Europe
	"	1910-1912	North America
	"	1913-1931	Europe
116	Maj. G. P. Evans	1906-1910	Burma
117	Vilhjalmur Stefansson	1906-1918	Arctic America
118	Richard Tjader	1906-1910	East Africa
119	Maj. H. C. Maydon	1906-1915	India-Malaya
	"	1916-1917	Port. E. Africa
	"	1920-1923	Abyssinia
	"	1924-1926	Asia Minor-Persia
	"	1927-1929	India
	"	1930-1937	Africa
120	H. F. Wallace	1906-1907	N. America
	"	1907-1908	India
	"	1908-1909	Africa
	"	1910-1932	Scotland
121	Capt. A. H. E. Mosse	1907-1912	Somaliland
122	Col. A. E Stewart	1907-1927	India
123	Percy C. Madeira	1907-1908	East Africa
124	Kermit Roosevelt	1908-1910	East Africa
	"	1921-1922	Korea
	"	1923-1924	India
	"	1925-1926	Central Asia
	"	1927-1928	China-Indo China
125	Edgar B. Bronson	1908-1909	East Africa
126	Jack O'Connor	1909-1946	N. America
127	John T. McCutcheon	1909-1910	East Africa

APPENDIX D

PART IV—1906-1946—The High Velocity Small Bores

ANIMALS HUNTED	RIFLES USED
113 Tiger, Panther, Bear, Markhor, Ibex, Sheep	9mm Mannl., .318 Jeffery,* .280 Ross
114 Tiger, Sambur, Panther	.500 DB Express,* .303 SS Lee
115 Elephant, Lion, Antelope	.400 DB Jeffery*, .303 SS Jeffery, .450 DB Holland
Chamois, Moufflon, Red Deer, Roebuck	.450 DB Holland, .303 SS Jeffery*
Sheep, Bear, Goat, Caribou, Moose	.303 SS Jeffery*, .303 DB Holland
Chamois, Deer, Elk, Reindeer	.30-06 DB Merkel, 8 x 60 Mauser, 8 x 60 SS Gibbs,* 9.3mm Mauser
116 Elephant, Gaur, Banteng, Tiger, Sambur, Serow	10 bore Paradox, .400 DB Army & Navy*
117 Muskox, Caribou, Walrus, Bear, Seal	.256 Mannl. Schoe., .256 Gibbs Mannl.*
118 Elephant, Lion, Rhino, Buffalo, Antelope	.577 DB, 50-110 Win., .405 Win.,* 11.2 Mauser, .256 Mannlicher
119 Markhor, Ibex, Tiger, Panther, Bear, Bison	.577 DB,* .400 DB, .500 SS, .256 Mannl.
Buffalo, Antelope	.470 DB*, 9mm Mannlicher
Ibex, Antelope	7.9mm Mauser*
Wild Goat, Ibex	7.9mm Mauser*
Markhor, Ibex, Burrhel, Thar	7.9mm Mauser*
Lion, Antelope	.470 DB, 7.9mm Mauser*
120 Elk, Sheep, Goat	.225 Rigby Mauser*
Deer, Black Buck	.225 Rigby Mauser*
Lion, Rhino, Buffalo, Antelope	.450 DB, .275 Rigby Mauser *
Red Deer	.275 Rigby Mauser*
121 Lion, Antelope	12 bore Paradox, .400 DB Watson,* .318 Westley Richards
122 Tiger, Markhor, Ibex, Oorial	.475 DB Holland,* .375 M Holland
123 Lion, Rhino, Buffalo, Antelope	.450 DB Army & Navy, 8mm and 9mm Mannlicher*
124 Elephant, Lion, Rhino, Buffalo, Antelope	.450 DB Rigby, .405 Win.,* .30-06 Springf.
Tiger, Boar, Deer	.405 Win., 30-06 Springfield*
Tiger, Gaur, Sambur	.30-06 Springfield*
Sambur, Poli, Yak, Burrhel, Gazelle	.375 M Hoffman, .30-06 Springfield*
Sambur, Wapiti, Takin, Serow, Panda	.375 M Hoffman, .30-06 Springfield*
125 Elephant, Rhino, Buffalo, Antelope	.450 DB, .405 Win.,* 9mm Mauser
126 Moose, Elk, Bear, Sheep, Deer	.30-06 Springf., 7mm Mauser, .270 Win.*
127 Elephant, Lion, Rhino, Antelope	.475 DB Jeffery, 9mm Mannl., .256 Mannl.

* The asterisk indicates the favorite rifle.

1906-1946—High-Velocity Small Bores

NAME	WHEN	WHERE
128 E. Marshall Scull	1909-1910	Alaska
129 George Agnew Chamberlain	1909-1917	Port. E. Africa
"	1922-1923	Port. E. Africa
130 William M. Newsom	1909-1940	N. America
131 James L. Clark	1909-1911	East Africa
"	1912-1921	N. America
"	1921-1922	East Africa
"	1923-1925	N. America
"	1926-1927	Central Asia
"	1928-1931	East Africa
"	1935-1936	Indo-China
132 Maj. L. M. H. Handley	1910-1932	India-Burma
133 J. Leslie Simpson	1910-1925	East Africa
134 Capt. W. T. Shorthose	1910-1922	Africa
135 Maj. Gerald Burrard	1910-1920	India
136 Maj. C. Court Treatt	1911-1930	Central Africa
137 Capt. Paul A. Curtis	1911-1929	N. America
"	1930-1932	Scotland
"	1933-1940	N. America
"	1941-1942	Scotland
138 R. S. Meikle	1912-1913	East Africa
139 Ben Burbridge	1912-1927	Central Africa
140 Kenneth Fuller Lee	1912-1938	N. America
141 Wilfred Robertson	1912-1931	South Africa
142 Roy Chapman Andrews	1912-1913	Korea
"	1916-1917	China
"	1918-1920	Mongolia
"	1921-1926	Central Asia
143 Harry A. Auer	1913-1914	Yukon
144 Commandant Augieras	1913-1933	Central Africa

1906-1946—High-Velocity Small Bores

ANIMALS HUNTED	RIFLES USED
128 Walrus, Bear, Sheep, Caribou	9mm Mauser*
129 Lion, Antelope	.450 DB Evans,* .22 HP Savage
Elephant, Lion, Antelope	.470 DB Churchill, .318 Westley R,* .256 Mannlicher
130 Moose, Bear, Deer	.450 DB Purdey, .38-55 Win.,* .256 Mannl.
131 Elephant, Lion, Rhino, Antelope	.470 DB Evans, 7.9mm Mauser*
Elk, Bear, Deer	.30-06 Springfield*
Lion, Gorilla	.470 DB Evans, .30-06 Springfield*
Caribou, Bear, Goat, Sheep	.30-06 Springfield*
Yak, Ammon, Ibex	.30-06 Springfield*
Elephant	.470 DB Evans, .30-06 Springfield*
Seladang, Banteng	.470 DB Evans, .465 DB Holland,* .318 Rigby M., .30-06 Springfield
132 Elephant, Tiger, Bison, Sambur	.470 DB,* .318 Westley Richards
133 Lion, Buffalo, Rhino, Antelope	.577 DB, .405 Win., .416 Rigby, .315 Westley, .30-06 Win.*
134 Elephant, Lion, Rhino, Buffalo, Antelope	.470 DB Lancaster, .318 Westley R, .280 Lancaster Mauser*
135 Sambur, Bear, Markhor, Ibex, Sheep, Yak	.577 DB Holland, .400 DB, .256 Mannl., .280 SS Lancaster*
136 Elephant, Lion, Antelope	.303 Lee Metford
137 Moose, Caribou, Bear, Goat, Sheep	.30-06 Springfield, .256 Mannlicher*
Red Deer	.30-06 Springfield*
Moose, Bear, Deer	.30-06 Springfield*
Red Deer	.30-06 Springfield*
138 Lion, Antelope	.465 DB, .360 DB Fraser*
139 Elephant, Lion, Rhino, Buffalo, Antelope, Gorilla	.405 Win.,* .30-40 Win.
140 Moose, Deer, Bear	.45-90, .38-40, .30-30 Win., .303, .250 Sav., .32 Rem. A., .256 Mannl.*
141 Lion, Rhino, Buffalo, Antelope	.400 DB Jeffery,* .303 Lee Metford
142 Tiger, Bear, Deer, Boar	.256 Mannlicher*
Tiger, Goral, Serow, Gazelle	.256 Mannlicher*
Elk, Sheep	.250-3000 Sav.,* .256 Mannl.
Gazelle	.250 Savage*
143 Moose, Caribou, Bear, Sheep	8mm Mannlicher*
144 Elephant, Lion, Rhino, Buffalo, Antelope	.405 Win.,* 10.75 Mauser, .32 Win., 8mm Rival

* The asterisk indicates the favorite rifle.

1906-1946—High-Velocity Small Bores

	NAME	WHEN	WHERE
145	A. B. Hepburn	1913-1914	East Africa
146	Arthur H. Carhart	1915-1945	N. America
147	Harold McCracken	1916-1942	Alaska
148	C. E. Hagie	1916-1946	N. America
149	Commander David E. Blunt	1919-1933	East Africa
150	Edison Marshall	1920-1928	N. America
	"	1929-1930	East Africa
	"	1931-1946	Indo China-India
151	Elmer Keith	1920-1936	U. S.-Canada
	"	1936-1937	Alaska
	"	1938-1946	United States
152	Herbert E. Bradley	1920-1924	Central Africa
	"	1928-1929	Malaya
153	Mary Hastings Bradley	1920-1924	Central Africa
	"	1928-1929	Malaya
154	Major James E. Corbett	1920-1940	India
155	Martin Johnson	1921-1935	East Africa
156	Osa Johnson	1921-1935	East Africa
157	Monroe H. Goode	1921-1937	N. America
158	Dr. Richard L. Sutton	1923-1924	East Africa
	"	1925-1926	Indo-China
	"	1929-1930	Africa-Indo China
	"	1931-1932	Spitzbergen
	"	1933-1946	North America
159	John M. Holzworth	1923-1929	Canada-Alaska
160	Vivienne de Watteville	1923-1927	East Africa
161	William J. Morden	1923-1925	India
	"	1926-1927	Central Asia
162	Martin Stephens	1924-1925	India
	"	1933-1934	N. America
	"	1935-1936	East Africa

1906-1946—High-Velocity Small Bores

ANIMALS HUNTED	RIFLES USED
145 Lion, Rhino, Buffalo, Antelope	.450 DB, .256 Mannl., .35 Rem. Auto.*
146 Elk, Bear, Deer	.25-35 Win.*
147 Moose, Bear, Caribou, Sheep	.303 Savage, .30-40 Win.*
148 Moose, Elk, Bear, Sheep, Deer	.25-35 & .30-30 Win., .303 & .250 Sav., 7.9 Mauser,* .30-06 Spr., .270 Win.
149 Elephant, Buffalo, Hippo, Antelope	12 bore DB, .416 Rigby,* .318 Westley R., .303 Lee Metford
150 Moose, Caribou, Bear	.35 Remington
Lion, Rhino, Antelope	.470 DB, 9.5mm Mannl.*
Seladang, Bison, Tiger	.404 Gibbs Mauser, .404 DB Gibbs,* 9.5mm Mannlicher
151 Elk, Bear, Sheep, Goat, Caribou, Deer	.38-55 Win., .30-06 Spr., .400 Whelen,* .35 Whelen
Bear, Sheep	.35 Whelen*
Elk, Bear, Goat, Deer	.280 Dubiel, .300 H&H Magnum*
152 Elephant, Lion, Rhino, Buffalo, Antelope	.475 DB Jeffery, .30-06 Springfield*
Tiger, Rhino	.475 DB Jeffery, .30-06 Springfield*
153 Elephant, Lion, Buffalo, Antelope	.30-06 Springfield*
Tiger	.30-06 Springfield*
154 Tiger, Panther, Bear, Goral	.450 Martini, .400 DB,* .275 Mauser
155 Elephant, Lion, Rhino, Buffalo, Antelope	.470 DB Bland, .405 Win.,* .30-06 Spingfield
156 Elephant, Lion, Rhino, Buffalo, Antelope	.405 Win., .30-06 Springfield*
157 Moose, Elk, Bear, Deer, Sheep	.30-06 Spr., .315 Hoffm., .300 H&H, .270 Win.*
158 Elephant, Lion, Rhino, Buffalo, Antelope	.577 DB Westley R., .465 DB Purdey,* .30-06 Win.
Elephant, Tiger, Seladang, Banteng, Sambur	.465 DB Holland, .400 DB Jeffery, .375 Hoffm., .300 H&H
Lion, Rhino, Antelope, Tiger, Bantung	.577 DB Westley R., .465 DB Holland, 9.3 Mauser
Walrus, Seal, Polar Bear	9.3 Mauser
Moose, Caribou, Bear, Elk, Sheep	.348 Win., .300 H&H, 9.3 Mauser
159 Caribou, Bear, Sheep, Goat	.405 DB Griffin & Howe, .30-06 Mauser
160 Elephant, Lion, Rhino, Antelope	.416 Rigby Mauser, .318 Westley Richards
161 Markhor, Ibex, Ammon	.30-06 Springfield
Poli, Burrhel, Yak, Gazelle	.30-06 Springfield
162 Tiger, Markhor, Ibex, Ammon, Shapoo	.375 M Holland*
Goat, Sheep	.375 M Holland*
Elephant, Rhino, Lion	.450 DB Holland,* .375 M Holland

* The asterisk indicates the favorite rifle.

1906-1946—High-Velocity Small Bores

	NAME	WHEN	WHERE
163	Capt. E. T. L. Lewis	1924-1928	East Africa
	"	1929-1931	India
	"	1932-1934	N. America
164	Count Vasco da Gama	1925-1930	Central Africa
165	John P. Holman	1925-1931	Alaska-Canada
166	Paul L. Hoefler	1925-1929	Central Africa
167	Theodore Roosevelt, Jr.	1925-1926	India-C. Asia
	"	1927-1928	China-Indo China
168	A. R. Siedentopf	1926-1941	East Africa
169	Mrs. John Borden	1927-1928	Alaska
170	John W. Eddy	1927-1928	Alaska

1906-1946—High-Velocity Small Bores

ANIMALS HUNTED	RIFLES USED
163 Elephant, Lion, Buffalo, Antelope	.465 DB Holland,* .375 H&H Magnum, .303 Lee Metford
Tiger, Bear, Sambur	.465 DB Holland,* .375 H&H Magnum, .303 Lee Metford
Bear, Deer, Sheep	.375 H&H Magnum,* .303 Lee M.
164 Elephant, Lion, Rhino, Buffalo, Antelope	.465 DB Holland, 9 Mannl., 7.9 Mauser, .275 Rigby Mauser*
165 Moose, Bear, Sheep	.45-90 Win., .30-06 Springf.,* .256 Mannl.
166 Lion, Buffalo, Antelope	.505 Gibbs, .30-06 Rem., 7mm Mauser*
167 Sambur, Poli, Burrhel, Yak	.375 M Hoffman, .30-06 Springfield*
Wapiti, Sambur, Serow, Takin, Panda	.375 M Hoffman, .30-06 Springfield*
168 Elephant, Lion, Rhino, Buffalo, Antelope	9mm Mauser, .30-06 Springfield,* 7mm Mauser
169 Sheep, Bear, Walrus	.30-06 Springfield*
170 Bear	.35 Whelen,* .405 Winchester

* The asterisk indicates the favorite rifle.

1906-1946—Summary of The High Velocity Small Bores

Large Bore Muzzle Loaders

LARGE BORES	USED BY	TOTAL
10 bore Paradox	116	1
12 bore Paradox	121	1
12 bore DB	149	1
Total		3

Medium Bore Muzzle Loaders

MEDIUM BORES	USED BY	TOTAL
.577 DB	118, 119, 133, 135, 158	5
.505 M	166	1
.500 DB	114	1
.500 SS	119	1
.50-110 M	118	1
.475 DB	122, 127, 152	3
.470 DB	119, 129, 131, 132, 134, 150, 155	7
.465 DB	131, 138, 158, 163, 164	5
.450 DB	115, 120, 123, 124, 125, 129, 130, 145, 162	9
.450 SS	154	1
.45-90 M	140, 165	2
11.2 M	118	1
10.75 M	144	1
.416 M	133, 149, 160, 170	4
.405 DB	159	1
.405 M	118, 124, 125, 133, 139, 144, 155, 156	8
.404 DB	150	1
.404 M	150	1
.400 DB	115, 116, 119, 121, 135, 141, 154, 158	8
.400 M	151	1
Total		62

Small Bore Breech Loaders

SMALL BORES	USED BY	TOTAL
.38-55	130, 151	2
.38-40	140	1
.375 M	122, 124, 157, 158, 162, 163, 167	7
9.5 M	150	1
93mm M	115, 158	2

Small Bore Breech Loaders

SMALL BORES	USED BY	TOTAL
.360 DB	138	1
9mm M	113, 119, 123, 125, 127, 128, 164, 168	8
.35 Whelen	151, 170	2
.35 Rem.	145, 150	2
.348 Win.	158	1
.32 Win.	144	1
.32 Rem.	140	1
.318 M	113, 121, 129, 131, 132, 134, 149, 160	8
8 x 60mm M	115	1
8 x 60 SS	115	1
8 x 56mm M	123, 143, 144	3
7.9 x 57mm M	119, 131, 148, 164	4
.303 M Lee	136, 141, 149, 163	4
.303 DB	115	1
.303 SS	114, 115	2
.303 Sav.	140, 147, 148	3
.300 H & H	151, 157, 158	3
.30-06 M	124, 126, 131, 137, 148, 151, 152, 153, 155, 156, 157, 158, 159, 161, 165, 166, 167, 168, 169	19
.30-06 DB	115	1
.30-40 M	139, 147	2
.30-30 M	140, 148	2
.280 M	113, 134, 151	3
.280 SS	135	1
7mm M	120, 126, 154, 164, 166, 168	6
.270 M	126, 148, 157	3
.256 M	117, 118, 119, 127, 129, 130, 135, 137, 140, 142, 145, 165	12
.250 Sav.	140, 142, 148	3
.25-35 M	146, 148	2
.22 Sav.	129	1
Total		114

SUMMARY

Rifles Large bore	3
Rifles Medium bore	62
Rifles Small bore	114
Total	178

Hunters 58—Rifles per hunter, 3.1

PART V
CONCLUSION

CHAPTER 9

IS THERE AN ALL ROUND RIFLE?

*E*VERY hunter starting on a trip to hunt some new species of big
game, wants to know the best type of rifle to use in such hunting.
He also wants to know the best bullet, and where game must be hit to
secure it.   Nine times out of ten it will be the expert's pet rifle that is
recommended, and in each case it will probably differ from that of some
other "old hand" who is equally expert and successful.   This has been true
for every land and every species of game.   Usually the tyro takes no
notice of the experience which may have dictated one choice over the
other, or of the fact that the expert is a far better rifle shot and hunter
of that particular type of game than he can hope to be.   If the expert
speaks with authority and conviction, the novice rushes off to purchase a
rifle of the exact specification, with ammunition to fit, and is off to the
hunt, with every confidence that he can be just as successful as the men
he has read about.   Much disappointment from such hunting is a natural
result.   If the tyro had been accustomed to a weapon which was not
greatly inferior in power to the rifles recommended, and had been fairly
successful with it, he would probably have secured better results than
with a new and untried weapon.

Yet the opinion of the experts as represented by the outstanding big
game hunters is valuable as it sets a general pattern of the type of rifle
and the killing power needed for the various types of game.   In this
book the development of the rifle in big game hunting has been followed
through the accounts given by the hunters themselves of their actual
hunting experiences. *The best hunters have not found an all round rifle,*
but the rifles used do show certain definite preferences.   These preferences may even be surprising in the light of the advice that has been
often given through question and answer columns of the sporting magazines.   The .256 Mannlicher has been rated by the magazine experts as
too light for anything but deer, yet among big game hunters, the world
around, it has been the most popular of all rifles, having been used by
thirty five men or 20 per cent of the total reported.   Of these, ten used
nothing else for all their hunting after it was introduced.   Littledale,

Loder, Pease, Millais, Radcliffe, Stigand, Prichard, Sheldon, Percival and Stefansson proved that the .256 would kill anything, including lion, brown bear, moose, rhino, and elephant when properly handled.

Second to the .256 is our own .30-'06 Springfield used by thirty men. Having grown to this popularity in about fifteen years less time than the Mannlicher, this may indicate that it has supplanted it as the general purpose rifle, and that it perhaps has strong claim to being the all round weapon. But of that more later.

The third rifle in popularity, listed thirty times and thus tied with the Springfield, is the .450 double barrel. Apparently the introduction of the near sizes of .465, .470 and .475 because of the prohibition against the .450's entry to India, except by special permission, has not seriously affected its continued popularity as a heavy second rifle for dangerous game.

Following the .450 comes the .303 Lee Metford used by twenty-seven hunters, the .500 double rifle in use by twenty-two, the .400 double barrel by eighteen men, the 7mm Mauser magazine rifle, as adapted by various makers, used by sixteen men, and the .577 double rifle and .405 Winchester rifle tied with fourteen users each.

Some rifles which have been highly advertised, such as the Newton, the .280 Ross, the .333 Jeffery, the .300 Magnum, the .404 Jeffery, the .425 Westley Richards, the .505 Gibbs and the .600 Jeffery have not been noticeably popular in the hunting field. This is perhaps unfair as the period covered in this book stops at about 1935, and these calibres may not have had sufficient time to develop by then. But more probably there was some inherent quality in the older calibers, such as the Mannlicher, the Springfield, the Lee-Metford or the 7 and 7.9 millimeter Mausers, the .30-30 and .30-40 Winchesters and even in some instances the .250 Savage, which none of the newer cartridges could improve upon. Sheldon used the .256 for ten years on sheep, caribou, moose and bear. Pease used a similar rifle for eighteen years hunting lion and other African game. Bell used a 7mm Rigby Mauser with the 173 grain military bullet for fifteen years and bagged most of his 1000 elephants with it. Maydon shot a 7.9 Mauser for twenty years. All of these men had other greatly improved "Magnums," "Ultras," and "Supers" available to them, but stuck to the one rifle and caliber, or returned to it after trying out some of the newer experiments. This choice of one rifle corresponds to the requisites for effective work on big game, which are a knowledge of the

.375 HOLLAND AND HOLLAND MAGNUM.

.350 RIBGY MAGNUM MAUSER.

9MM MAUSER OR MANNLICHER.

.318 WESTLEY RICHARDS ACCELERATED EXPRESS.

.300 HOLLAND AND HOLLAND MAGNUM.

8MM MAUSER

.30-'06 SPRINGFIELD.

.30-40 KRAG.

.303 LEE-METFORD.

.30-30 WINCHESTER.

.280 ROSS.

7MM MAUSER.

.270 WINCHESTER, 150 GRAIN BULLET.

.256 or 6.5MM MANNLICHER.

.250-3000 SAVAGE.

.25-35 WINCHESTER.

ARTHUR SAVAGE. INVENTOR AND RIFLE MANUFACTURER.

From Mr. Arthur T. Ward.

ROY CHAPMAN ANDREWS WITH A .250-3000 SAVAGE USED ON
MONGOLIAN BIG HORN HUNT WITH H. R. CALDWELL.

From H. R. Caldwell's book *Blue Tiger*.

SIR CHARLES ROSS. SCOTCH BARONET, LANDED
PROPRIETOR, RIFLE INVENTOR, MANUFACTURER
AND CONSULTING ENGINEER.

From Mr. Arthur T. Ward.

MANEATER KILLED WITH A .22 HIPOWER SAVAGE BY H. R. CALDWELL, BIG GAME HUNTER, MISSIONARY AND AUTHOR. ONE OF THE FEW WRITERS ON CHINESE BIG GAME HUNTING.

A CHARGING RHINO. THIS ANIMAL WAS PHOTOGRAPHED BY A. RADCLIFFE
DUGMORE AND DROPPED A FRACTION OF A SECOND LATER
BY JAMES L. CLARK.

From Clark's *Trails of the Hunted*.

game and rifle, accuracy, handiness, reliability and penetration. The successful rifleman-hunter had to have all of these in a high degree.

In some of these writings on big game rifles there are detailed discussions of the rifles needed for big game hunting, and definite considerations of the question of all round rifles. Such is the following in a communication from Major C. H. Stigand to Colonel Townsend Whelen:

It is a noticeable fact that most men who have had the greatest experience have been the first to appreciate the benefits of modern rifles. The people who are most adverse to them are men who have shot their game with the old black powder weapons, and without having properly tested the powers of the new weapons, at once condemn them. The advantage of the new rifles are as follows:

1. Flatter trajectory (due to greater velocity).
2. Absence of smoke and noise.
3. Slight recoil.
4. Lightness of rifle and ammunition.
5. Greater accuracy (especially at unknown ranges).

We should most certainly advise the sportsman to use magazine or single loaders, for, as we have said, they are handier and cost much less, for the best magazine or single loader can be purchased for less than £25, whereas a really good double would cost from £40 to £60. Cordite rifles can be had in all small bores from .256 to .600. The .600's, .577's and .450's are made solely for the ponderous game such as elephant, rhino, and buffalo. The .400's, .375's, .360's and .350's are intended for use against all game, but most makers would never think of recommending a man to start away on a trip with only a .303, .275, or .256 Mannlicher, but it is a fact that not only buck and lion, but animals such as elephant, rhino, and buffalo can be easily killed with them, provided a suitable projectile is used, and they are hit in a vital part.

The larger bores are certainly safer, especially to a nervous man or a bad shot, but it does not make much difference to the elephant whether his brain has been punctured by a .577 or .256 bullet. When a man has a weapon like a .500 bore cordite in his hand he is apt to think that he has only got to hit the beast to bring it to bag; but this is not always the case, though there would certainly be more likelihood of finding it if only wounded. There is undoubtedly one advantage, which the larger bores possess, and that is the quantity of the blood spoor; but in our opinion this is a minor advantage when the handiness and other advantages of the smaller bores are taken into account. The ammunition for the larger bores is much more costly and bulky to carry. At present the .303 cannot be taken into India without special permission, though an officer can pass it as part of his kit; but this rule does not apply to Africa, and .303 cartridges can be bought in a number of stores in that country. There are a great number of fanciful bullets (expanding type) made by the gunmakers for the .303, in fact every prominent maker has his own bullet, but we do not think that more than two types need be taken, viz., expanding and solid. The best expanding .303 bullet that we know is the Mark V, with a hollow $\frac{3}{8}$ inch deep in the nose, the hole having a slight taper and left open. This bullet is ample for all buck, and for lion, leopard, wart-hog, etc. The solid (full jacketed) is best for elephant, rhino, hippo, and for raking shots at buffalo and eland. The best shot for elephant is the head one, and if the animal is broadside on, a few inches forward of the ear hole in a line with the eye, low if anything. If the bullet strikes here it will reach the brain.

For the .256 and the .275 Mauser the best form of expanding bullet is one with the lead just exposed at the point, with a small hole drilled in the nose. The lead ought not to project but to be cut off flush. If there is a projection of lead and it becomes dented, as often happens in carriage, they will sometimes jam in the breech shoulder of a magazine form of rifle.

Very much depends upon the man behind the rifle, his faith in the rifle he uses, his nerve, the spot the projectile hits, the angle the animal is turned at, and the state of the heart or other vital organs when they are hit. We think people are often too much inclined to praise or condemn a rifle on a few single instances, whereas no two animals or bullets behave exactly in the same way. To quote two instances: we have dropped a charging elephant on his knees at ten yards with one shot from a Mannlicher, and with the same weapon failed to stop a charging lion at two yards. The inference drawn from the first instance is that the Mannlicher is all that can be desired for the most ponderous game, and from the second that the same rifle is utterly useless, even for comparatively small game, neither of which inferences are of the least value unless compared with hundreds of other cases. In the first case, had we had a heavy bore we might not have been able to get in such a deadly shot, whereas in the second case, with a heavy bore or even a shotgun, the shock of impact would in probability have turned the animal.

The great advantage of a double barrelled rifle is the rapidity with which a second shot can be got in, which is a very serious consideration in a tight place. The first shot is the all-important one, and if this only wounds, the animal must be stopped by sheer weight of lead and blow of impact. For the first shot we wish to use all the accuracy at our disposal, and something that we can always have in our hand through a long and tiring day, hence we advocate the small bore. If after firing this we had an automaton to hand us our big bore it might be useful to have one in reserve to meet a possible charge, but gunbearers are only human, and rather than run the risk of having to look for it up a tree or some yards in the rear, perhaps it is as well to depend on your magazine and accurate shooting and save yourself sixty guineas by not having a rifle which may be in the way when you don't want it, and very possibly not available when you want it mighty badly.

While Stigand was provided with a double .450 he carried the Mannlicher most of the time and one is impressed when reading his hunting experiences with the number of times he used the small rifle for elephant or any other game that appeared. But after he was nearly trampled by a rhino and later badly mauled by a lion, he wrote D. D. Lyell:

I told you that I wouldn't lose faith in my Mannlicher till I had been mauled by a lion. Now I have modified my opinion. A small bore is still what I shall shoot with, for all the reasons given . . . i. e. light to carry, magazine, light cartridges, more accurate, especially for shooting standing, cheaper, etc., etc.
BUT for a springing or charging lion (wounded) and for the violent animals at very close quarters one wants a 15 pounder, or large bore howitzer; or 12 inch wire gun would be safer. The difficulty is how to exchange your small bore for a large at a critical moment."

Another remarkable East African hunter was an American Leslie Simpson whose singlehanded score on lion was estimated at over 300 by Colonel Hamilton. The following is from a letter as to the best possible all round rifle for East Africa. After describing the .416 Rigby as very good but heavy, he says:

Secondly the .318 Westley Richards 250 grain round nose bullet starting at about 2500 f.s., I gave this cartridge a long and good tryout and it seems to me as near as possible to the ideal. The long bullet with small lead point (not the patent capped which I thought not so good) gave excellent penetration, mushroomed O.K. on small and soft-skinned game, but held together sufficiently to do good work on shoulder shots and raking shots on big animals. Its velocity is high enough to render accurate shooting without too much guessing of distance at the ranges over which most of the shots must be taken. The rifle which I had made to shoot this cartridge weighed eight pounds and gave no unpleasant recoil. It is a popular cartridge among men who have lived in Africa and had much experience *and who use only one rifle and dispense with the double.*

Thirdly, we come to the .30 Springfield cartridge. I started to use this cartridge in 1910, and have done most of my shooting with the 220 grain bullet since that date. This bullet speeded up to about 2300 f.s., satisfies me and I am at home with it under all conditions. This bullet in the lungs or paunch will not kill as well as the 180 grain going faster, but it will break both shoulders of big animals and is better than the 180 on raking shots and large animals. Two years ago I took with me the open point 180 grain Western ammunition and have used it continuously since. While I have not the confidence in it that I have in the 220 when in a corner with my back against the wall, still results were much better than I had been led to expect after using a few pointed soft point bullets on a previous trip, which went to pieces like smoke. I like the Western 180 so much that I am taking it with me on this trip.

What I think the average American coming out to shoot in Africa should bring is a rifle taking a .350 cartridge with a heavy bullet and as high a velocity as possible compatible with pressure and weight of rifle. My idea would be a 275 grain bullet at 2500 f.s., or if this gives too much pressure or would necessitate the rifle being too heavy, then cut down the velocity rather than the bullet weight. I think that any rifle which can be developed above the .350 approaches the big bores too much and should be left at home. On this point my .416 is just a fifth wheel of a rifle crank and has no place in one's battery on a single shooting trip.

Going back to the big stopping rifle, I think one should use just as large a caliber and as heavy a bullet as he can handle, and nothing smaller than the .450 caliber with 480 grain bullet. I have for twenty-three years used a .577-1-750 and find no trouble from recoil or slowness when using it on game. It has also been forcibly impressed upon me that one's big rifle should be a double ejector, and not a magazine rifle, for a magazine becomes a single shot in certain cases.

If you could develop a .350 cartridge with heavy bullet yet fair velocity, which could be used in a medium weight rifle, I think you will have solved the problem for an all round rifle for Africans as well as a very useful one in America, perhaps with lighter bullets.

The comment on the .35 caliber rifle with about a 275 grain bullet at 2500 foot seconds is undoubtedly what prompted Whelen, and Griffin and Howe to bring out the .35 and .400 Whelen which have reached some degree of popularity among American hunters. Of the .35 Whelen, Elmer Keith has this to say in *Big Game Rifles and Cartridges*:

I consider the .35 Whelen the best of all our larger caliber rifles for all species. While the bolt action is not as fast as the lever, pump, automatic, or double-barreled rifles, it is, nevertheless, a very fine rifle and cartridge for timber hunting by the man who tries his best to plant that first shot where it belongs. Recent group shooting at 200 yards . . . produced five shot groups averaging 2¾ inches . . . Such accuracy is good enough for me for big game hunting, and if I were forced to use just one rifle for all species of big game, I would certainly choose this .35 Whelen rifle. It is not only a beautiful example of gun making but a very effective rifle on anything found on this continent.

The .35 Whelen was used by Elmer Keith in his hunting in Alaska in 1936-37 for brown bear and by John W. Eddy in an earlier hunt in 1927-1928 on the north side of the Alaskan Peninsula. In both cases the rifle performed excellently. But there are other opinions of the all round rifle which must be considered. One authority which has already been quoted is from Major Gerald Burrard's *Notes on Sporting Rifles* in which the question is discussed as follows:

Most big game shots, particularly novices, desire an all-round rifle; but in reality there is no such thing. How can the qualities which are essential to rifles for jungle and hill shooting be combined in one weapon? A favorite, so called, all-round rifle is the .400 H.V., but this is only a compromise. It lacks the power of a larger bore so essential for jungle shooting and the necessary handiness and flat trajectory of a small bore for hill shooting.

No rifle that is not a double can be considered an all-round rifle.

The best plan is to decide on which kind of shooting you intend to take up, buy a rifle perfect for that kind, and try and make it do for the other kind. A .470 H.V. would be very useful in the Himalayas, although somewhat heavy, and a .375 Magnum would be a very serviceable weapon in the jungles. In fact, this last seems to more nearly approach the ideal all-round weapon than any other. With 235 grain bullet it is perfection for the hills and the comparatively heavy bullet of 300 grains with its high velocity would deal a tremendous blow at close quarters.

The .404 and .360 are really very similar, although neither has quite such a flat trajectory as the .375 Magnum with the 235 grain bullet, while the .404 is only made in magazine form. The .350 Magnum, .333 and .318 are also somewhat similar weapons, but their ballistics are not quite so good, although the .318 is a very favorite weapon in Africa. The .416 and .425 are heavy for hill shooting, and lack bullet weight for jungle shooting. They seem to be perfect for neither.

And since sportsmen in all parts of the world are always discussing the question of the best type of all-round rifle to select I hope I may be forgiven if I offer some suggestion as to how the problem may be approached:

Big game country may be classified as follows:

1. Absolutely open country entirely devoid of cover such as the slopes above the tree line on mountains, table-lands, plateaus, open plains and desert.

2. Scattered scrub jungle interspersed with open spaces.

3. Dense forest or jungle.

In the first type of country long shots, that is, long shots from the sporting point of view, must be the rule rather than the exception, and the usual range will be anything from 150 to 300 yards, and sometimes possibly even more. Except in very exceptional cases, however, I would always place 300 yards as the normal limit at which sporting shots should be taken. The game usually found in such country is of the non-dangerous thin-skinned variety, and consequently great weight of metal is not of primary importance. In this form of shooting the chief difficulty to be overcome is judging distances and for this reason a flat trajectory is a desideratum in any suitable rifle. On this account the choice must always fall on a magnum small bore, and the flatter the trajectory the better. As has already been seen, a flat trajectory naturally demands a very high muzzle velocity, and for this reason a rifle developing a muzzle velocity of 2800 foot seconds should always be selected. It is, however, a mistake to sacrifice bullet weight wholly to velocity as a very light bullet breaks up all too easily when it strikes a bone, and I would regard 140 grains as the absolute minimum limit below which it is not safe to go.

To sum up, the most suitable form of rifle in this form of shooting is one which develops a muzzle velocity of from 2800 to 3100 foot seconds and which carries a bullet of at least 140 grains.

In our second type of country, that is what I have termed scrub jungle, the majority of shots will probably be taken at ranges which lie between 100 and 200 yards. Further the game animals will frequently be heavier and larger than those found in open country, and they will quite often include dangerous game, both thin-skinned and thick-skinned. In this form of shooting one should never stir without a rifle in ones hand. Any moment may give its chance, so it is not sufficient to have a man carrying a rifle just behind one. Such men cannot always be depended upon and even if they can, there may not be time to seize the proffered rifle before the chance of a lifetime is gone.

After the question of weight the next question is stopping power. Game may be both heavy and dangerous, and on this account plenty of weight of bullet is essential. Here I regard 220, or better still 250 grains, as the lightest weight which should be used, and the more increase over 300 grains the better from the point of view of killing power.

Since shots are very seldom taken at over 200 yards a very high velocity is not necessary. In fact, so far from being necessary, I regard it as a mistake because high velocities are only obtained at the expense of bullet weight. I have for years been inclined to believe that the whole tendency in recent development of sporting rifles was too great in the direction of velocity at the expense of bullet weight. And in this type of country, I am sure that a velocity of from 2300 foot seconds to 2500 foot seconds is as high as is needed.

To sum up, in this type of shooting—which includes the greater part of African shooting—the most suitable rifle is a light weapon which the sportsman can carry all day and every day himself without undue fatigue which carries a bullet of at least 220 to 250 grains (or better still 300 grains) and which develops a muzzle velocity of from 2300 to 2500 foot seconds.

We now come to the third type of country, namely, thick jungle. Here game is usually dangerous, and a human life may depend on getting in a second shot without movement or noise.

The hammerless, ejector, double rifle is the best and quickest to reload; next comes the hammerless non-ejector, and then the double hammer rifle; but I regard the double as a *sine qua non*. For use against really dangerous game a rifle must be extremely powerful, and power means weight. It is true that the rifle must always be carried in the hand, and the weight is conseqently limited to a certain extent by the owner's strength. Nevertheless facts must be faced, and I regard a double rifle as an essential. Dangerous game must not only be given a mortal wound, but must be "knocked down flat" so to speak, so that, even if the wound is not mortal time is allowed for a second shot . . . For this reason I am certain that a double medium powered nitro-rifle is the best, provided it is not beyond the owner's strength.

The only exception which I would make is in the case of the elephant, which I think would be placed in a category by itself. Although I am, and have always been, a firm believer in the shock delivered by a heavy bullet, I would be the last to deny that in the case of such huge animals shock is of little use without accuracy of aim. In the case of elephant the first essential is penetration as unless a vital organ is reached and penetrated no serious harm will be done. These vital organs are comparatively small, and for this reason a rifle with which extremely accurate shooting can be made is of primary importance.

. . . I am inclined to think that the rifle most suitable for the second class of shooting, that is, a light weapon which fires a bullet of about 250 grains, with a muzzle velocity of about 2300 foot seconds, is the weapon with which the majority of men are most likely to be successful.

The above is from the third edition of his book and is a considerable concession from the big bore for all ponderous game advocated in Burrard's earlier works. His criticism of the East African small bore men such as Lyell, Stigand, Bell, etc., created a good deal of adverse comment about his being "ratty about small bores for big stuff" and Burrard changed his tune somewhat in this later edition. For one who advocated such an extreme high velocity small bore as the Ross .280 for hill shooting he went overboard at first for the double .470's, .500's, and .577's for jungle shooting and some of the jungle shooters thought he was cock-eyed. Or as Bell himself said:

What sustains the big bore men is the thought that weight of metal will cover deficient accuracy, allowing them another chance to blot the fellow out, and they should admit it, instead of trying to make out that it is not "sporting" to use small bores.

But in order to get the full picture of the argument for the small bore magazine versus the big bore double barrelled rifle on jungle game, the views of Count Vasco da Gama contained in an article in *The American Rifleman* for December 1929, are pertinent:

The advantage of the magazine rifle over the express is the possibility of firing quite rapidly a few shots in succession. This advantage ceases with large cartridges because then the recoil does not permit you to operate the bolt almost at the same instant that the bullet is fired.   I have tried in London, since my return from Africa, several high powered magazine rifles like the .375 from Hollands, and I find that the recoil, throwing my shoulder back, delays reloading; as does also the great length of brass case, which calls for a longer movement of the bolt. The .318 from Westley Richards seems very satisfactory, from the point of view both of absence of recoil and shortness of movement of the bolt to expel the fired case. The .350 from Rigby would be about the heaviest magazine I would care to use, while the 275 Rigby is as good a light rifle as can be made. The 333 from Jeffery's is excellent as far as ballistics go, but there is too much recoil and the case is too long to permit taking full advantage of the repeating action.

Extra heavy magazines such as the .416 from Rigby are recommended only in the case of a sportsman wanting at all costs a very large bullet, and balking at the price of an express. I am afraid that once on the field not much satisfaction will be derived from such a heavy and clumsy weapon.

It is a good plan to take along in addition to one of these English rifles, an original Mauser rifle firing the same cartridge. Being much cheaper this second rifle can be used to finish the animals, and can eventually be put in the hands of a gun bearer.

The advocates of the double rifle have a right to state the case for that type of weapon, since there must be logical reasons why it has survived through over one hundred years of big game hunting in the hands of the most expert hunters of Africa and India. Capt. E. T. L. Lewis presented the case excellently in an article in the *American Rifleman* in 1936:

It may be asked what the advantages of a double-barrel rifle are over a single-barrel weapon with magazine action. The principal advantages are fairly obvious, particularly to the big-game hunters, and are, first, that one has a second shot in immediate reserve should the first one fail to hit, or be badly placed. A second advantage is the handiness and balance of a double rifle for snap-shooting or quick work at close quarters. There is also the accuracy, not only as regards the separate grouping of each barrel, but also the grouping of both barrels together at the various ranges. We have as a total the advantages of light weight, magnificent balance, superb accuracy together with the handling qualities of a fine shotgun, speed of getting the weapon into action because of the shotgun safety, tang peep-sight in the correct position to obtain the best in optical efficiency, locks that can be taken out instantly and are so designed as to give perfect trigger release or single trigger if desired, and a second shot in split-second time, which is a great advantage and in the African and Indian gamefields may mean all the difference between the demise of the hunted or the hunter.

Only two points in the above seem to be stretched a bit in the double rifle's favor, the accuracy of double rifle barrels will be subject to the added difficulties of regulating two converging barrels to shoot together and to the third plane of the sight line, and the obviously increased weight for two barrels, of safe dimensions, to the one for a magazine rifle. There should be no question that the second shot with a double rifle can be fired more quickly and with less disturbance of aim than with a magazine rifle and everything is lovely *if two shots are enough*. Shots 3, 4 and 5 will be measurably quicker with the magazine rifle.

The above opinions on all-round rifles represent, with one exception, the ideas of big game hunters familiar largely with English and Continental rifles and Indian or African game. The following statement is from an American who has already been quoted as to the importance of American conditions in studying big game hunting. Discounting his low opinion of such conclusions derived from purely American hunting, and American types of game, the argument is interesting and tends to explain the increasing popularity of the Springfield. Says Capt. E. C. Crossman in *The Book of the Springfield*:

To me the answer to all of these claims and counterclaims of the two schools, high velocity and heavy bullet, is simple and obvious. It is— both high velocity and heavy bullet. There is a limit, of course, a compromise, but no necessity for extremes either way.

The prescription should be merely: a bullet heavy enough or slow enough in break-up qualities to get into the vitals of the animal before going to pieces. And this keeping in mind the possibility of a raking shot from the rear which means that much more solid substance must be penetrated before the 'middlins' of the game can be reached.

In my opinion this claim that a bullet should go through an animal is as silly as the other one that blowing a saucer-sized hole four inches deep is enough. It is obvious to anybody with enough intelligence to come in out of the rain that initial diameter of the bullet has little to do with the price of eggs.

A big diameter bullet of short stubby proportions is the best possible form—except a round one—to waste velocity trying to displace air. A long slender bullet with the same weight can be expanded to double its size, or it can be blown to pieces if the shooter prefers and depending on the type of point and the velocity.

The paralyzing effect of the shock of a high speed expanding or even exploding bullet has been too well demonstrated to need argument. This, however, should be in the form of enough bullet material to blast well into the vitals of the animal. I believe that a bullet which goes nearly intact, through the animal, is all wrong, basing this on the evidence of my own eyes and my own shooting, not to mention the much better evidence of scores of other hunters.

I followed out the wound channel of a .38-55 soft-nose bullet in a bear shot out of the top of a tree and which came down still able to give the dogs a fight, and I followed out the channel of a heavy 236 grain 8 mm. bullet in a deer, both bullets going through. Neither the effect nor the wound channel itself compared with the frightful work of such a bullet as the .280 Ross, or the 150 grain or 180 grain Springfield, or even the .250. I would rather shoot the .250 on any game found in this country than the stubby .38-55. The 8mm is, of course, a far more effective bullet on heavier game or longer ranges than normal.

We have no problem in this country of stopping 400-pound cats of unparalleled ferocity and tenacity of life, nor armored pachyderms. Wherefore it seems to me that a lot of the recommendation of ultra-heavy bullets at the expense of velocity is uncalled for.

If we could keep the high velocity and still have the heavy bullet, fine, but there is no use in throwing away velocity for the sake of pushing more lead through the air than is necessary for adequate penetration. And this term does not mean going through the quarry and blasting down trees on the other side. The business of the bullet is with that animal and the animal 'lives' in the middle of his body, not on the far side. This 'high penetration' stuff is as uncalled for as arranging a delayed action fuse on a battleship shell so it will explode on the far side of the ship instead of its interior, or not explode at all. . .

With the evidence all in, and ranging back over 23 years, there is no question that the .30 Springfield and rifles firing this ammunition constitutes the nearest approach there is to the all-round game rifle. It is a bit strenuous for woodchuck and a bit light for lion but no other arm comes so near to this non-existent universal hunting rifle.

In the hands of Stewart White the Springfield proved practically as effective on lions as the .405, while there is, of course, no comparison in the long range killing ability of the two, in the flat flight, the accuracy, and the superior balance and lines of the Springfield. . .

The 220 grain Western Short Exposed Point, boat-tailed to reduce friction in the bore—and more useful ballistically with the lower initial velocity of the bullet—2385 feet per second—shares with the Remington full jacket 'delayed mushroom' 220 grain bullet the credit of first putting the Springfield into the class of a lion rifle.

The testimony of another expert on the all-round rifle possibility is given in the following statement by Colonel Caswell in his book *Sporting Rifles and Rifle Shooting*:

For many years we have heard of the all-round rifle. There is no such thing. True there are rifles that may be used for both target and sporting purposes, but with the exception of the U. S. Springfield '03 and rifles of that type which have been introduced in recent years, few, if any, fulfill adequately both requirements, and these are mainly for long-range target work. Many times one is asked which is the best rifle, and the questioner seems rather put out at the answer: "What for?" Now each rifle is made for some specific purpose and then adapted to others.

But Col. Caswell did have some ideas as to an all purpose rifle for non-dangerous game and elsewhere in his book he indicates what they should be:

Now let us take the gun that will be the most used in hunting game of any size, non-dangerous. Here we are limited in size of bore from 256 to 300 thousandths of an inch and have open to our choice the Mannlicher, Mauser, Ross, and Springfield. First let me say that the seven millimeter or 275 bore is the nearest approach to the ballistic ideal, both as to wind cutting and range. We have the seven millimeter Mauser with a charge of 42½ grains and bullet of 139 grains, velocity at the muzzle 2784 foot-seconds, energy at 100 yards, 2057 foot-pounds. The weak point is our energy, which falls nearly 500 foot-pounds below the required standard and puts this rifle out of consideration for all but deer and lighter game. With the 280 Ross we have a bullet of 145 grains, muzzle velocity, 3050 foot-seconds, and energy at 100 yards, 2595 foot pounds, but we encounter another problem in this gun. The bullet is too light to sustain the velocity and therefore breaks up badly before it can penetrate far enough into the body of game for its energy to be effective on the vital organs. The 280 with the 180 grain bullet and 2700 foot seconds velocity is beside the question as I know of no action that will feed it through the magazine and function. Then too, its energy is not as great as the 145 grain bullet, being only 2584 foot pounds, although it is very much more effective on account of the heavier bullet.

He was undoubtedly in error about the Ross 180 grain as it was manufactured and used through the magazine in the Canadian team's match rifles used at Bisley, England, from 1908 to 1914.

But indeed, when you come right down to it, who wants or would buy an all-round rifle. Not the American deer hunter or the European mountaineer after chamois. Probably only one man in thousands ever gets the opportunity to hunt more than one or two types of big game, and his idea of an all-round rifle wouldn't mean much to the African hunter or the man in the jungles of India. This has probably been the experience of the few gunmakers that have manufactured what they thought were rifles of this type. Certainly there is no evidence from the hunting experiences of representative big game hunters that the .350 Rigby, the .35 and .400 Whelen or the .375 Hoffman are becoming more than slightly popular. It is usually as Colonel Caswell says a matter of utilizing different rifles for different types of game, where such rifles are particularly adapted to the range and terrain hunted over.

And now having cited these opinions, one might be pardoned for attempting to arrive at an average of the favorite rifles of the most noted hunters of the later, or so-called small bore periods, and in suggesting that such a rifle, even if it could not lay claim to the title of an all-round rifle, was at least representative of a personal or general purpose rifle, supported, when occasion requires, with special tools for special tasks.

Name	Favorite Rifle Make	Caliber	Bullet	Velocity	Energy
Pease	Mannlicher	6.5mm.	156	2380	1950
Whelen	Springfield	.30-06	180	2700	2910
Millais	Mannlicher	6.5mm	156	2380	1950
Lyell	Rigby-Mauser	7.9mm	227	2050	2120
Sheldon	Jeffery-Mannlicher	6.5mm	156	2380	1950
Bell	Rigby-Mauser	7mm	173	2300	2060
Stigand	Mannlicher	6.5mm	156	2380	1950
Prichard	Mannlicher	6.5mm	156	2380	1950
Cottar	Winchester	.405	300	2700	3210
Melland	Rigby-Mauser	.350	310	2000	2750
Rosenberg	Mauser	8 X 60	227	2350	2770
Evans	Army & Navy	.400	400	2150	4100
Maydon	Mauser 8 X 7.9mm		227	2050	2120
O'Connor	Winchester	.270	130	3160	2880
Clark	Springfield	.30-06	220	2410	2840
Burrard	Ross	.280	140	3010	2820
Robertson	Jeffery	.400	400	2150	4100
Blunt	Rigby-Mauser	.416	410	2300	4700
Marshall	Gibbs	.404	400	2125	4010
Keith	Holland	.300	180	2700	2920
Goode	Winchester	.270	130	3160	2880
Sutton	Holland	.465	480	2125	4800
Da Gama	Rigby-Mauser	7mm	173	2300	2060
Simpson	Winchester	.30-06	220	2410	2840
24-men	Average	.320	238	2400	2860 (3040)

The actual energy, computed from the average bullet weight and velocity, is 3040 foot pounds rather than 2860, the average of the energy figures. This rifle is equivalent to the German 7.9mm with the old 1888 bullet, or perhaps more nearly the .318 Westley Richards with its 250 grain bullet at 2340 feet per second. It would undoubtedly be a very effective weapon and would meet the requirements of weight and handiness if kept below 8 lbs. but the recoil would run up to about 25 foot pounds and be very definitely more noticeable than the Springfield.

However, it is probably well that there can be no agreement on an all-round rifle, since the requirements vary so widely and the physical ability of the hunter may vary just as widely. An 18 pound elephant rifle is not a snap shot weapon for a man of 150 lbs., although Sir Samuel Baker

thought nothing of manipulating a rifle of 21 pounds. The super accurate game shot who is also an expert stalker can use a very small bore
if the bullet has accuracy and penetration. A different approach would be
to state the requisites of the big game rifle for the two types of hunting,
one for dangerous game and the other for non-dangerous game as follows:

	Dangerous Game	Non-dangerous Game
Caliber	Medium to large	Small
Bullet weight	Heavy	Medium
Velocity	Medium	High
Penetration	Deep	Medium
Accuracy	Medium	High
Weight	To absorb recoil	Light

In each case the characteristics are interdependent. A large caliber with
a heavy bullet at medium velocity would require a heavy rifle but the type
of bullet and its velocity would not be conducive to great accuracy. On
the other hand, high velocity with a long bullet is possible in a lighter
rifle with a greater degree of accuracy. One of the early experiments with
barrel vibration conclusively proved that this vibration had less time to take
effect with high velocities and therefore accuracy was improved. This
is probably the one significant gain by the development of ultra high velocity rifles but is offset by the lighter less effective bullets, and increased
barrel wear.

And finally before leaving the discussion of the all-round rifle one piece
of advice in the following passage from *Hunting Among The Thongas*
by George Agnew Chamberlain adds confirmation to the idea that a rifle
with which the hunter is familiar, providing it is otherwise equal to the
task, is far preferable than an untried weapon, no matter how remarkable
it may be:

A few weeks later we were together in London, sweating blood over
the choice of batteries. That hyperbole is just barely an exaggeration, for
there is no battle of experts more baffling than the endless discussion as
to the proper armament for tackling the heavy and dangerous game of
Africa.

It would take a book to describe the evolution of the sporting rifle, the
ups and downs of bores, and calibers, the reactions of a dozen styles of
bullet, the astonishing ascendancy and recent collapse of the needle-gun in
the estimation of the great hunters, and the weighing of the rough and

ready American product against the exquisite finish of the most expensive heavy English guns compared, in turn, with the lightness of the asplike cordite French weapons.

An old hand at the game invariably starts in with what he is convinced is a perfect battery; just as invariably he comes out saying "Well, I carried this and that; but *if I were you—!*" Only one admonition can never go wrong; if you have a rifle which gets results, what is known as a "lucky" gun, hang on to it as you would your back teeth. There is an old and ugly stock-model .318 of the vintage of 1910, and a more ancient double barreled .450 by Evans, for the repossession of which, could they be traced, I would give their weight in liquor.

Written, of course, during Prohibition in the United States when liquor *was* expensive. The reference to "needle guns" undoubtedly refers to the ultra small bores and not to the "chassepot."

CHAPTER 10

AMMUNITION, SIGHTS, OUTFIT, TRANSPORT AND THE FUTURE

*O*NLY experience in the field can determine what is needed in hunting. While the choice of a proper rifle is of prime importance, there are other items of equipment and details of outfitting for hunting expeditions to various parts of the world, that must not be overlooked. Even with a perfect battery, the sportsman may find, too late, that some piece of equipment or some detail of his outfit is deficient or lacking, and that it may seriously affect the success of his hunt. This may occur in regard to the quality of ammunition, proper sights for the rifle, the right clothing, suitable and complete camp equipment, or means of transport. Each of these things has varied with the development of the science of weapons and hunting, and between the various regions hunted. The ammunition must be proper for the rifle, the game hunted and the ranges shot over; sights will be different for open plain or mountain hunting from those used in the forest or jungle; clothing of a type proper for the jungle or bush of the tropics would be quite out of place in Northern America or Tibet. The amount of camp equipment considered necessary for comfort and the amount and cost of transport will be affected by the climate and the distance and difficulty of reaching the game fields. On that account these details will vary as between hunting in North America for deer and moose or for Alaskan game, for a trip to Africa, or hunting in the Indian jungles or the Himalayas; and as far as possible these variations will be shown by quoting from experienced hunters in these various fields.

First as to the quality of ammunition, and here a litttle history will assist in explaining preferences and developments. The early big game hunter bought his Curtis and Harvey powder by the keg and his bullets as block lead. If his flint was good and he had sufficient wadding and patch material he was independent of the ammunition manufacturer. In fact, if we except the powder makers and the shot tower operators, there were no ammunition companies. The advent of the breechloader, which depended on the cartridge to seal the chamber, changed this situation. The first cartridges of paper and cloth were made by the manufacturers

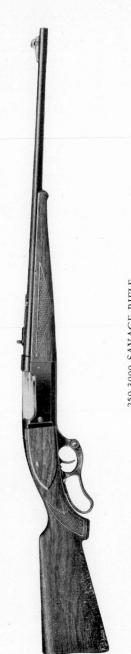

.250-3000 SAVAGE RIFLE.

Courtesy Moser & Cotin, and Savage Repeating Arms Co., Utica, N. Y.

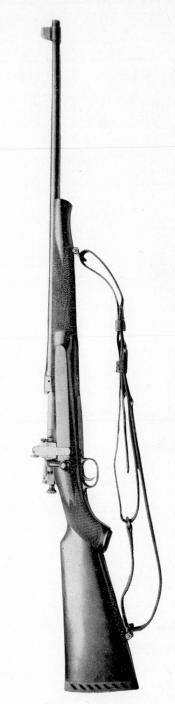

DR. R. L. SUTTON'S 30-'06 SPRINGFIELD.

JOHN M. BROWNING, AMERICA'S
GREATEST INVENTOR OF
FIREARMS.

From *Hatchers Notebook*, by Maj. Gen.
Julian S. Hatcher.

CHARLES NEWTON. LAWYER,
PROMOTER, RIFLE DESIGNER.
FATHER OF THE 22 "IMP," HI-
POWER SAVAGE, THE .250-3000
SAVAGE AND THE .256 AND .35
NEWTON RIFLES.

By courtesy of A. D. Bissell.

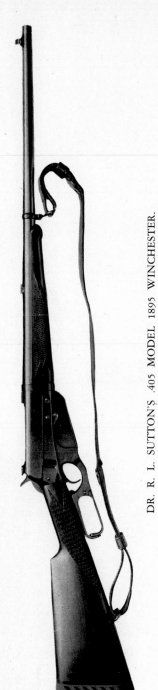

DR. R. L. SUTTON'S .405 MODEL 1895 WINCHESTER.

HOLLAND AND HOLLAND .465 DOUBLE EXPRESS RIFLE.

DR. R. L. SUTTON. EMINENT
MEDICAL SPECIALIST, BIG GAME
HUNTER AND AUTHOR

COL. TOWNSEND WHELEN. BIG
GAME HUNTER, ARMS EXPERT
AND AUTHOR.

From *Hatcher's Notebook*, by Maj. Gen.
Julian S. Hatcher.

DR. JAMES L. CLARK. BIG GAME
HUNTER, COLLECTOR, CURATOR,
AUTHOR.

From the American Museum of Natural
History.

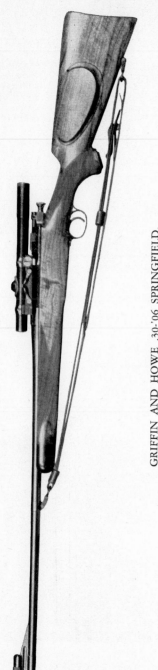

GRIFFIN AND HOWE .30-'06 SPRINGFIELD.

Courtesy of Abercrombie and Fitch, New York.

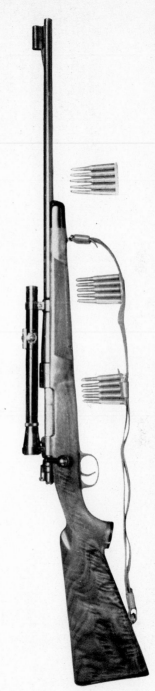

7MM MAUSER RESTOCKED BY AUTHOR WITH SELECTED AMERICAN WALNUT. THE RIFLE IS A WAFFENFABRIK OBERNDORF A/N (Am NECKAR) MODEL 98 ACTION WITH A WINCHESTER 24 INCH MODEL 70 BARREL MOUNTED BY NIEDNER AND A HOME-MOUNTED LYMAN ALASKAN SCOPE.

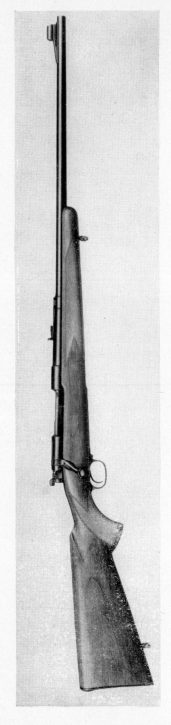

WINCHESTER .270 BOLT ACTION MODEL 70.

Courtesy of Winchester Repeating Arms Company.

VICKERS' MAUSER .404 EXPRESS WITH 25-INCH BARREL WEIGHING 9¼ POUNDS.

THE SAFARI.

From Blayney Percival's *A Game Ranger on Safari.*

and supplied with the weapons.   When the metallic cartridge came in as a result of Pauli's experiments in 1816, Houillier's French patents between 1847 and 1850, Lefaucheux's pin fire cartridge of 1836, Col. Boxer's wrapped foil cartridge of 1855, Maynard's and Gen. Burnside's rifle cartridges in America and finally the drawn brass case accredited to Col. Berdan in 1869, cartridge making became an industry by itself. However, if it had not been for the general adoption of the American machine methods of drawing brass, the breech loading rifle might have suffered a serious setback in its progress.   One of the early objections of the U. S. Army to the Spencer rifle was that the rifle could not be used as a muzzle loader when its cartridges were exhausted.   Consequently cartridges had to be available everywhere at a reasonable cost, made to accurate dimensions, and this could only be secured through machine production using standard gages of the American type.   Until cartridges manufactured in this manner were available, sportsmen at a distance from the sources of supply continued to cast their own spherical or conical bullets and reload the crude paper or brass shells that had been supplied with their rifle.

The English and other Continental manufacturers were not long in adopting American methods of cartridge manufacture in addition to those for gun making, and Greener in 1873 refers to a plant in Birmingham equipped to make the drawn brass cartridges of Col. Berdan's, although it was not until 1882 that the British Army finally gave up the inferior foil wrapped Boxer cartridge for the Martini.   This Birmingham plant was Kynoch's which with Eley's Cartridge Company became the leading British manufacturers specializing in the heavy large and medium bore cartridge demanded by African and Indian sportsmen.   On the Continent, outside of the government arsenals manufacturing military cartridges, Germany had two private factories, the Deutsche Waffen und Munitions Fabriken originally located at Berlin, manufacturing Mauser rifles and ammunition, and later moved to Karlsruhe and specializing in cartridge manufacture, and the Rheinisch-Westfalische Sprengstoff Aktien Gesellschaft at Nuremburg.   The tradmarks of DWM and RWS or R were well known in Continental circles before the last war.   These, and the four American companies, Winchester (with its H for Henry on rim-fire cartridges), Peters, Union-Metallic Cartridge, and Western Cartridge Company constituted the leading sources of all sporting cartridges after the advent of the breechloader.   The size and number of American plants came about from the immense war orders received between 1870 and 1885 to supply the Russian, Turkish and Spanish armies equipped with American rifles, and the fact that cartridge manufacture was developed as a private industry in this country.

As a result of this lineup of the cartridge making industry, the English specialized in the large caliber straight or bottlenecked shells for custommade English double rifles, the Americans supplied the long straight shells for their single shot rifles or the short blunt-nosed cartridges for their tubular magazines repeaters, while the Germans specialized in the bottle necked military cartridge for Mauser and Mannlicher bolt action rifles. And it has not been until the last 25 years, or since World War I that there has been any particular intermingling of the manufacture of these types of cartridges. The exceptions have been for a few calibers such as the 6.5, 7 and 8 millimeter cartridges taken over bodily by the English custom gun makers before 1900, and in this country the 7mm cartridges made for South American republics when they replaced Remington rifles with Mausers in the nineties. Before the last war, D.W.M. was making two or three rimmed cartridges for the English big bores, and we in this country had adopted the 6.5, 7 and 8 millimeter German cartridges and the English .300 and .375 Holland magnum cartridges.

The components used in cartridge manufacture have varied somewhat with the amount and type of scientific research on these materials in the various countries. As has already been stated, the English pioneered the development of smokeless powder derived from nitroglycerine, and loaded this product in the form of cordite in practically all their sporting and military cartridges. The United States and Germany were more interested in the development of nitrocellulose powder and non-corrosive primers because of the injurious effect of the hotter nitroglycerine powders and mercuric primers on barrels. Where rifle shooting was a sport for the masses economy was of prime consideration and new barrels were expensive. The English big game hunter who might use only three or four hundred cartridges in a year and who had a gun bearer to clean his rifles was more interested in the higher velocity secured with cordite in spite of the fact that storage or heat might cause irregularities in its performance.

Bullets have been pretty much the same, with each country developing particular types of metal jackets, soft points, hollow points, etc., although latterly in the years before World War II, Germany and the United States had brought out some singularly successful bullets for shooting game. The German types were called strong jacket or "Stark-Mantel" and the American types were called "controlled expansion" bullets, both types having much thicker jackets at the base to resist complete breaking up of the bullet at high velocities. However, there has hardly been experience enough, as yet, with these types to determine how much improvement they have been over the older soft, open, or copper-tube pointed bullets such as the 87 grain .250-300 or the Ross 140 grain bullet, which at times seemed to disintegrate on hitting game.

This matter of bullet design has been of increasing importance with the trend to higher velocities and before leaving it the opinion of two American experts will be of value. Elmer Keith and Major Charles Askins have had long experience with all types of high velocity rifles both in the hunting field and in target work. Major Askins is quoted from *The American Rifleman* of November 1930:

Of course, what apparently is needed is bullet weight, and the penetration that is guaranteed by that weight. Again quoting Mr. Riggs, he has suggested that probably in time to come, if we keep on increasing bullet velocities, we will have to use solid bullets on big game, with some modification of the jacket at the point or elsewhere. We have all been afraid of solid bullets, and, as a matter of fact, we have all been afraid of penetration. Let a man tell what he considers ideal penetration, and he will state that is where a bullet goes through the animal, lodging in the skin on the opposite side. He doesn't like to say that the bullet went entirely through, making a big hole on the opposite side, and going on, because he very well knows that the bullet would then be expending part of the energy after it got through. He is obsessed with the conviction that the missile must expend all of its energy within the beast, or else it is a defective bullet. Now, with some misgivings I question the wisdom of all this. I believe that if we could have a bullet which would pass entirely through the game—a brown bear, say—and make a hole on the other side as big as your two fists, we'd get that bear. Same thing with anything else we shot . . .

The modern tendency in cartridge building is to leave the bullets as they are and to speed them up. The bullet that was designed and well designed, for a velocity of 2300 feet is speeded up to the velocity of 2800 feet, with no change in the bullet jacket. I question the wisdom of this, and question whether the high velocity bullet is going to prove a better killer than the same missile at lower velocity. In like manner—still worse and more of it—bullet speed has been obtained by lightening the missile. This has been done with the .30-06, the 7mm, the .256, and the .250, and the results are in grave doubt where animals are to be shot above a certain size. In very large game shooting I'd far rather trust the

220 grain in .30-06, the 175 grain in 7mm, the 160 grain in .256, the 117 grain in .250, the 350 grain in .375 to any of the lighter missiles that are made for these calibers. The thing lies partly in weight of lead, but still more in keeping the speed of the bullet down to its working velocity.

Although he has competed as a member of his state rifle team at Camp Perry, Elmer Keith is better known as a big-game hunter, an experimenter with all types of rifled firearms and an author of many books and articles on hunting with the rifle. While his views may have changed somewhat in the past ten years his ideas of an effective big-game bullet are well stated in the following from *The American Rifleman* published in January 1936:

Over twenty years of hunting American big game, especially our heavier species, has convinced me that for reliable results under all conditions in timber and brush, with raking and running shots, only long heavy bullets with thick jackets, and at velocities of from 2000 to 2400 feet, will surely produce reliable results. These same bullets I prefer to be of not less than .35 caliber, and they must be so constructed that they will always expand, yet retain most of their weight and give good penetration. High velocity is a fine thing in its place, especially in shooting mule-deer, sheep and goat and coyotes at long range where flat trajectory is absolutely necessary; but the bullets of such cartridges are apt to expand entirely too soon on heavy game at close ranges, producing a bad wound but one that often is not deep enough to reach the vitals of the animal. A velocity of from 2300 to 2400 feet is ample to insure vital hits on game the size of elk, large bear and moose up to 400 yards . . .

As to the performance of certain types of ammunition in the field Stewart Edward White's comments from his African trips between 1909 and 1914 have already been quoted. On the later trip in 1925 with Pope and Young they used .220 grain pin-point soft-point and 180 grain open-point boat-tail bullets in the .30-06. The .220 grain bullet was Leslie Simpson's choice for everything that didn't require his .577 double rifle. But not all experiences have been commendatory of some types of ammunition as, for example, Bell's experience with British ammunition:

I have never heard any explanation of the undoubted fact that our British ammunition manufacturers cannot even yet produce a reliable rifle cartridge head, anvil and cap, other than that of the service .303. On my last shoot in Africa two years ago, when W. and I went up to Bahr Aouck, the very first time he fired at an elephant he had a misfire and I had identically the same thing. We were using .318's with English made cartridges. Then on the same shoot I nearly had my head blown off and my thumb severely bruised by an English loaded .256. There was no misfire there. The cartridge appeared to me almost to detonate. More vapour came from the breech end than from the other. I have since been told by a great authority that it was probably due to a burst case, due to weak head. On my return I complained about this and was supplied with a new batch, said to be all right. But whenever I fire four or five rounds I have a jamb, and on investigating invariably find a cap blown out and lodging in the slots cut for the lugs of the bolt head. Luckily these cartridges are wanting in force; at one time they used fairly to blast me with gas from the wrong end. The fact that these faults are not conspicuously apparent in this country may be traced to the small number of rounds fired from sporting rifles, or, more probably, to the pressures increasing in a tropical temperature.

In speaking of his .275 Rigby Mauser with which he did the bulk of his elephant shooting Bell has this also to say about his ammunition:

Then again the ballistics of the .275 cartridge, as loaded in Germany at any rate, are such as to make for the very greatest reliability. In spite of the pressures being high, the cartridge construction is so excellent that trouble from blowbacks and split cases and loose caps in the mechanism are entirely obviated. Why the caps should be so reliable in this particular cartridge I have never understood. But the fact remains that, although I have used almost every kind of rifle, the only one which never let me down was a .276 with German (DWM) ammunition. I never had one single hang-fire even. Nor a stuck case, nor a split one, nor a blow-back, nor a misfire. All these I had with other rifles.

A somewhat different experience with ammunition is described by Vilhjalmur Stefansson in *The Friendly Arctic:*

Just at this time I suffered a slight injury through an accident with defective ammunition. On my expedition of 1908-1912 I used the Austrian 6.5mm Mannlicher-Schoenauer rifle and found it most satisfactory. The advertised muzzle velocity was 2560 feet. For the present expedition I was using the Mannlicher-Schoenauer as remodeled by Gibbs of Bristol, said to have a muzzle velocity of 3160 feet, attained through a considerable increase of the powder charge. I found the Gibbs modification excellent, if the blame for the sort of accident which happened to me September 22nd (1915) is put upon the ammunition rather than the rifle.

This day I was sealing and had already killed and secured six seals. When the seventh appeared in the water a hundred yards away I fired but never knew whether I hit him, for as I fired I saw a flash of light and for several days thereafter saw very little more with my right eye. The shell had cracked from the primer out to the edge and about a quarter of an inch up the side. It seems unbelievable in examining the Mann-licher-Schoenauer that powder could come back through the bolt but it did. The black spots made by it were on my nose and cheek and fore-head. They were so conspicuous and hurt so much that I can only explain the slight injury to the eye itself by supposing that it was partly closed and protected. It was about a week before the inflammation disappeared.

Accidents of this sort occurred to our rifles about twice per thousand rounds of ammunition. I had two similar experiences in later years but in neither case did so much powder come through, and there was no real injury except on this occasion. Storkerson had one or two accidents of the same sort but his eye was not hurt. It seems possible, therefore, that the rifle which I had at the time of the first accident was in some respects slightly different from the others. We had about half a dozen of these rifles and as I made no record of which one I was using at the time, I cannot say whether a second shell ever cracked in the same rifle.

But wherever or whenever sportsmen speak of ammunition they are of one mind, that it must be packed secure from weather and temperature, in air tight tins, not to be opened until used. This is especially true of English cordite cartridges as is pointed out in the following statement from *Wild Game in Zambezia* by R. C. F. Maugham, published in 1914:

Ammunition must be fresh. I do not know whether the last year may have produced a cordite impervious to the considerable variations of tem-perature inseparable from the African climate, but I fear not. That the efficiency of one's cordite ammunition is thus varied there can be no shadow of doubt, in fact I have had occasion to observe it on more occa-sions than one. I would, therefore, impress upon the newcomers—and some old ones for the matter of that—the advisability of conveying as much of the stock of cartridges as possible in their original stout tin-lined ammunition case . . . But a most important and one I fear too frequently neglected is the golden rule, not of keeping your powder dry, but of keeping it cool.

The amount of ammunition used by big game hunters will be greater on longer trips, farther away from outfitting points. The average African sportsman overestimates his needs for fear of running short, not realizing that cartridges can be secured locally. Steward Edward White took 1500 cartridges to Africa and used 500. Powell-Cotton used about 2.5 cartridges per day and per animal with the ratio of small to large-bore of 4 to 1. Kittenberger estimated 400 cartridges for the small-bore and 150 for the large bore for a three to four months' hunting trip. In each case the ratio of small bore solid to soft-nose was about 3 to 1, and for the large bore one solid to 2 soft-nose cartridges. This is for African hunting.

In Asia, Morden and Clark took 1000 Springfield 180 grain open-point cartridges for two rifles on their nine month trip from India through Central Asia to China, an average of about two cartridges per rifle per day. Darrah recommends, for a six months Himalayan trip after sheep, markhor, ibex and bear, 300 soft-nosed small-bore cartridges, which is somewhat under two cartridges per day. Dr. Sutton in his book *Tiger Trails in Southern Asia* recommends 100 small-bore and 50 large-bore cartridges per man for the usual hunting trip such as he took to Indo-China in 1925, but as this was in company with other shooters, using similar calibers, the supply was undoubtedly somewhat reduced. For the eighties when the sportsmen were using black powder express rifles, and cartridges were quite expensive, the *Sportsmans' Vade Mecum for the Himalayas* by K.C.A.J., whoever that may have been, advised 150 rifle cartridges for a six months' trip or rather less than one a day.

Now as to rifle sights, which seemingly, to the man in the field, have been an item of lesser importance than the rifle, ammunition, and outfit, since little is said about sight equipment in the books they have written. And this is not to be wondered at, as the average shot at game is probably under, rather than over 100 yards. In the jungle the average, from all accounts, is much shorter than this, or from 10 to 50 yards, while in open country it will be from 75 to 300 yards with occasional shots up to 500 yards. So the rifle sights for jungle work, from the point of view of the target shooter, are coarse, made with the sole view of being quickly and accurately alined on a vital spot at short range. Hence, the wide V and bright bead foresight. Dr. Christy hunting in the Congo forest recommends the wide V rear sight and set for 100 yards and the 45 degree sloped bead foresight, as has already been quoted. Blunt says an elephant rifle should have no "extraneous fittings, such as leaf sights, fittings for a sling, etc., and that leaf sights should never be necessary for big game, as one should always be well within the hundred yards before firing." For this type of shooting the telescope or aperture sight would be dangerous as they too severely restrict the eye's visual angle.

On the other hand for open mountain and plains work Burrard is strong for the aperture sight as being more accurate and easily alined. He also recommends a wide V sight for jungle work, and for either occasion, a small platinum or silver bead, with a vertical face and undercut, to reduce the glare. Lt. Col. C. H. Stockley also a Himalayan and Indian jungle hunter differs in some ways from this point of view in his book *Stalking in the Himalayas and Northern India*:

The sighting of a rifle is very important, and is often far from satisfactory when it leaves the makers. Narrow V's to backsight and enormous raised blocks to the foresight are all very well for deliberate shooting at bull's-eyes on a rifle range in good light, but inimical to good shooting in the field.

The whole sighting should be as near flush with the barrel as possible, or eye and hand will not work together. If the V of the backsight is too narrow its definition will be blurred, often forming a double image. The V should be wide and shallow giving a view of the whole target, and with a small nick, or silver line, below the centre.

The bead of the foresight should be suited to the individual, but to normal sight one of medium size, ivory-tipped and sloped forward to catch the light, is most suitable. A fine bead is difficult to pick up in a bad light or against an ill-defined target. A coarse bead is suitable for quick shooting at close range, and may well be substituted for the usual foresight if shooting in forest.

A gloaming sight is little use; it is liable to tempt people to take shots in light too bad for certainty of aim.

Personally, I think a rifle should have only one standing backsight, for 150 yards range, and no extra flaps. The same amount of foresight should always be taken, and the aim directed a little lower if the animal is closer than 150 yards. The rise of the bullet above the line of sight at 150 yards is so small with modern rifles, that the difference never amounts to aiming below even the smallest beast's body.

"Peep" or "aperture" sights are liked by some, but are unnecessary and unsuited to most. Telescopic sights are easily knocked out of adjustment, unnecessary to normal sight, and unsporting if used over 180 yards.

The American sportsman has come to use the aperture sight from its almost universal use in target work, but it has never been very popular among foreign big game hunters, and on that account has had very limited use in any African or Asian hunting. As has already been stated, this is because in jungle or forest hunting the aperture is a serious handicap in light barely sufficient for accurate shooting with the easily pointed open sights.

This is true also of the telescope sight. So far as can be determined from the written accounts of their hunting only four African sportsmen have used the telescopic sight, Foa, Powell-Cotton, Kittenberger and da Gama. Powell-Cotton had used one on his Mannlicher rifle, shooting in the Himalayas in 1897-98 and brought it with him to Africa on his trip through Abyssinia in 1899. But he never mentions its use either favorably or unfavorably. Kittenberger has the following comment in his *Big Game Hunting in East Africa* published in 1929:

I would use a telescope sight only on the 6.7mm. I only began using one during my last trip, and to be honest, I am rather sorry that I got into the habit. If I had to tackle dangerous game the telescope quickly came off the rifle.

Of course, only the best telescope sight ought to be used. Such a rifle must always be carried by hand, because the great heat and shaking it goes through during the caravaning can influence the delicate cross wires with disastrous effects.

Vasco da Gama whose remarks on rifles are quoted elsewhere, contributed a second series of articles to *The American Rifleman* in 1929-30 on African equipment in which he says apropos of telescope sights:

A magazine rifle is not complete without a detachable telescope. In this line no telescope, of which I tried many, is as good as the Zeiss Zielvier. The telescopic sight has manifold advantages, among which we can say that it lengthens the shooting hours of the day by at least one hour. Long before you will be able to aim in the dew of the early morning with ordinary sights, you will be able to shoot perfectly with a Zeiss telescope. This happened to me the first time I went buffalo hunting in the prairies with a magazine rifle with telescope. I was carrying this rifle in a leather case, while my express from Holland's was ready for action. A native pointed out in the morning mist a buffalo over 150 yards away. I could hardly see the horns, but nevertheless put the Holland to the shoulder. Firing was impossible as I could not see anything through the sights of my express. I took the Mauser from the cover, and through the telescope could see the buffalo perfectly, and a single bullet going through the heart disposed of the beast.

At very long distances, in open prairies, I have shot with the aid of the telescope, as far as 450 yards, which under the then existing conditions of visibility I could not have done with ordinary sights. At night also (with the moon out, of course) I have shot buffalos and elephants at distances which otherwise I would have considered entirely out of range.

There are several different sights or reticules for the telescopes. No matter which one you choose, be sure it is of the cross or semi-cross type. At night, when aiming, for instance at an elephant's head, you will not be able to see the point of intersection of the two lines but you will find that you can see fairly well the beginning of these cross lines, which will permit you to make out exactly the place where your bullet will go.

The fitting of the telescope is a very delicate operation, which should never be attempted on an already made rifle. In other words, the telescope must be ordered and placed when the gun is being manufactured. It must allow sidewise and lengthwise adjustment; also, shooting with the ordinary sights from underneath the telescope, in case of a charge. The original Mauser fitting is most satisfactory, as is also the Westley-Richards mounting.

Avoid telescopes magnifying more than four times, as then the trembling of your rifle while aiming will produce a movement of the point of aim, transforming the shooting of a standing animal to something like shooting at the ball in a fair shooting gallery."

This is similar to the comment made by Phillips-Wolley (later Sir Clive Phillips-Wolley) in his article on *Deer Stalking* (in Scotland) in *Big Game Shooting* of the *Country Life Library* published in 1905:

The peep-sights help the eyes of middle-age, and for the long, standing shot—that is when the deer is standing—the telescope sight is a wonderful help. But it is of no use for quick work, and Mr. Fremantle is very right in insisting that it should be arranged alongside the barrel for sporting purposes, not over the barrel. If in the latter position, it prevents the use of ordinary sights for a quick or running shot.

Major Gerald Burrard now Major Sir Gerald Burrard devoted much of his chapter on Sights in the third edition of his *Notes on Sporting Rifles* published in 1932 to telescopic sights but makes no mention of using such sights on big game, either in that book, or his *Big Game Hunting in the Himalayas* published in 1925. In the first edition of the *Notes* after three short paragraphs on telescopic sights he had this to say:

On the whole I do not care for telescope sights nor has their use ever seemed to me to be quite cricket.

However, there has been of late years, a definite trend toward greater use of telescopic sights for hunting certain types of big game. Where the terrain is open, with little cover for stalking, shots must be taken at longer ranges. For the smaller types of big game, such shots are, at times, beyond the power of normal eyesight and open sights, to direct at vital spots. In these cases the use of telescopic sights has become quite popular. This development has been well described by Julian Feiss in an article in *The American Rifleman* for June 1934:

In the last analysis, the scope for big game hunting has not been a thorough success for the practical hunter, especially when used under tropical conditions. Frankly, I am of the opinion that this is not always the fault of the instrument, the rifle, or the mount, for there are really very few men who know how to use a hunting scope to best advantage . . .

In Africa, India and perhaps occasionally in this country when shooting certain classes of game, one must be ready for a possible charge, and anyone who has tried to center a rapidly moving object in the sights of a movie camera, or even a small Kodak, will realize the difficulties involved in trying to pick up a charging beast in the field of a telescope. Imagine trying to stop a charging lion or grizzly at a hundred feet with a rifle equipped with a five power scope and no iron sights to use as an alternative. In the first place, it would be almost hopeless to try to find the moving animal with the sights. This is particularly true if the scope were of high power and had a small field of view. After you finally got the animal in the field of vision, you would have to center him on the cross-hairs or post, and pick a vital spot. And remmber that with a five power scope every movement that you make is magnified five times. Again, the animal might charge so close that he would be out of focus in the glass. Under these conditions the hunter is distinctly out of luck . . .

. . . Personally I never take a shot with or without the scope if the animal is much beyond 300 yards, unless I have plenty of time and am shooting prone. Too much game is wounded by long shots. After a number of years of hunting experience of all types under all conditions, from nearly the Arctic to the Antarctic, and through the Tropics in Two hemispheres, I have noticed that ninety per cent of the game that I have killed has been shot at under 150 yards.

Making a kill in one shot should be the goal of every hunter. It is not only economical, but it is also humane, and saves much hard work. The big game scope is an ideal adjunct for antelope, deer, goat and sheep hunting, because many of the shots offered are at long distances.   For the dangerous members of the cat family, before taking the shot the hunter of experience invariably tries to get as close to his target as possible, and here a scope is not necessary.   These opinions are not arbitrary, but are based upon observation; and I am certain from what I heard that many hunters have suffered mistaken ideas when it comes to big-game hunting with a telescope sight.   The limitations of this type of sight are many, but with proper use a good detachable telescope for hoofed animals is very hard to beat.

This with Foa's remarks about the telescope on his .303 double already quoted, is the extent of the evidence of the use of telescopic sights, outside of some American advocates, even though such sights have been in use in this country for target work, according to Chapman, since 1848; were supplied up to 20 power for the western hide-hunters between 1870 and 1885; and were manufactured commercially for sporting rifles by Zeiss and Aldis prior to 1900.   The American popularity of telescope sights as used in big game hunting by its leading exponents Keith, Lee, Goode, and O'Connor will be further discussed at the end of the chapter.

The other items of a hunters outfit and the means of transport, which are the usual topic of the last chapter of any hunting book, with weight, costs, and source, are only important here as they may cast some light on the means and ability of big game hunters to experiment with weapons and the weight such experiments may have on the development of the rifle. The hunting of big game has become increasingly expensive throughout the world.   Where transportation is well developed and cheap, outfits are smaller, the length of hunting trips shorter, and the number of hunters greater.   Being shorter, with smaller outfits, the time spent on planning a trip is less and the importance of wholly reliable and effective weapons is also less.   In this country, the man equipped with a .30-30 will go hunting deer, elk, or moose and if he fails to find game or down it with a fusillade of shots after he finds it, he can always go again next year.   But with the overseas trip of two to six months duration the size of outfit and its transportation are an indication of the importance of the expedition and of the supreme necessity for efficient and reliable weapons.   It is highly fortunate, that because of this importance, interest in the outfits and weapons has been greater and has encouraged publication of full accounts of these trips.   As an indication of the minimum type of outfit for hunting in Africa the following is quoted from an article by Wilfred Robertson, a resident of Northern Rhodesia, which appeared in *The American Rifleman* for January 1931:

The average person of means, contemplating going out to Africa with the idea of getting some shooting, usually knows nothing whatever about the country or conditions, and, instead of going out first and picking up locally the things he needs, taking advice from disinterested local men, he goes first to some large emporium before sailing, and informs the man behind the counter that he is contemplating going to Africa, shooting. This is the shopman's chance. He rubs his hands, and proceeds to introduce his bewildered client to a vast array of folding beds, folding tents, folding furniture—Heaven knows what besides! He insists that all these are essential to a gentleman proceeding to Africa.

After a couple of hours the prospective voyager staggers out of the shop, and begins to mentally contemplate the huge array of "essentials"; camp furniture *ad lib,* clothes, helmets, stores ranging from sugar to champagne that he has purchased. All this useless "kag" is duly shipped, and when he gets to the point where ships and trains will no longer carry him and his mountain of luggage, he finds he will want about 300 carriers to lug all his rubbish along. He may get them; if he does he has to pay "through the nose" to an "agent" for them, and, having quite forgotten to arrange for the carrying of food for his army, probably most of them bolt before the week is out . . .

The first thing is to cut down everything to an irreducible minimum, at the same time forgetting nothing that is absolutely essential. First a tent is unnecessary, except when an expedition has to be made in the rainy season. As no one, unless he were forced, would undertake an expedition in the rains, a tent can be put aside at once. A big tree makes splendid shade, far better than a stuffy tent. Even in the dry season there is a chance of a rare thunderstorm, but in case one is seen working up, it takes but a few minutes for the carriers to run up a pole and grass shelter. Provided it doesn't leak, what better canopy is there to sleep under than the star-spangled sky?

There is generally a light fall of dew at night; but this is a very small point. The top blanket may get damped, but it is easily dried in a few minutes in the blazing midday sun. As regards clothes, I always put them under my pillow, where they remain dry from any chance of dew. The rifles lie by my side, under a flap of the blankets, free from dew, and handy in case they are needed in the night to choke off a prowling lion or rhinoceros.

The next thing to discard is all camp furniture, with the exception, perhaps, of a light deck chair. For a table I use one of the food boxes, emptied of its contents, and inverted. The box thereby serves a double purpose—a table in camp, and a receptacle for stores, travelling on a carrier's head on the march. I always carry a small galvanized iron bath, which is most useful. When on the march, this bath forms a receptacle for the kitchen utensils, and travels on the cook boy's head.

Dry grass, freshly cut each night, under the blankets serves as a mattress, and very comfortable if it is properly laid. A mattress is a useless encumbrance to drag along. The dry grass keeps one's blankets off the ground, and out of the way of any damp. A camp bed, or stretcher, is only useful if traveling in the rainy season. A good mosquito net is essential as are boots and a helmet (I prefer the khaki quilted kind), a change of clothes (khaki shirt and shorts), pajamas, and in case of a chill evening, an old tweed jacket. A sweater is very useful for slipping on in camp after the sun goes down, and also for sleeping in over the pajama jacket. It keeps the body from getting chilled in case of having to turn out in a night alarm, to fire at and drive off some prowling lion or disgruntled rhino. Slippers, towel, soap, shaving tackle and so on, must not be forgotten.

Now for the question of stores. The absolute essentials are flour, sugar, tea and salt. To these I add a few odd tins of jam and condensed milk. Also a tin or two of "bully," and packets of dessicated soup, for use while traveling through the country where there is neither game, nor native villages where fowls and eggs can be obtained. A little dried fruit is useful. A hurricane lamp and a little parafin (kerosene), washing soap, matches, tobacco, and a few small oddments complete the list, with the exception of a flask of brandy in case of accidents. A nightly "sundowner" of whiskey is very nice, but it is too heavy to carry; therefore, all liquor except the medicinal brandy must be taboo. For the rest, the rifle must supply that—either direct, in the shape of meat, or by trading meat at the villages for native produce, i. e., fowls, eggs, tomatoes, sweet potatoes, maize meal, etc. I reckon to carry flour at the rate of 20 pounds per month for self; more, of course, if I have a white companion.

By far the more serious problem is that of considering the food for the carriers. The ordinary ration is reckoned at 2 pounds of meal per head per day; but once the expedition is in the shooting country, and there is plenty of meat for them this can be considerably reduced. Personally I always try to carry a ration of meal working out at not less than half-pound per head, per day, for some time, with the expedition, so as to have a good supply to fall back upon in the case of being unable to trade meat for meal with the local natives. Usually, provided one travels with a small party of carriers, a certain amount can be purchased—eked out, if necessary, with the meal carried with the column.   It must be remembered that, however much meat the carriers are getting, they must have meal.   Meal is food to the African savage, the rest-meat and vegetables—are dubbed "flavorings."   Feed him on meat alone, and he will die in a week or two from malnutrition.

The cooking utensils, etc., need be of the simplest description. A couple of saucepans, a frying pan, a kettle, enameled (or better still, aluminum) plates and mugs, knives, forks and spoons—not forgetting a tin-opener—a basin and bucket, are all that are needed.   Do not forget needle and thread for clothes repair.

A very important item is that of medicines, which thanks to the tabloid, can be easily packed in small space.   Quinine, asperin, Epsom salts, and chlorodyne are essential, also a supply of bandages, boracic lint, and permanganate.   Scissors, fine tweezers, and a clinical thermometer should also be added.   Being prepared for accident or sickness is the best way to avoid it.   There is not only oneself to be considered, there is also one's carriers. Also, in the wild parts in which I have done most of my traveling, I used to get quite a number of natives coming to me asking for "white man's medicine" to cure them.   Apart from the humanity side of the question, I have found that timely medical assistance sometimes comes very advantageously.   Giving a head man a dose of quinine to cure him of a sharp attack of malaria may produce food and extra carriers, where none were forthcoming previously.   Some knowledge of first aid—wounds, burns, and so on—is very useful, and it is a knowledge that sometimes comes in very opportunely.

The net result of the above forethought in the matter of kit is a small party of contented carriers, fast travelling; and freedom from worry.

Carrier management is a matter that repays study.   To begin with, I always weigh all loads before leaving on an expedition, and no carrier's load is allowed to exceed 50 pounds.   Loads naturally lighten as the food is eaten.   As regards what one might describe as permanent loads—that is, loads like blankets, cooking utensils, and so on—that will not vary on the trip, I make these loads weighing decidedly less than the 50 pounds. If they add stuff of their own to the load, that's their own business.   I remember one carrier who had only about a 20 pound load of my stuff to carry, staggering along under fully 70 pounds of dried Zebra meat of his own.   Being his own, he was quite cheerful over his 90 pound load; had I asked him to carry it, there would have been many groans and *sotto voce* mutterings.

The above is outfitting by an "old hand" who can put up with many discomforts that the average Englishman, and Americans as well, would

not consider for a moment. It does not include a "Pigskin Library"
or cases of Scotch and Champagne and so would not qualify with the
gentleman sportsman, but it certainly should be easily managed and
produce some real hunting even though all transport is by native carriers.
For hunting in India or the Himalayas the same care should be exercised
as the transport is of the same type in the hunting fields, although pack
animals, ponies, yaks, or elephants may be used to reach the edge of "the
wilds."   A short description of Indian outfitting is the following by
Major C. S. Cumberland in *Big Game Shooting* in the *Country Life
Library*:

The outfit for all parts of high Asia is practically the same for any one
who means business and yet likes to be comfortable—one square, double
poled, single fly tent with three foot walls made of green Willesden canvas. For servants, what Edgington calls a patrol tent, which is simply the
same as the former, only on a smaller scale, is very suitable. One more
of these may also be carried for light marching order when small expeditions are made from the main camp. For the large tent a camp-bed and
folding table and chair may be taken, and for light-marching order an
air-bed of the stoutest make and largest size should be taken, for besides
being a most comfortable bed to sleep on when camped on hard or wet
ground, if two be carried in the outfit they will be found most useful in
negotiating unfordable rivers where no boats are available. A framework
can be made of tent poles, willow, tamarisk or what not, lashed on to the
two inflated air-beds, and a raft good enough to cross most rivers can be
made. Rafts of this sort are made by Asiatics, who use inflated goat-skins
instead of air beds for flotation. Ground sheets and kit-bags of Willesden
canvas are also most useful and durable.

For shooting in India, where camel cart or elephant transport can be
procured, double fly tents which can be made better in India than anywhere else, can be taken. The sportsman should always bear in mind
that the more comfortable he is in camp, the more work he can do when
he is out, and the longer he can go on with it. For the same reason, he
should outfit himself well in the way of food. If a horse is worked hard
he should be well fed and stabled, and this rule applies equally to man
and beast. The system of roughing it is all very well on emergency, but
in the long run it does not pay.

Food supply is an all-important matter. Tibet, Turkestan, Mongolia
may be termed a mountainous desert region—at all events the parts of it
frequented by the wild sheep. Anything like fruit, berries or green food
is not to be found. A good supply of California dried fruit and vege-

tables should be taken, plenty of bacon, tinned butter, tea and sugar, rice and flour. Baking powder is most important for a course of unleavened bread will soon upset the stomach of the ordinary white man. Tinned milk is also very useful; if not taken with tea it is always good to make puddings. Sardines and potted meat, macaroni, cheese, and a good supply of jam and marmalade are needed.

As for dress, a Norfolk jacket and knickerbockers of good Scotch tweed or Cashmir "puttoo," a Terai or double wide-awake hat, with a cap in the pocket for stalking, are all wanted. Boots are very important for Asiatic shooting. The best in the world are Scafe's patent.* They can be put on any boots. Care should be taken that the India-rubber tabs should project well from the sole, otherwise they do not grip the ground sufficiently. On grass slopes, wet or dry, loose rubble and rocky debris, flat rock, cliff climbing, snow or ice, there is nothing better. A pair of knee-boots lined with fur or sheepskin, to wear in camp at night, are absolutely essential, for in most parts of Asia wood for a camp fire is not procurable. On some occasions a hot-water bottle, made of India-rubber which is nothing to carry comes in very useful. A folding bath of the same material is also necessary. As for cooking pots, etc., this should be left to a certain extent to the cook. Those made of aluminum are the lightest and cleanest.

Even so Cumberland's outfit, with his companion Bowers, into the Pamirs for Ovis Poli took over 20 ponies or 10 yak loads—over a ton of impedimenta and supplies. For American outfitting the best outline is from C. E. Hagie's *How to Hunt North American Big Game*:

For a hunter who wants at least a minimum of civilized comforts and the more valuable of the auxiliary gadgets, the following is a list in the order of their importance; sleeping bag or two or three wool blankets, skillet, tin plate, cup, knife, fork, and spoon, salt, pair of binoculars of 6 to 8 power, sheath knife, camp axe, shovel, light tent, extra handkerchiefs, extra suit of underwear and socks, compass (for those who need one), 15 feet of heavy sash cord, cake of soap and towels. The soap will make life seem more civilized, although ordinary silt or soil will remove dirt or grease almost as well as the best of soap.

If the hunter wants to go beyond these primary conveniences, he may add two or three pans or a nested camp-kit of utensils, an extra shirt and pair of pants, a pair of light shoes for wear in camp, a small meat saw, an air mattress, an electric or gasoline lantern, a collapsible sheet-metal wood-burning stove or a gasoline camp-stove (by turning large tin or

---

*Scafe's patent shoes were double soled. The inner sole of rubber had round lugs like football cleats which projected through holes in the outer leather sole giving two kinds of purchase for slippery going on grass or rock.

sheet-metal pans upside down over each burner, it will make a first-class heating unit for the tent), nails, a small pillow, a 7 x 9 foot tarpaulin, folding camp-chairs, a collapsible table, pajamas, toilet articles, including toilet paper (better leave the shaving equipment at home, for the beard will protect the face from sun, wind, and weather), a small-caliber pistol or revolver, snake-bite kit (if in snake country), an alkalizer (baking soda will do the trick), small first-aid kit, fishing tackle (if it is legal to fish in your hunting country), and pills if you need them.

Don't take any of the following items on a hunting trip: hard liquor, bed springs, (boughs, grass, or twigs are better), heavy mattress, coal or heavy wood-burning stove, more than one change of clothes unless the trip is to be a month or more in length and transportation is not a major item, more than one rifle, a shotgun unless it is the primary hunting weapon, more than two pairs of shoes or boots for field use (one of leather and one of rubber), quilts (use wool blankets), golf clubs, cots or bedsteads, chairs or tables that are not collapsible, mirror, hair tonic, trunks, chests of drawers, framed pictures, bath tub, dogs (where their use is prohibited), your wife (unless she is one in a thousand and can really enjoy roughing it—and then don't expect her to do the cooking), anyone as a member of the party who is unlikely to carry his full share of the camp drudgery cheerfully . . .

For most North American big game hunting it is pretty safe to plan a wardrobe made up somewhat as follows: heavy soft wool shirts, light weight fine wool underwear, wool socks (over light silk socks if one prefers), wool pants of the soft-finish type, all-wool jacket of mackinaw cloth (moisture-proofed), rubber-bottomed pacs with 10-inch top, leather-soled pacs for dry weather, lined mittens for very cold days, wool cap with visor for ordinary wear or soft felt hat and knitted cap that can be pulled well down over ears and back of neck in extreme cold (never a cap of leather), a slicker for riding in the rain.

The weight of such an outfit for hunter, guide and cook might run, with supplies, from 500 to 1000 pounds for a three-weeks trip by pack horse.

As to transport, this can be figured at 50 lbs. per pack for porters although the North American packers carry at times up to 150 pounds for short portages on canoe trips, 100 pounds for pony travel in the Himalayas, 200 pounds is the average for pack horse or yak travel, a camel is considered well loaded with 375 to 400 pounds, and an elephant will carry fairly easily from 800 to 1000 pounds. In 1924-25, the Bradley expedition of about three months (although it was over five months including steamer and rail travel) to the Belgian Congo and Lake Kivu, required 175 porters for 6 people, between four and five tons of outfit, food, and trophies and must have cost about $4,000 per month. R. C. F. Maugham, estimates for a two months' shooting trip in Nyassa-land for two sportsmen, 30 porters and a cost of £128 or $575 per man including big game licenses. These costs were in 1906, not including steamer or rail fare, so it will be seen that a hunt of this type can contemplate no failure as to outfit or weapons carried—it is not an everyday jaunt for the sportsman who undertakes it. Maugham's distribution of the porter loads is interesting:

```
10 Provision cases numbered ..................   10 men
 1 Service box ............................    2 men
 1 Tent with fly and poles ....................    2 men
 2 Hold-alls of clothing ......................    2 men
 2 Beds, chairs, tables, bath ..................    2 men
 2 Ammunition cases .........................    2 men
 2 Loads—Bedding, blankets, etc. ..............    2 men
 1 Load—Kitchen utensils ....................    1 man
 3 Loads—Guns and rifles ....................    3 men
 1 Load—Buckets and water demijohn ..........    1 man
Leaving available for transport of wines, etc. ......    3 men
                                            ──────
        Total porters .......................   30 men
```

The extension of automobile roads has greatly reduced the amount of pack transport but these various other mediums are still required to reach really good hunting territory, and the costs have increased, so that over-all there has been no great increase in the amount of long distance big game hunting. Locally, the automobile has made it possible for a great many casual hunters to hunt deer and other of the lesser types of big game close to settled communities. The opening of roads across Africa, into Central Asia and across the wilderness of Canada, such as the Alaskan Highway will very seriously threaten the remaining haunts of the larger big game of the world.

Conclusion

This study was undertaken to find out what the general consensus was, among big game hunters of the past, as to their choice of weapons. It is far from complete but is probably an excellent sample. There are other more recent developments, especially in this country, which are not completely covered for several reasons. Number one is that these are too recent to be fully understood, the second is that they are generally a mass development in which no one man can have had sufficient experience to assay the value. Hunters and their opinions are legion, out of which it is difficult to draw conclusions that are of any value. Yet for what they may be worth, to the student of rifle development for big game hunting in this country, the following conclusions will be stated for consideration:

1. The wide adoption of telescopic sights, at least in the western sections of the continent, has replaced stalking, as an art, and the absolutely sure shots at game from within 100 yards.

2. The game of these western hunting grounds will suffer more from this trend than the species that frequent the forested and cut-over regions of the eastern parts of the continent.

3. The telescopic hunting in the West will tend to make long range rifles of larger bore or improved ballistics a necessity in order to supply greater energy at the longer range.

4. However, the lighter, more easily handled small-bore rifles, with adequate open sights, which are now in general use, will continue to fill all requirements for Eastern hunting in brush and forest country, for years to come, providing game conservation in its present form continues or increases.

5. There is no evidence, past or present, that the power represented by the Kentucky rifle with its ball of 130 grains or less at 2000 feet per second, was not entirely adequate for all conditions and game in the Eastern Sections of the continent, provided the hunter had a reasonable knowledge of stalking, was a good shot and knew the vital spots of the game hunted.

BIBLIOGRAPHY AND APPENDICES

NOTE: *The information contained in these appendices was secured from the published writings of the men listed, or from contemporary sources, and is as accurate as possible under the circumstances. In a few cases the dates and territories hunted are approximate. Because of the length of hunting careers of such men as Baker, Rainsford, Selous, Hornaday, Littledale, Loder, Roosevelt, Millais, etc., the periods overlap and this must be considered in their later choice of rifles. The favorite rifle of each hunter is indicated by an asterisk where any preference was displayed.*

The following abbreviations have been used:

ML: Muzzle Loader. BL: Breech Loader. DB: Double Barrel. SS: Single Shot. M: Magazine. SP: Smokeless Powder. BP: Black Powder.

BIBLIOGRAPHY

THIS BIBLIOGRAPHY FOLLOWS THE ORDER IN WHICH THE HUNTERS ARE PRESENTED IN THE APPENDICES

Hunting Experiences, 1834 to 1874

Author	Title	Publisher	Date
Capt. Henry Shakespear	Wild Sports of India	Ticknor & Fields	1859
Capt. Wm. Cornwallis Harris	Sport and Travel in S. Africa	John Murray	1839
W. E. Oswell	The Life of Wm. Cotton Oswell	Doubleday	1900
Roualeyn Gordon-Cumming	A Hunter's Life	Derby & Jackson	1857
Sir Samuel W. Baker	Rifle and Hound in Ceylon	Lippincott	**1869**
	Wild Beasts and Their Ways	Frederick Warne & Co.	n. d.
Major Leveson	Sport in Many Lands	Macmillan	1891
Lt. Col. Wm. Gordon-Cumming	Wild Men and Wild Beasts	Scribners	1888
C. J. Andersson	Exploration and Discoveries in S. W. Africa	Harpers	1856
Maj. Gen. William Rice	Indian Game	W. H. Allen	1884
William C. Baldwin	Hunting in South Africa	Bentley	1863
Col. F. T. Pollok	Sport in British Burmah	Chapman Hall	1879
Maj. Gen. Donald Macintyre	Wild Sports of Burma and Assam	Hurst & Blackett	1900
	Hindu Koh	Blackwood	1891
Capt. J. H. Baldwin	Large and Small Game of Bengal	Henry King	1876
Capt. James Forsyth	The Sporting Rifle and its Projectile	Smith, Elder	1863
	The Highlands of Central India	Dutton	1871
O. Leslie Stephen	Sir Victor Brooke-Sportsman and Naturalist	John Murray	1894
James Inglis	Sport and Work on the Nepaul Frontier	Macmillan	1878

Author	Title	Publisher	Date
George P. Sanderson	Thirteen Years Among the Wild Beasts of India	John Grant	1878
Gen. Alex A. A. Kinloch	Large Game Shooting	Thacker	1885
W. A. Baillie Grohman	Camps in the Rockies	Scribners	1884
	Sport in the Alps	Scribners	1896
	Sport and Life in Western America	Horace Cox	1900
Wm. Henry Drummond	The Large Game of S. E. Africa	Johnston Douglas	1875
Arthur Neumann	Elephant Hunting	R. Ward	1898
Rev. W. S. Rainsford	The Land of the Lion	Doubleday	1909
Frederick Courtenay Selous	A Hunter's Wanderings in South Africa	Macmillan	1881
	Travel and Adventure in S. E. Africa	R. Ward	1893
	Sunshine and Storm in Rhodesia	R. Ward	1896
	Sport and Travel	Longmans	1900
	Hunting Trips in North America	Scribners	1907
	African Nature Notes	Macmillan	1908
Col. V. M. Stockley	Big Game Shooting in India, etc.	Horace Cox	1913

Hunting Experiences, 1875 to 1892

Author	Title	Publisher	Date
Sir Alfred Pease	Edmund Loder, a Memoir	John Murray	1923
John R. Cook	The Border and the Buffalo	Crane	1896
S. J. Stone	In and Beyond the Himalayas	Arnold	1896
T. S. Van Dyke	The Still Hunter	Macmillan	1882
	The Rifle, Rod and Gun in California	Ford, Howard & Hulbert	1881

Author	Title	Publisher	Year
C. E. M. Russell	Bullet and Shot in Indian Forests, etc.	Thacker	1900
W. T. Hornaday	Two Years in the Jungle	Scribners	1885
	Campfires in the Canadian Rockies	Scribners	1906
	Campfires in Desert and Lava	Scribners	1914
	Our Vanishing Wild Life	N. Y. Zool. Soc.	1913
	A Wild Animal Roundup	Scribners	1925
Col. Wm. D. Pickett	Memories of a Bear Hunter (from Hunting at High Altitudes—Boone & Crockett Club)	Harpers	1913
Clive Phillips-Wolley	Sport in the Crimea and the Caucasus	Bentley	1881
	A Sportsman's Eden	Bentley	1888
	Big Game Shooting, 2 vols. Bedminton Library	Longmans	1894
Sir Henry Seton-Karr	Ten Years Travel and Sport	Chapman Hall	1890
George O. Shields	Hunting in the Great West	Belford Clark	1883
Clarence E. Edwords	Campfires of a Naturalist (L. L. Dyche)	Appleton	1895
Major C. S. Cumberland	Sport on the Pamir Steppes	Blackwood	1895
Edouard Foa	After Big Game in Central Africa	Black	1899
Edward North Buxton	Short Stalks	Stanford	1893
	Short Stalks—Second Series	Stanford	1898
	Two African Trips	Stanford	1902
William H. Wright	The Grizzly Bear	Laurie	1909
Theodore Roosevelt	Hunting Trips of a Ranchman	Putnam	1885
	The Wilderness Hunter	Putnam	1893
	Outdoor Pastimes of an American Hunter	Scribners	1905
	African Game Trails	Scribners	1910
	Through the Brazilian Wilderness	Scribners	1914
	A Booklover's Holidays in the Open	Scribners	1916
F. Vaughan Kirby	In the haunts of Wild Game	Blackwood	1896
	Sport in East Central Africa	R. Ward	1889

Author	Title	Publisher	Date
Lt. Col. H. G. C. Swayne	Seventeen Trips Through Somaliland	R. Ward	1895
Frederick J. Jackson	Big Game Hunting—Badminton Library	Longmans	1894
Sir Nigel Woodyatt	My Sporting Memories	Jenkins	1922
Stewart Edward White	The Forest	McClure Phillips	1904
	Camp and Trail	Outing	1906
	The Land of Footprints	Doubleday	1912
	African Campfires	Doubleday	1913
	The Rediscovered Country	Doubleday	1915
C. E. Gouldsbury	Tiger Slayer by Order (Digby Davies)	Dutton	1915
W. S. Thom	Wild Sports of Burma and Assam (with Col. Pollok)	Hurst & Blackett	1900
A. Bryan Williams	Game Trails in British Columbia	Murray	1925
Warburton Pike	The Barren Grounds of Northern Canada	Macmillan	1892
F. W. F. Fletcher	Sport on the Nilgiris	Macmillan	1911
Capt. B. W. Robinson	With Shotgun and Rifle in N. American Game Fields	Appleton	1925
Capt. A. I. R. Glasfurd	Rifle and Romance in the Indian Jungle	Lane	1896
Harry Storey	Hunting and Shooting in Ceylon	Longmans	1907
Caspar Whitney	On Snowshoes to the Barren Grounds	Harpers	1896
	Muskox, Bison, Sheep and Goat	Macmillan	1904
	The Flowing Road	Lippincott	1912

Hunting Experiences, 1893 to 1905

Author	Title	Publisher	Year
Sir Alfred Pease	The Book of the Lion	Murray	1913
	Travel and Sport in Africa	Humphreys	1902
Col. Townsend Whelen	The American Rifle	Century	1918
	Big Game Hunting	Outers Book	1923
	Wilderness Hunting and Wildcraft	Small Arms Technical Pub. Co.	1927
	The Hunting Rifle	Stackpole	1940
Major R. L. Kennion	Sport and Life in the Further Himalaya	Blackwood	1910
	By Mountain, Lake and Plain	Blackwood	1911
John G. Millais	Newfoundland and Its Untrodden Ways	Longmans	1907
	Wanderings and Memories	Longmans	1919
	Life of Frederick Courtenay Selous	Longmans	1919
	Far Away Up the Nile	Longmans	1924
E. P. Stebbing	Jungle Byways in India	John Lane	1911
	Stalks in the Himalayas	John Lane	1912
	The Diary of a Sportsman Naturalist	John Lane	1920
Maj. P. H. G. Powell-Cotton	Sporting Trip Through Abyssinia	R. Ward	1902
	In Unknown Africa	Hurst & Blackett	1904
Denis D. Lyell	Hunting Trips in Northern Rhodesia	H. Cox	1910
	Wild Life in Central Africa	H. Cox	1913
	Memories of an African Hunter	Maynard	1923
	The African Elephant and Its Hunters	Maynard	1924
	The Hunting and Spoor of Central African Game	Lippincott	1926
	African Adventure	Dutton	1935
Capt. B. R. M. Glossop	Sporting Trips of a Subaltern	Harpers	1906
Gen. R. G. Burton	Sport and Wild Life in the Deccan	Seeley	1928
	A Book of Maneaters	Hutchinson	1931
	The Book of the Tiger	Houghton	1933
	The Tiger Hunters	Hutchinson	1936

Author	Title	Publisher	Date
Maj. Gen. A. E. Wardrop	Modern Pig-Sticking	Macmillan	1914
	Days and Nights with Indian Big Game	Macmillan	1923
H. Z. Darrah	Sport in the Highlands of Kashmir	Rowland Ward	1898
R. C. F. Maugham	Portuguese East Africa	Murray	1906
	Wild Game in Zambesia	Scribner	1914
James Sutherland	The Adventures of an Elephant Hunter	Macmillan	1912
Carl E. Akeley	In Brightest Africa	Doubleday	1920
Mary Jobe Akeley	Carl Akeley's Africa	Dodd Mead	1936
Archibald Rutledge	Plantation Game Trails	Houghton, Mifflin	1921
	Days Off in Dixie	Doubleday	1924
	An American Hunter	Stokes	1937
Marcus Daly	Big Game Hunting and Adventure	Macmillan	1937
Charles Sheldon	The Wilderness of the Upper Yukon	Scribners	1911
	The Wilderness of the N. Pacific Coast Islands	Scribners	1912
	The Wilderness of Denali	Scribners	1930
Col. John Caswell	Sporting Rifles and Rifle Shooting	Appleton	1920
Lt. Col. J. H. Patterson	Maneaters of Tsavo	Macmillan	1907
	In the Grip of the Nyika	Macmillan	1909
W. D. M. Bell	The Wanderings of an Elephant Hunter	Country Life	1923
Paul Niedieck	With Rifle in Five Continents	R. Ward	1908
T. R. Hubback	Elephant and Seladang Hunting in Malaya	R. Ward	1905
	To Far Western Alaska for Big Game	Scribners	1929
Dr. Cuthbert Christy	Big Game and Pygmies	Macmillan	1924

Edward J. House	A Hunter's Campfires	Harpers	1909
John A. McGuire	In the Alaska-Yukon Gamelands	Steward-Kidd	1921
Horace Kephart	Guns, Ammunition and Tackle	Macmillan	1904
	Sporting Firearms	Outing	1912
	Camping and Woodcraft	Macmillan	1917
Malcolm S. Mackay	Cow Range and Hunting Trail	Putnam	1925
Rev. Harry Caldwell	Blue Tiger	Abingdon	1924
Maj. C. H. Stigand & D. D. Lyell	Central African Game and Its Spoor	H. Cox	1906
Maj. C. H. Stigand	The Game of British East Africa	H. Cox	1909
	Hunting the Elephant in Africa	Macmillan	1913
Maj. Charles Askins	Rifles and Rifle Shooting	Outing	1912
	Shooting Facts	Outdoor Life	1928
A. Blayney Percival	A Game Ranger's Notebook	Doran	1929
	A Game Ranger on Safari	Nisbet	1928
Maj. Hesketh K. H. Prichard	Through the Heart of Patagonia	Appleton	1902
	Hunting Camps in Wood and Wilderness	Heineman	1910
	Through Trackless Labrador	Heineman	1911
	Sniping in France	Hutchinson	n. d.
Eric Parker	Hesketh Prichard—A Memoir	Dutton	n. d.
Col. J. Stevenson Hamilton	Animal Life in Africa	Dutton	1912
Capt. H. A. Wilson	A British Borderland	Murray	1913
Lieut. A. W. Hodson	Trekking the Great Thirst	Scribners	1912
Kalman Kittenberger	Big Game Hunting in East Africa	Longmans	1929
C. E. R. Raddiffe	Big Game Shooting in Alaska	Rowland Ward	1904

Author	Title	Publisher	Date
W. S. Chadwick	Mankillers and Marauders	Witherby	1929
	Life Stories of Big Game	Witherby	1930
	Giants of the Forest	Bobbs, Merrill	1928
	Hunter and the Hunted	Witherby	1931
T. Alexander Barns	The Wonderland of the Eastern Congo	Putnam	1922
	Across the Great Craterland to the Congo	Benn	1923
	An African Eldorado	Methuen	1926
	Angolan Sketches	Methuen	1928
Frank Melland	Elephant in Africa	Scribners	1938
William J. Schaldach	Carl Rungius—Big Game Painter	Countryman	1945

Hunting Experiences, 1906 to 1947

Author	Title	Publisher	Date
Lt. Col. C. H. Stockley	Big Game Shooting in the Indian Empire	Constable	1928
	Shikar	Constable	1928
	Stalking in the Himalayas and Northern India	Jenkins	1936
Frantz Rosenberg	Big Game Shooting	Hopkinson	1928
Maj. G. P. Evans	Big Game Shooting in Upper Burma	Longmans	1911
Vilhjalmur Stefansson	My Life With the Eskimo	Macmillan	1913
	The Friendly Arctic	Macmillan	1921
	Hunters of the Great North	Harcourt	1922
Richard Tjader	The Big Game of Africa	Appletons	1920
Major H. C. Maydon	Simen, Its Heights and Abysses	Witherby	1925
	Big Game Shooting in Africa (Lonsdale Library)	Lippincott	n. d.
	Big Game of Africa	Scribners	1935
	Big Game of India	Scribners	1937

Author	Title	Publisher	Year
H. F. Wallace	Stalks Abroad	Longmans	1908
	Big Game of Central and Western China	Murray	1913
Capt. A. H. E. Mosse	My Somali Book	Sampson Bow	1913
Col. A. E. Stewart	Tiger and Other Game	Longmans	1927
Percy C. Madeira	Hunting in British East Africa	Lippincott	1909
Kermit Roosevelt with T. R., Jr.	East of the Sun and West of the Moon	Scribners	1926
	Trailing the Giant Panda	Scribners	1929
	Cleared for Strange Ports	Scribners	1927
Theodore Roosevelt, Jr.	Three Kingdoms of Indo China	Crowell	1933
Edgar B. Bronson	In Closed Territory	McClurg	1910
Jack O'Connor	Hunting in the Southwest	Knopf	1939
	Hunting in the Rockies	Knopf	1947
E. Marshall Scull	Hunting in the Arctic and Alaska	Winston	1914
George Agnew Chamberlain	African Hunting Among the Thongas	Harpers	1923
William M. Newsom	White-tailed Deer	Scribners	1926
James L. Clark	Trails of the Hunted	Cornwall	1928
Maj. L. M. H. Handley	Hunter's Moon	Macmillan	1933
Capt. W. T. Shorthose	Sport and Adventure in Africa	Lippincott	1923
Maj. Gerald Burrard	Notes on Sporting Rifles	Arnold	1920
	Notes on Sporting Rifles (2nd Ed.)	Arnold	1925
	Notes on Sporting Rifles (3rd Ed.)	Arnold	1932
	Big Game Hunting in the Himalayas and Tibet	Stokes	1925
Maj. C. Court Treatt	Out of the Beaten Track	Dutton	1931

Author	Title	Publisher	Date
Capt. Paul A. Curtis	Sporting Firearms of Today in Use	Dutton	1922
	American Game Shooting	Dutton	1927
	Guns and Gunning	Penn	1934
R. S. Meikle	After Big Game	Laurie	n. d.
Ben Burbridge	Gorilla	Century	1928
Kenneth Fuller Lee	Big Game Hunting and Marksmanship	Samworth	1941
Ray Chapman Andrews	Whale Hunting with Gun and Camera	Appleton	1918
	Camps and Trails in China	Appleton	1921
	Across Mongolian Plains	Curtis	1929
	Ends of the Earth	Steward-Kidd	1916
Harry A. Auer	Camp Fires in the Yukon		
Commandant Augieras	La Grande Chasse en Afrique	Comitie L'Afrique Francais	1935
A. B. Hepburn	The Story of an Outing	Harpers	1913
Arthur H. Carhart	Hunting North American Deer	Macmillan	1946
Harold McCracken	Alaska Bear Trails	Doubleday	1931
C. E. Hagie	The American Rifle	Macmillan	1946
	How to Hunt North American Big Game	Macmillan	1946
Commander David E. Blunt	Elephant	Houghton	1933
Edison Marshall	Shikar and Safari	Farrar	1947
Elmer Keith	Big Game Rifles and Cartridges	Samworth	1936
	Rifles for Large Game	Standard	1946
Mary Hastings Bradley	On the Gorilla Trail	Appleton	1922
	Caravans and Cannibals	Appleton	1926
	Trailing the Tiger	Appleton	1929

Lt. Col. James E. Corbett	Maneaters of Kumaon	Oxford	1946
Martin Johnson	Camera Trails in Africa	Century	1924
Osa Johnson	Four Years in Paradise	Garden City	1941
	I Married Adventure	Halcyon	1942
Dr. Richard L. Sutton	An African Holiday	Mosby	1924
	Tiger Trails in Southern Asia	Mosby	1926
	The Long Trek	Mosby	1930
	An Arctic Safari	Mosby	1932
John M. Holzworth	The Wild Grizzlies of Alaska	Putnam	1938
Vivienne de Watteville	Out in the Blue	Methuen	1927
	Speak of the Earth	Smith Haas	1935
William J. Morden	Across Asias Snows and Deserts	Putnam	1927
Martin Stephens	Fair Game	Murray	1936
John P. Holman	Sheep and Bear Trails	Walters	1933
Paul L. Hoefler	Africa Speaks	Winston	1931
A. R. Siedentopf	The Last Stronghold of Big Game	McBride	1946
Mrs. John Borden	Adventures in a Man's World	Macmillan	1933
John W. Eddy	Hunting the Alaskan Brown Bear	Putnam	1930

Other Books Consulted

J. R. Chapman	Improved American Rifle		1848
Deane	Manual of the History and Science of Firearms	Longmans	1858
Hans Busk	The Rifle and How to Use It	Routledge	1858

Author	Title	Publisher	Date
Lieut. C. M. Wilcox	Rifles and Rifle Practice	Van Nostrand	1861
H. W. S. Cleveland	Hints to Riflemen	Appleton	1864
W. W. Greener	Modern Breech Loaders	Cassell	1873 (?)
Col. William C. Church	American Guns and Ammunition	Scribners Magazine	1880
K. C. A. J.	The Sportsman's Vade Mecum for the Himalayas	Cox	1891
British War Office	Textbook of Small Arms	Harrison	1894
	Textbook of Small Arms	Harrison	1909
	Textbook of Small Arms	Harrison	1929
Boone and Crockett Club	Hunting in Many Lands	Forest & Stream	1895
	Trail and Campfire	Forest & Stream	1897
	American Big Game in Its Haunts	Forest & Stream	1904
	Hunting at High Altitudes	Harpers	1913
	Hunting and Conservation	Hale	1925
	Hunting Trails on Three Continents	Windward	1933
	North American Big Game	Scribners	1938
G. T. Teasdale-Bucknell	Experts on Guns and Shooting	Low-Marston	1900
T. F. Fremantle	The Book of the Rifle	Longmans	1901
Jean de Bloch	The Future of War	Ginn	1903
Horace G. Hutchinson	Big Game Shooting, 2 vols.	Country Life	1905
Henry Sharp	Modern Sporting Gunnery	Kent	1906
N. S. Shaler	Man and the Earth	Chautauqua	1907
W. W. Greener	The Gun and Its Development	Cassell	1907

J. C. Grew	Sport and Travel in the Far East	Houghton, Mifflin	1910
L. R. Tippins	Modern Rifle Shooting in Peace, War and Sport	Phillips	1912
M. I. Newbegin	Animal Geography	Oxford	1913
Chas. Winthrop Sawyer	Our Rifles—Firearms in American History	Cornhill	1920
Capt. E. C. Crossman	The Book of the Springfield	Small Arms Technical Pub. Co.	1932
Edgar N. Barclay	Big Game Shooting Records	Witherby	1932
Rawdon Malet	Unforgiving Minutes	Hutchinson	1934
Copley & Mayer	The East African Sportsman's Book	Standard	1934
Martin S. Garretson	The American Bison	N. Y. Zool. Soc.	1938
Philip B. Sharpe	The Rifle in America	Morrow	1938
	Complete Guide to Handloading	Funk & Wagnall	1942
Satterlee & Gluckman	American Gun Makers	Ullbrich	1940
Harry P. Davis	A Forgotten Heritage	Standard	1941
Prof. A. M. Low	Musket to Machine Guns	Hutchinson	1942
Johnson & Haven	Ammunition	Morrow	1943
Lynn Montross	War Through the Ages	Harpers	1944
Col. Townsend Whelen	Small Arms Design and Ballistics, Vol. 1	Samworth	1945
Walter H. B. Smith	Mauser Rifles and Pistols	Military Service Pub.	1947
	Mannlicher Rifles and Pistols	Military Service Pub.	1947
James J. Grant	Single Shot Rifles	Morrow	1947
W. O. Smith	The Sharps Rifle	Morrow	1943

APPENDIX A

The Development of the Rifle in Big Game Hunting

NAME	WHEN	WHERE
1 Capt. Henry Shakespear	1834-1859	Central India
2 Capt. Wm. Cornwallis Harris	1835-1836	South Africa
3 William Cotton Oswell	1837-1852	South Africa
4 Roualeyn Gordon-Cumming ·	1843-1848	South Africa
5 Sir Samuel W. Baker	1845-1855	Ceylon
"	1861-1873	Sudan
"	1880-1882	North America
"	1882-1886	India
6 Maj. Henry A. Leveson	1845-1854	India
"	1856-1869	Europe, Africa
"	1870-1871	North America
7 Lt. Col. Wm. Gordon-Cumming	1847-1871	India
8 C. J. Andersson	1850-1854	South Africa
9 Maj. Gen. William Rice	1850-1884	India
10 William C. Baldwin	1852-1860	South Africa
11 Col. F. T. Pollok	1853-1879	Burma
12 Maj. Gen. Donald Macintyre	1853-1897	Himalayas
13 Capt. J. H. Baldwin	1859-1876	India
14 Capt. James Forsyth	1861-1871	Central India
15 Sir Victor Brooke	1862-1863	India
"	1869-1881	Spain-Sardinia
16 James Inglis	1863-1878	India
17 George P. Sanderson	1864-1877	India

APPENDIX A

Part I—1834 to 1874—The Large Bores

	ANIMALS HUNTED	RIFLES USED
1	Elephant, Tiger, Panther, Bison, Bear	ML 10 bore DB Westley Richards, ML 10 bore DB Wilkinson*
2	Elephant, Lion, Rhino, Buffalo, Antelope	ML 8 bore DB
3	Elephant, Lion, Rhino, Buffalo, Antelope	ML 10 bore (Smooth) DB Purdey*, ML 12 bore DB Westley-R
4	Elephant, Lion, Rhino, Buffalo, Antelope	ML 4 and 12 bore SS, ML 12 bore DB Purdey*
5	Elephant, Tiger, Sambur	ML 4 bore SS Gibbs, ML 8 bore SS Blisset, ML 10 bore DB Beattie*
	Elephant, Lion, Rhino, Buffalo, Antelope	ML 8 and 10 bore DB Reilly, BL .577 DB Holland*
	Bear, Buffalo, Elk	BL .577 DB Holland*
	Tiger, Bear, Sambur	BL .577 DB Holland*, BL .400 DB Holland
6	Elephant, Tiger, Bear, Bison, Sambur	ML 8 bore DB Westley R, ML 10 bore DB Westley Richards
	Chamois, Lion, Rhino, Buffalo, Antelope	ML 8 bore DB Westley R, ML 10 bore DB Westley Richards*
	Buffalo, Bear, Elk, Deer	BL 12 bore DB Westley Richards*
7	Tiger, Panther, Bear, Bison, Sambur	ML 12 bore DB Sam Smith*, ML 14 bore DB
8	Elephant, Lion, Rhino, Buffalo, Antelope	ML 14 bore DB Powell, ML 17 bore DB
9	Tiger, Bison, Bear, Panther, Sambur	ML 18 bore DB, .577 SS Snider, BL 12 bore DB Henry*
10	Elephant, Lion, Rhino, Buffalo, Antelope	ML 7 and 9 bore DB Burrow, ML 10 bore DB Witten*
11	Elephant, Tiger, Rhino, Gaur, Bear	ML 10 bore DB Lang*, BL 8 bore DB Westley Richards
12	Bear, Sambur, Markhor, Ibex, Ammon	ML .577 SS Enfield, ML .450 DB Whitworth*, BL .360 DB Rigby
13	Elephant, Tiger, Bison, Sambur, Ammon	ML 6 bore DB, BL 12 bore DB Powell*, BL .500 DB
14	Tiger, Bear, Bison, Sambur	ML 8 and 12 bore DB, BL 12 and 14 bore, DB BL .500 SS Henry*
15	Elephant, Bison, Ibex	ML 8 bore DB Purdy*
	Moufflon, Ibex, Chamois	BL .360 DB Lancaster*
16	Tiger, Bear, Deer	12 bore DB Greener, .500 DB Murcott
17	Elephant, Tiger, Bison	BL 4 bore SS Lang, BL 8 and 12 bore DB Greener, 16 bore DB Purdy, .450 DB Lang*

* The asterisk indicates the favorite rifle.

1834-1874—The Large Bores

NAME	WHEN	WHERE
18 William Finaughty	1864-1875	Central Africa
19 Gen. Alex A. A. Kinloch	1864-1900	India-Assam
20 W. A. Baillie-Grohmann	1865-1878	Bavaria
"	1879-1898	North America
21 William H. Drummond	1867-1875	Southeast Africa
22 Arthur H. Neumann	1868-1906	Central Africa
23 Rev. Wm. S. Rainsford	1868-1883	North America
"	1906-1909	East Africa
24 J. M. Murphy	1870-1880	North America
25 Frank Mayer	1871-1882	North America
26 Frederick Courtenay Selous	1871-1894	South Africa
"	1895	Asia Minor
"	1897-1901	North America
"	1902	Sardinia
"	1902-1903	East Africa
"	1904-1906	North America
"	1907	Norway
"	1908-1913	East Africa
27 Col. V. M. Stockley	1874-1898	India, Burma
"	1899-1910	Africa

1834-1874—The Large Bores

	ANIMALS HUNTED	RIFLES USED
18	Elephant, Lion, Rhino, Buffalo, Antelope	ML 4 bore SS, BL 12 bore DB*, .450 SS Westley Richards
19	Elephant, Tiger, Rhino, Gaur	ML 12 bore DB, BL 12 bore DB Rigby
20	Ibex, Chamois, Roedeer	ML 24, bore SS, BL .450 DB Holland*
	Elk, Bear, Sheep	BL .450 DB Holland*, .450 SS Holland
21	Elephant, Lion, Rhino, Buffalo, Antelope	BL 10 bore DB, BL 6 bore SS
22	Elephant, Lion, Rhino, Buffalo, Antelope	10 bore DB Holland, .577 DB Gibbs*, .303 Lee, .450 DB Rigby*, .256 Mannlicher
23	Bear, Elk, Sheep, Deer, Buffalo	ML 8 bore DB Rigby, .50-110 Bullard*
	Elephant, Lion, Rhino, Buffalo, Antelope	.450 DB Rigby, .350 M Rigby,* .256 Mannl.
24	Buffalo, Elk, Bear, Moose, Sheep, Deer	.50 SS Springfield, .500 DB Expr.,* .45-75 Winchester
25	Buffalo, Elk, Bear, Deer	.50-70 SS Sharps, .40-90 SS Sharps, .45-120 SS Sharps*
26	Elephant, Lion, Rhino, Buffalo, Antelope	ML 4 and 10 bore SS Roer, BL 450 SS Gibbs*
	Moufflon, Ibex, Red Deer	.450 SS Gibbs, .256 Mannl., .303 SS Holland*
	Elk, Moose, Caribou, Bear, Sheep	.303 SS Holland*, .256 Mannlicher
	Moufflon	.303 SS Holland*
	Elephant, Lion, Rhino, Buffalo, Antelope	.450 SS Gibbs, .303 SS Holland*
	Moose, Caribou, Bear, Sheep, Goat	.303 SS Holland, .375 SS Holland*
	Elk, Reindeer	.375 SS Holland*
	Elephant, Lion, Rhino, Buffalo, Antelope	.375 M Holland*, .256 Mannlicher
27	Elephant, Tiger, Bison, Markhor, Ibex	8 bore DB, .577 DB Westley R.*
	Ibex, Lion, Buffalo	.577 DB Westley R.,* .405 Win., .303 Lee, .256 Mannlicher

* The asterisk indicates the favorite rifle.

1834-1874—Summary of Large Bore Rifles

Large Bore Muzzle Loaders

LARGE BORES	USED BY	TOTAL
4 SS	4, 5, 18, 26	4
8 SS	5	1
10 SS	26	1
12 SS	4	1
24 SS	20	1
6 DB	13	1
7 DB	10	1
8 DB	2, 5, 6, 14, 15, 23	6
9 DB	10	1
10 DB	1, 3, 5, 6, 10, 11	6
12 DB	3, 4, 7, 14, 19	5
14 DB	7, 8	2
17 DB	8	1
18 DB	9	1
Total		32

Medium Bore Muzzle Loaders

MEDIUM BORES	USED BY	TOTAL
.577 SS	12	1
.450 DB	12	1
Total		2

Large Bore Breech Loaders

LARGE BORES	USED BY	TOTAL
4 SS	17	1
6 SS	21	1
8 DB	11, 17, 27	3
10 DB	21, 22	2
12 DB	6, 9, 13, 14, 16, 17, 18, 19	8
14 DB	14	1
16 DB	17	1
Total		17

1834-1874—Summary of Large Bore Rifles

Medium Bore Breech Loaders

MEDIUM BORES	USED BY	TOTAL
.577 DB	5, 22, 27,	3
.577 SS	9	1
.500 DB	13, 16, 24	3
.500 SS	14	1
.50 Bullard	23	1
.50 SS Spr.	24	1
.50-70 SS	25	1
.450 DB	17, 20, 22, 23	4
.450 SS	18, 20, 26	3
.45-120 SS	25	1
.45-75 M	24	1
.405 M	27	1
.400 DB	5	1
.40-90 SS	25	1
Total		23

Small Bore Breech Loaders

SMALL BORES	USED BY	TOTAL
.375 M	26	1
.375 SS	26	1
.360 DB	12, 15	2
.350 M	23	1
.303 M	22, 27	2
.303 SS	25, 26	2
.256 M	22, 23, 26, 27	4
Total		13

Summary

	ML	BL	TOTAL
Large bores	32	17	49
Medium bores	2	23	25
Small bores	—	13	13
Total			87

Hunters—27   Rifles per hunter—3.2

APPENDIX B

PART II—1875 to 1892—The Medium Bores

	NAME	WHEN	WHERE
28	St. George Littledale	1874	North America
	"	1875-1876	India
	"	1887-1889	Russia-Asia
	"	1890-1891	Europe
	"	1892-1895	Central Asia
29	Sir Edmund Loder	1874-1875	India-Sumatra
	"	1876-1877	North Africa
	"	1887-1888	North America
	"	1891-1896	Europe-North Africa
	"	1906-1907	East Africa
30	John R. Cook	1874-1878	North America
31	S. J. Stone	1875-1895	India-Tibet
32	Theodore S. Van Dyke	1875-1902	North America
33	C. E. M. Russell	1876-1896	India
34	Wm. T. Hornaday	1876-1877	India-Malaya
	"	1886-1906	United States-Canada
	"	1907-1908	Mexico
35	Col. William D. Pickett	1876-1883	North America
36	Clive Phillips-Wolley	1876-1877	North America
	"	1878-1886	Europe-Russia
	"	1887-1893	North America
37	Sir Henry Seton-Karr	1877-1889	Europe-Asia
	"	1886-1898	North America
38	George O. Shields	1878-1887	North America
39	L. L. Dyche	1879-1891	North America
40	Maj. C. S. Cumberland	1880-1910	India-Central Asia
	"	1911-1912	East Africa
41	Edouard Foa	1880-1890	North Africa
	"	1891-1900	Central Africa

APPENDIX B

1875 to 1892—The Medium Bores

ANIMALS HUNTED	RIFLES USED
28 Elk, Sheep, Bear, Deer	.500 DB Henry
Tiger, Bison, Sambur, Markhor,Ibex, Sheep	.500 DB Henry
Bison, Bear, Poli, Yak	.500 DB Henry
Bison, Bear, Chamois	.500 DB Henry
Yak, Sheep, Ibex	.256 Roum. Mannl.*, .256 Mannl. Schon.
29 Tiger, Rhino, Bison, Sambur, Markhor	8 bore DB Reilly, 12 bore DB Reilly*
Moufflon, Gazelle	12 bore DB Reilly, .450 DB Express*
Elk, Sheep, Goat, Buffalo	.450 DB Express
Moufflon, Chamois, Ibex, Gazelle	256 Roum Mannlicher*
Rhino, Buffalo, Antelope	.256 Mannl.
30 Buffalo, Bear, Deer, Antelope	.577 SS Enfield, .44 SS Sharps*, .44-40 Win.
31 Yak, Bear, Sheep, Markhor, Ibex	.450 SS Henry*, .500 and 450 DB Henry, .50-110 Winchester
32 Elk, Bear, Deer	.40-60 Winchester
33 Elephant, Tiger, Bison, Bear, Sambur	4 bore DB Dixon, 12 bore DB Holland*, .500 DB Holland
34 Elephant, Tiger, Bison, Sambur	Ml 8 bore DB Westley, .40-70 SS Maynard*
Buffalo, Moose, Elk, Bear, Sheep, Goat	.40-70 SS Maynard, .303 Savage, .405 Win.*
Sheep, Deer	.303 Savage, .405 Win.*
35 Bear, Elk, Sheep	.45-102 SS Sharps, .45-90 SS Sharps*
36 Elk, Sheep, Goat, Bear	12 bore DB Paradox, .450 DB Express*
Bison, Bear, Deer, Ibex, Chamois	12 bore DB Paradox, .450 DB Express*
Moose, Elk, Bear, Sheep	12 bore DB Paradox, .450 DB Express*
37 Elk, Moufflon, Goat, Antelope	.500 DB Purdey, .400 DB Purdey*
Elk, Deer, Antelope, Goat	.500 DB Purdey, .256 Mannlicher*
Buffalo, Elk, Bear, Sheep, Goat, Deer	.32-35 SS Stevens, .45-75 Win., .40-75 SS Sharps*
39 Moose, Elk, Bear, Sheep, Goat, Antelope	.45-100 SS Sharps, .40-75 SS Rem., .40-82 Winchester*
40 Tiger, Bison, Yak, Sheep, Markhor, Ibex	12 bore DB Dougal, .500 DB Henry*, .303 Lee Metford
Elephant, Lion, Antelope	.500 DB Henry*, .303 Lee Metford
41 Moufflon, Gazelle, Antelope	8 bore DB, .577 DB Galand
Elephant, Lion, Rhino, Buffalo, Antelope	.577 DB Galand, .303 DB Lee Metford*

* The asterisk indicates the favorite rifle.

1875-1892—The Medium Bores

	NAME	WHEN	WHERE
42	Edward North Buxton	1881-1890	Sardinia-N. Africa
	"	1891-1892	N. America
	"	1893-1897	Europe, Asia Minor
	"	1898-1901	North Africa
43	William H. Wright	1893-1909	N. America
44	Theodore Roosevelt	1883-1907	N. America
	"	1908-1910	East Africa
	"	1911-1912	N. America
	"	1913-1914	S. America
45	F. Vaughan Kirby	1884-1899	S. E. Africa
	"	1900-1903	Central Africa
46	Lt. Col. H. G. C. Swayne	1884-1897	Somaliland
	"	1898-1927	India
47	Frederick J. Jackson	1884-1891	East Africa
48	Sir Nigel Woodyatt	1884-1922	India
49	Stewart Edward White	1884-1909	N. America
	"	1909-1914	East Africa
	"	1924-1925	East Africa
50	Digby Davies	1885-1915	India-Africa
51	John B. Burnham	1887-1893	N. America
	"	1898-1900	Alaska
	"	1905-1906	Mexico
	"	1919-1921	Siberia-Alaska
52	W. S. Thom	1887-1900	Burma
53	Maj. N. H. Roberts	1887-1934	N. America
54	Bryan H. Williams	1888-1924	British Columbia
55	Warburton Pike	1889-1891	Canada
56	Richard J. Cunninghame	1889-1924	East Africa

1875-1892—The Medium Bores

ANIMALS HUNTED	RIFLES USED
42 Moufflon, Antelope	.500 DB Express
Elk, Sheep, Bear	.500 DB Express
Ibex, Chamois, Moufflon	.500 DB Express, .256 Mannlicher*
Lion, Rhino, Antelope	.500 DB Express, .256 Mannlicher*
43 Grizzly Bear	.45-100 SS Win.*, .44-40 Win., .30-30 Win.
44 Buffalo, Elk, Bear, Sheep, Deer	.40-90 SS Sharps, .45-75 Win., .45-90 Win.*, .30-30 Winchester
Elephant, Lion, Rhino, Buffalo, Antelope	.450 DB Holland, .405 Winchester*, .30-06 Springfield
Moose, Bear, Cougar, Wolves	.30-06 Springfield*
Tapir, Deer, Agouti	.30-06 Springfield*
45 Lion, Rhino, Leopard, Buffalo, Antelope	.500 SS Westley-R., .450 SS Gibbs*
Elephant, Lion, Rhino, Buffalo, Antelope	.450 SS Gibbs*
46 Lion, Elephant, Rhino, Antelope	8 and 12 bore Paradox, .577 DB Holland*, .450 Martini, .303 Lee Metford
Elephant, Tiger, Sambur	.577 DB Holland*, .303 Lee Metford
47 Elephant, Lion, Rhino, Buffalo, Antelope	8 bore DB, 10 bore DB*, .500 DB Express, .450 SS Express
48 Tiger, Bison, Bear, Panther, Markhor, Ibex	.500 DB Jeffrey, .303 DB Fraser, .400 DB Jeffrey*, .280 Ross
49 Elk, Bear, Sheep, Goat, Deer	.44-40 Win., .30-30 Win., 30-40 Win.*
Elephant, Lion, Rhino, Buffalo, Antelope	.465 DB Holland, .405 Win., .30-06 Springfield*
Lion, Buffalo	.465 DB Holland, .405 Win., .30-06 Springfield*
50 Elephant, Tiger, Lion, Bison, Bear, Antelope	10 bore DB Dickson, 10 bore Paradox, .500 DB Rigby*, .303 Lee Metford
51 Moose, Deer, Antelope	.40-82 Winchester
Moose, Bear, Caribou, Sheep	.40-65 Winchester
Sheep	.30-30 Winchester
Sheep, Walrus	.35 Newton
52 Elephant, Tiger, Rhino, Bison, Sambur	8 bore DB Westley, 12 bore DB Dickson*, .450 Martini, .303 Lee Metford
53 Moose, Caribou, Bear, Deer	.40-60 Win., .44-40 Win., .38-55 Marlin*, .30-40 Krag, 7mm Mauser
54 Moose, Caribou, Bear, Sheep, Goat	.45-90 Winchester*
55 Moose, Caribou, Muskox	12 bore Paradox, .50-95 Winchester*
56 Elephant, Lion, Rhino, Buffalo, Antelope	.465 DB Holland*, .450 DB Express, .30-06 Springfield

* The asterisk indicates the favorite rifle.

1875-1892—The Medium Bores

	NAME	WHEN	WHERE
57	F. W. F. Fletcher	1890-1909	Southern India
58	Capt. Beverly W. Robinson	1891-1922	North America
59	Capt. A. I. R. Glasfurd	1891-1906	India
60	Leslie Tarlton	1891-1926	East Africa
61	Harry Storey	1891-1906	Ceylon
62	Carl Larsen	1892-1909	Portuguese East Africa
63	Caspar Whitney	1892-1895	North America
	"	1903-1905	Sumatra-Malaya
	"	1910-1911	South America

1875-1892—The Medium Bores

ANIMALS HUNTED	RIFLES USED
57 Elephant, Tiger, Bison, Bear, Sambur, Ibex	.500 and 400 DB Tolley, 12 Paradox, .450 DB Westley, .600 DB Jeffery*
58 Elk, Sheep, Goat, Bear, Moose, Caribou, Antelope	.45-90 Win., .30-40 Win., .30-06 Spr.*
59 Tiger, Panther, Bear, Bison, Sambur	.577 DB Holl., .450 DB Rigby, .400 DB Jeffery*, .276 Mauser; .303 Lee
60 Elephant, Lion, Rhino, Buffalo, Antelope	.465 DB Holland, .276 Rigby*, .350 Rigby, .30-06 Springfield
61 Elephant, Buffalo, Elk, Panther, Bear, Deer	12 bore Paradox, .303 SS Lee, .303 Lee M., .303 Savage*
62 Elephant, Lion, Rhino, Antelope	.600 DB Jeffery*
63 Moose, Caribou, Muskox	.45-90 Win.*
Tiger, Rhino, Seladang, Panther	12 bore DB, .50-110 Win.,* .45-90 Win.
Tapir, Jaguar, Deer, Agouti	9mm Mannlicher*

* The asterisk indicates the favorite rifle.

1875-1892—Summary of Medium Bore Rifles

LARGE BORES		USED BY	TOTAL
ML	8 DB	34	1
BL	4 DB	33	1
	8 DB	29, 41, 47, 52	4
	10 DB	47, 50	2
	12 DB	29, 33, 40, 52, 63	5
Paradox	8 DB	46	1
	10 DB	50	1
	12 DB	36, 46, 55, 57, 61	5
Total			20

MEDIUM BORES	USED BY	TOTAL
.600 DB	57, 62	2
.577 DB	41, 46, 59	3
.577 SS	30	1
.500 DB	28, 31, 33, 37, 40, 42, 47, 48, 50, 57	10
.500 SS	45	1
.50-110 Win.	31, 55, 63	3
.465 DB	49, 56, 60	3
.450 DB	29, 31, 36, 44, 56, 57, 59	7
.450 SS	31, 45, 46, 47, 52	5
.45-102 SS	35, 39, 43	3
.45-90 Win.	44, 54, 58, 63	4
.45-90 SS	35	1
.45-75 Win.	38, 44	2
.44-40 Win.	30, 43, 49, 53	4
.44 SS Sharps	30	1
.405 Win	34, 44, 49	3
.400 DB	37, 48, 57, 59	4
.40-90 SS	44	1
.40-82 Win.	39, 51	2
.40-75 SS	38, 39	2
.40-65 Win.	51	1
.40-60 Win.	32, 53	2
.40-70 Maynard	34	1
Total		66

1875-1892—Summary of Medium Bore Rifles

SMALL BORES	USED BY	TOTAL
.38-55 Marlin	53	1
9 mm	63	1
.350 Rigby	60	1
.35 Newton	51	1
.32-35 Stevens	38	1
.303 DB Lee	41, 48	2
.303 Lee	40, 46, 50, 52, 59, 61	6
.303 SS Lee	61	1
.303 Sav.	34, 61	2
.30-30 Win.	43, 44, 49, 51	4
.30-40 Krag	53	1
.30-40 Win.	49, 58	2
.30-06 Spr.	44, 49, 56, 58, 60	5
.280 Ross	48	1
7 mm Mauser	53, 59, 60	3
.256 Mannl.	28, 29, 37, 42	4
Total		36

SUMMARY

Large bores	20
Medium bores	66
Small bores	36
Total Rifles	122

Hunters—36 Rifles per hunter—3.4

APPENDIX C

PART III—1893-1905—The Small Bores

	NAME	WHEN	WHERE
64	Sir Alfred Pease	1892-1895	North Africa
	"	1896-1924	East Africa
65	Col. Townsend Whelen	1892-1910	North America
	"	1911-1914	Panama
	"	1915-1946	N. America
66	Maj. R. L. Kennion	1893-1905	India
	"	1906-1910	Persia
67	John G. Millais	1893-1894	South Africa
	"	1906-1909	Newfoundland-Alaska
	"	1913-1914	East Africa
	"	1916-1917	Norway
	"	1920-1922	Scotland
	"	1922-1924	East Africa
68	E. P. Stebbing	1894-1914	North India
69	P. H. G. Powell-Cotton	1895-1898	Himalayas
	"	1899-1901	Abyssinia
	"	1902-1904	Central Africa
70	Denis D. Lyell	1895-1896	India
	"	1897-1903	South Africa
	"	1903-1920	East Africa
71	Capt. B. R. M. Glossop	1895-1897	India
	"	1897-1905	Somaliland
72	Gen. R. G. Burton	1895-1933	India
73	Maj. Gen. A. E. Wardrop	1895-1923	India
74	H. Z. Darrah	1896-1897	Himalayas

APPENDIX C

PART III—1893-1905—The Small Bores

ANIMALS HUNTED	RIFLES USED
64 Moufflon, Boar, Gazelle	10 bore Paradox, .256 Mannlicher*
Elephant, Lion, Rhino, Buffalo, Antelope	10 bore Paradox, .350 Rigby, .333 Jeffery, .404 Jeffery, .256 Mannlicher*
65 Moose, Elk, Bear, Sheep, Deer	.40-72 Win., .30-40 SS Winchester*
Deer	.30-06 Springfield
Moose, Caribou, Elk, Bear, Sheep, Goat	.35 Whelen, .30-06 Springfield, .270 Winch.*
66 Tiger, Markhor, Sheep, Ibex, Sambur	303 Lee M, .256 Mannlicher*
Ibex, Sheep, Gazelle, Deer	.280 Ross*, .256 Mannl., .303 Lee M.
67 Antelope	.256 Mannlicher*
Moose, Caribou, Elk, Sheep, Goat, Bear	.256 Mannlicher*
Lion, Antelope	.256 Mannlicher*
Elk, Reindeer	.256 Mannlicher*
Deer	.256 Mannlicher*
Ibex, Kudu, Eland	.256 Mannlicher*
68 Tiger, Bison, Bear, Sambur, Markhor	10 bore Paradox, .500 DB Holland*, .303 Lee Metford
69 Markhor, Ibex, Sheep, Bear	.400 DB Jeffery, .256 Mannlicher*
Ibex, Antelope, Elephant	8 and 12 bore Paradox, .400 DB Jeffery*, .256 Mannlicher* *
Elephant, Lion, Rhino, Buffalo, Antelope	12 bore Paradox, .600 DB Jeffrey, .400 DB Jeffery*, .256 Mannlicher*
70 Sambur	10 bore DB Purdey, .450 SS Henry, .303 Lee M., .303 SS Fraser*
Elephant, Lion, Antelope	.404 Jeffery, .303 SS Fraser, 7.9 Rigby*, .318 Westley R.
Elephant, Lion, Rhino, Buffalo, Antelope	.404 Jeffery, 7.9 Rigby, 7 Rigby, .256 Mannlicher*
71 Bear, Sambur, Goral, Thar, Serow	12 bore DB Paradox, .400 SS Holland*
Lion, Antelope	12 bore DB, .500 DB Express*
72 Tiger, Bear, Panther	.500 DB Holland*
73 Elephant, Tiger, Bear, Bison, Sambur	8 bore Paradox, .470 DB Tolley*, .400 DB .318 Westley
74 Bear, Sambur, Markhor, Ibex, Sheep	12 bore Paradox, .450 DB Rigby, .303 Lee Metford*

* The asterisk indicates the favorite rifle.

1893-1905—The Small Bores

NAME	WHEN	WHERE
75 R. C. F. Maugham	1896-1906	Port E. Africa
"	1907-1919	Central Africa
76 James Sutherland	1896-1932	Central Africa
77 Norman B. Smith	1896-1910	East Africa
"	1911-1912	Sudan
78 Carl E. Akeley	1896-1906	East Africa
"	1912-1926	Central Africa
79 Archibald Rutledge	1896-1946	N. America
80 Marcus Daly	1897-1936	Africa
81 Charles Sheldon	1897-1902	Mexico
"	1904-1909	Alaska-Yukon
"	1916-1921	Mexico-U. S.
82 Col. John Caswell	1897-1909	N. America
"	1910-1912	East Africa
83 Lt. Col. J. H. Patterson	1898-1908	East Africa
84 W. D. M Bell	1898-1921	Central Africa
85 Paul Niedieck	1898-1899	India-Ceylon
"	1900-1901	N. America
"	1902	Sudan
"	1903	Alaska-Canada
86 T R. Hubback	1898-1917	Malaya
"	1918-1921	Alaska
87 Dr. Cuthbert Christy	1898-1924	Central Africa
88 Edward J. House	1898-1899	Greenland
"	1900-1905	Canada-Newfoundland
"	1906-1907	East Africa
"	1907-1908	N. America
89 John A. McGuire	1898-1916	U. S.-Canada
"	1917-1918	Alaska

1893-1905—The Small Bores

ANIMALS HUNTED	RIFLES USED
75 Elephant, Lion, Rhino, Buffalo, Antelope	8 bore DB, 10 bore Paradox, .500 DB, .303 DB Holland*
Elephant, Lion, Rhino, Buffalo, Antelope	.450 DB Holland, .375 DB Holland*, .303 DB Holland
76 Elephant, Lion, Rhino, Buffalo, Antelope	.577 DB Westley*, 10.75 Mauser, .303 Lee M., .318 Westley
77 Elephant, Lion, Rhino, Buffalo, Antelope	10 bore DB, 10 bore Paradox, .475 DB Jeffery*, .500 DB, .400 DB
Lion, Antelope	.475 DB Jeffery*, .303 Lee M., .256 Mannl.
78 Elephant, Lion, Rhino, Buffalo, Antelope	.470 DB*, 9mm Mannl, .256 Mannl.
Elephant, Lion, Leopard, Gorilla	.475 DB Jeffery*, 7.9mm Mauser, .30-06 Spr., .275 Hoffman
79 Deer, Bear, Boar	12 ga. DB Parker*, .250-300 Savage
80 Elephant, Lion, Rhino, Buffalo	.450 Martini, .416 Rigby, 10.75 Mauser*
81 Sheep, Deer, Bear	.303 Mannl., .256 Mannlicher*
Moose, Caribou, Sheep, Bear	.256 Jeffery Mannlicher*
Sheep	.256 Jeffery Mannlicher*
82 Moose, Bear, Deer	.30-30 Win., .303 Win., .375 Holland*
Elephant, Lion, Rhino, Antelope	.465 DB Purdey, 375 DB Holland*, 30-06 Springfield
83 Lion, Elephant, Rhino, Antelope	.450 DB Exp., .303 Lee Mtford
84 Elephant, Lion, Rhino, Buffalo, Antelope	.400 DB, .318 Jeffery Mauser, .275 Rigby Mauser*
85 Elephant, Tiger, Buffalo, Bear, Sambur	10 bore Paradox, 11mm DB*, .500 DB Exp.
Caribou, Moose, Elk, Deer	.500 DB Express*, 11mm DB
Elephant, Lion, Rhino, Buffalo, Antelope	10 bore Paradox, 9mm Mauser*, .375 DB
Moose, Caribou, Bear, Sheep	.375 DB Cordite Exp.*
86 Elephant, Tiger, Seladang	8 bore DB Manton, .500 DB Evans*
Moose, Bear, Caribou, Sheep	.450 SS Bland, .375 DB Cogswell & Harrison, .400 DB Evans*
87 Elephant, Buffalo, Okapi, Bougo	12 bore DB, .500 DB Exp.*, .303 Lee M., 7mm Mauser
88 Walrus, Caribou	.30-40 Winchester*
Moose, Caribou, Elk, Sheep, Goat, Bear	.30-40 Winchester, 9mm Mauser*
Elephant, Rhino, Antelope	.450 DB Exp., 9mm Mauser*
Bear, Elk	9mm Mauser*
89 Bear, Cougar, Elk, Sheep, Deer	.30-40 Winchester, .30-60 Winchester*
Moose, Caribou, Sheep	.30-06 Winchester*

* The asterisk indicates the favorite rifle.

1893-1905—The Small Bores

	NAME	WHEN	WHERE
90	Malcolm S. Mackay	1899-1925	United States
	"	1925-1927	Alaska
91	Horace Kephart	1899-1927	United States
92	Rev. Harry Caldwell	1899-1918	South China
	"	1919-1920	Mongolia
93	Maj. C. H. Stigand	1899-1902	Somaliland
	"	1903-1919	Central Africa
94	James H. Kidder	1900-1901	Alaska
95	Maj. Charles Askins	1900-1917	United States
	"	1920-1940	United States
96	A. Blayney Percival	1900-1925	East Africa
97	Hesketh K. H. Prichard	1900-1901	S. America
	"	1903-1907	Newfoundland-Canada
	"	1908-1909	Sardinia
	"	1909-1910	Labrador
98	Col. J. Stevenson Hamilton	1900-1926	East Africa
99	F. H. Riggall	1902-1930	Br. Columbia
100	Capt. H. A. Wilson	1902-1913	East Africa
101	Lieut. A. W. Hodson	1902-1912	South Africa
102	Kalman Kittenberger	1902-1912	East Africa
	"	1925-1929	Central Africa
103	Charles Cottar	1902-1940	East Africa

1893-1905—The Small Bores

ANIMALS HUNTED	RIFLES USED
90 Elk, Sheep, Bear, Deer	50-110 Win., .45-90 Win.*, .33 Win.
Moose, Bear, Sheep	.405 Win.*, .30-06 Springfield
91 Deer, Bear	.30-40 SS Win.,* .30-40 Rem. Lee
92 Tiger, Serow, Takin, Boar	.303 Savage, .22 HP Savage*
Elk, Sheep	.250-3000 Savage*
93 Lion, Ibex, Addax, Kudu, Oryx	.450 DB, .256 Mannlicher*
Elephant, Lion, Rhino, Buffalo, Antelope	450 DB, .318 Jeffery, .256 Mannlicher*
94 Bear, Moose, Sheep, Caribou	.50-110 Winchester, .30-40 Winchester*
95 Bear, Elk, Deer	.45-90 W, .30-06 Spr., .22 HP, .250 Sav., .256 Newton*
Bear, Elk, Deer	7 mm Mauser, .276 Hoffman,* 35 Rem-Auto., .270 Winchester*
96 Lion, Elephant, Rhino, Antelope	.450 DB Rigby, 360 DB, .256 Mannlicher*
97 Guanaco, Wild Cattle, Deer	7 mm Mauser
Caribou Moose	.256 Mannlicher*
Moufflon	.256 Mannlicher*
Caribou	.256 Mannl., .350 Rigby Mauser*
98 Lion, Elephant, Antelope	.577 DB, .416 Rigby, .350 Rigby Mauser,* .303 Lee Metford
99 Bear, Deer, Goat, Sheep	.30-30 Win., .250 Savage, 7 mm Mauser*
100 Elephant, Lion, Rhino, Buffalo, Antelope	.450 DB Lang, .256 Jeffery Mannlicher*
101 Lion, Antelope	.450 SS Gibbs*, .303 Lee Metford
102 Elephant, Lion, Rhino, Buffalo, Antelope	.465 DB Holland, 8 mm Mannl.,* 7 mm Mauser, .256 Mannlicher
Elephant, Lion, Rhino, Buffalo, Antelope	.465 DB Holland, 8 mm Mannl., 9 mm Mannlicher*
103 Elephant, Lion, Rhino, Buffalo, Antelope	.470 DB Rigby, .405 Win.,* .35 Newton,* .250 Savage

* The asterisk indicates the favorite rifle.

1893-1905—The Small Bores

	NAME	WHEN	WHERE
104	C. E. R. Radcliffe	1903-1904	Alaska
105	Maj. Henry Darley	1903-1919	Abyssinia
106	Martin Ryan	1903-1917	East Africa
107	A. L. Barnshaw	1903-1907	Central Africa
108	W. S. Chadwick	1903-1928	South Africa
109	T. A. Barns	1903-1930	Central Africa
110	Frank Melland	1904-1930	Central Africa
111	Carl Rungius	1904-1906	Yukon
	"	1907-1946	United States
112	A. A. Dunbar Brander	1904-1923	India

1893-1905—The Small Bores

ANIMALS HUNTED	RIFLES USED
104 Moose, Bear	8 mm Mannl.*, .256 Mannlicher
105 Elephant, Lion, Rhino, Antelope	.450 DB Express*, .303 Lee Metford
106 Elephant, Lion, Rhino, Antelope	.416 Rigby Mauser, .375 M Holland, 7.9 mm Mauser*
107 Elephant, Lion, Rhino, Buffalo, Antelope	.303 Lee M, 7 mm Mauser, 7.9 mm Mauser,* 9 mm Mauser, .256 Mannlicher
108 Elephant, Lion, Rhino, Buffalo, Antelope	.450 DB, 9.3 Mauser*, .303 Lee Metford
109 Elephant, Lion, Rhino, Buffalo, Antelope	7.9 mm Mauser*
110 Elephant, Lion, Rhino, Buffalo	.450 DB Rigby, .350 DB Rigby*
111 Moose, Caribou, Sheep, Bear	.256 Mannlicher
Elk, Bear, Deer	.256 Mannlicher
112 Tiger, Elephant, Panther, Bison, Bear	12 bore DB, .577 DB

* The asterisk indicates the favorite rifle.

1893-1905—Summary of The Small Bores

LARGE BORES	USED BY	TOTAL
8 bore DB	75, 86	2
10 bore DB	70, 77	2
12 bore DB	71, 87, 112	3
8 bore Paradox	69, 73	2
10 bore Paradox	64, 68, 75, 77, 85	5
12 bore Paradox	69, 71, 74, 79	4
Total		18

MEDIUM BORES	USED BY	TOTAL
.600 DB	69	1
.577 DB	76, 98, 112	3
.500 DB	68, 71, 72, 75, 77, 85, 86, 87	8
.50-110W	90, 94	2
.475 DB	77, 78	2
.470 DB	73, 78, 103	3
.465 DB	82, 102	2
.450 DB	74, 75, 83, 88, 93, 96, 100, 105, 108, 110	10
.450 SS	70, 80, 86, 101	4
.45-90 M	90, 95	2
11mm DB	85	1
10.75mm M	76, 80	2
.416 M	98, 106	2
.405 Win.	90, 103	2
.404 M	64, 70	2
.400 DB	69, 73, 77, 84, 86	5
.400 SS	71	1
.40-72 Win.	65	1
Total		53

1893-1905—Summary of The Small Bores

SMALL BORES	USED BY	TOTAL
.375 DB	75, 85, 86	3
.375 M	82, 106	2
9.3mm M	108	1
.360 DB	96	1
9mm M	78, 85, 88, 102, 106	5
.350 M	64, 98, 97	3
.35 M	65, 103	2
350 DB	110	1
.35 Rem.	95	1
.333 M	64	1
.33 Win.	90	1
.318 M	70, 73, 76, 84, 93	5
8mm M	102, 104	2
7.9mm M	70, 106, 109	3
.303 M	66, 68, 70, 74, 76, 77, 81, 82, 83, 87, 98, 101, 105, 106, 108	15
.303 DB	75	1
.303 SS	70	1
.303 Sav.	92	1
.30-06 M	65, 78, 82, 89, 90, 95	6
.30-40 M	88, 89, 91, 94	4
.30-40 SS	65, 91	2
.30-30 M	82, 99	2
.280 M	66	1
.276 M	78, 95	2
7mm M	70, 84, 87, 95, 97, 99, 102	7
.270 M	65, 95	2
.256 Newton	95	1
.256 Mannl.	64, 66, 67, 69, 70, 77, 78, 81, 93, 96, 97, 100, 102, 104, 106, 111	16
.250 Sav.	79, 92, 95, 99, 103	5
.22 Sav.	92, 95	2
Total		99

SUMMARY

Large Bore	18
Medium Bore	53
Small Bore	99
Total	170

Hunters 49—Rifles per hunter 3.4

APPENDIX D

PART IV—1906-1946—The High-Velocity Small Bores

	NAME	WHEN	WHERE
113	Lt. Col. C. H. Stockley	1905-1933	India
114	S. Eardley Wilmot	1905-1930	India
115	Frantz Rosenberg	1906-1907	East Africa
	"	1908-1909	Central Europe
	"	1910-1912	North America
	"	1913-1931	Europe
116	Maj. G. P. Evans	1906-1910	Burma
117	Vilhjalmur Stefansson	1906-1918	Arctic America
118	Richard Tjader	1906-1910	East Africa
119	Maj. H. C. Maydon	1906-1915	India-Malaya
	"	1916-1917	Port. E. Africa
	"	1920-1923	Abyssinia
	"	1924-1926	Asia Minor-Persia
	"	1927-1929	India
	"	1930-1937	Africa
120	H. F. Wallace	1906-1907	N. America
	"	1907-1908	India
	"	1908-1909	Africa
	"	1910-1932	Scotland
121	Capt. A. H. E. Mosse	1907-1912	Somaliland
122	Col. A. E Stewart	1907-1927	India
123	Percy C. Madeira	1907-1908	East Africa
124	Kermit Roosevelt	1908-1910	East Africa
	"	1921-1922	Korea
	"	1923-1924	India
	"	1925-1926	Central Asia
	"	1927-1928	China-Indo China
125	Edgar B. Bronson	1908-1909	East Africa
126	Jack O'Connor	1909-1946	N. America
127	John T. McCutcheon	1909-1910	East Africa

APPENDIX D

PART IV—1906-1946—The High Velocity Small Bores

ANIMALS HUNTED	RIFLES USED
113 Tiger, Panther, Bear, Markhor, Ibex, Sheep	9mm Mannl., .318 Jeffery,* .280 Ross
114 Tiger, Sambur, Panther	.500 DB Express,* .303 SS Lee
115 Elephant, Lion, Antelope	.400 DB Jeffery*, .303 SS Jeffery, .450 DB Holland
Chamois, Moufflon, Red Deer, Roebuck	.450 DB Holland, .303 SS Jeffery*
Sheep, Bear, Goat, Caribou, Moose	.303 SS Jeffery*, .303 DB Holland
Chamois, Deer, Elk, Reindeer	DB 90-06 Merkel, 8 x 60 Mauser, 8 x 60 SS Gibbs,* 9.3mm Mauser
116 Elephant, Gaur, Banteng, Tiger, Sambur, Serow	10 bore Paradox, .400 DB Army & Navy*
117 Muskox, Caribou, Walrus, Bear, Seal	.256 Mannl. Schoe., .256 Gibbs Mannl.*
118 Elephant, Lion, Rhino, Buffalo, Antelope	.577 DB, 50-110 Win., .405 Win.,* 11.2 Mauser, .256 Mannlicher
119 Markhor, Ibex, Tiger, Panther, Bear, Bison	.577 DB.* .400 DB, .500 SS, .256 Mannl.
Buffalo, Antelope	.470 DB*, 9mm Mannlicher
Ibex, Antelope	7.9mm Mauser*
Wild Goat, Ibex	7.9mm Mauser*
Markhor, Ibex, Burrhel, Thar	7.9mm Mauser*
Lion, Antelope	.470 DB, 7.9mm Mauser*
120 Elk, Sheep, Goat	.225 Rigby Mauser*
Deer, Black Buck	.225 Rigby Mauser*
Lion, Rhino, Buffalo, Antelope	.450 DB, .275 Rigby Mauser *
Red Deer	.275 Rigby Mauser*
121 Lion, Antelope	12 bore Paradox, .400 DB Watson,* .318 Westley Richards
122 Tiger, Markhor, Ibex, Oorial	.475 DB Holland,* .375 M Holland
123 Lion, Rhino, Buffalo, Antelope	.450 DB Army & Navy, 8mm and 9mm Mannlicher*
124 Elephant, Lion, Rhino, Buffalo, Antelope	.450 DB Rigby, .405 Win.,* .30-06 Springf.
Tiger, Boar, Deer	.405 Win., 30-06 Springfield*
Tiger, Gaur, Sambur	.30-06 Springfield*
Sambur, Poli, Yak, Burrhel, Gazelle	.375 M Hoffman, .30-06 Springfield*
Sambur, Wapiti, Takin, Serow, Panda	.375 M Hoffman, .30-06 Springfield*
125 Elephant, Rhino, Buffalo, Antelope	.450 DB, .405 Win.,* 9mm Mauser
126 Moose, Elk, Bear, Sheep, Deer	.30-06 Springf., 7mm Mauser, .270 Win.*
127 Elephant, Lion, Rhino, Antelope	.475 DB Jeffery, 9mm Mannl., .256 Mannl.

* The asterisk indicates the favorite rifle.

1906-1946—High-Velocity Small Bores

NAME	WHEN	WHERE
128 E. Marshall Scull	1909-1910	Alaska
129 George Agnew Chamberlain	1909-1917	Port. E. Africa
"	1922-1923	Port. E. Africa
130 William M. Newsom	1909-1940	N. America
131 James L. Clark	1909-1911	East Africa
"	1912-1921	N. America
"	1921-1922	East Africa
"	1923-1925	N. America
"	1926-1927	Central Asia
"	1928-1931	East Africa
"	1935-1936	Indo-China
132 Maj. L. M. H. Handley	1910-1932	India-Burma
133 J. Leslie Simpson	1910-1925	East Africa
134 Capt. W. T. Shorthose	1910-1922	Africa
135 Maj. Gerald Burrard	1910-1920	India
136 Maj. C. Court Treatt	1911-1930	Central Africa
137 Capt. Paul A. Curtis	1911-1929	N. America
"	1930-1932	Scotland
"	1933-1940	N. America
"	1941-1942	Scotland
138 R. S. Meikle	1912-1913	East Africa
139 Ben Burbridge	1912-1927	Central Africa
140 Kenneth Fuller Lee	1912-1938	N. America
141 Wilfred Robertson	1912-1931	South Africa
142 Roy Chapman Andrews	1912-1913	Korea
"	1916-1917	China
"	1918-1920	Mongolia
"	1921-1926	Central Asia
143 Harry A. Auer	1913-1914	Yukon
144 Commandant Augieras	1913-1933	Central Africa

1906-1946—High-Velocity Small Bores

ANIMALS HUNTED	RIFLES USED
128 Walrus, Bear, Sheep, Caribou	9mm Mauser*
129 Lion, Antelope	.450 DB Evans,* .22 HP Savage
Elephant, Lion, Antelope	.470 DB Churchill, .318 Westley R,* .256 Mannlicher
130 Moose, Bear, Deer	.450 DB Purdey, .38-55 Win.,* .256 Mannl.
131 Elephant, Lion, Rhino, Antelope	.470 DB Evans, 7.9mm Mauser*
Elk, Bear, Deer	.30-06 Springfield*
Lion, Gorilla	.470 DB Evans, .30-06 Springfield*
Caribou, Bear, Goat, Sheep	.30-06 Springfield*
Yak, Ammon, Ibex	.30-06 Springfield*
Elephant	.470 DB Evans, .30-06 Springfield*
Seladang, Banteng	.470 DB Evans, .465 DB Holland,* .318 Rigby M., .30-06 Springfield
132 Elephant, Tiger, Bison, Sambur	.470 DB,* .318 Westley Richards
133 Lion, Buffalo, Rhino, Antelope	.577 DB, .405 Win., .416 Rigby, .315 Westley, .30-06 Win.*
134 Elephant, Lion, Rhino, Buffalo, Antelope	.470 DB Lancaster, .318 Westley R, .280 Lancaster Mauser*
135 Sambur, Bear, Markhor, Ibex, Sheep, Yak	.577 DB Holland, .400 DB, .256 Mannl., .280 SS Lancaster*
136 Elephant, Lion, Antelope	.303 Lee Metford
137 Moose, Caribou, Bear, Goat, Sheep	.30-06 Springfield, .256 Mannlicher*
Red Deer	.30-06 Springfield*
Moose, Bear, Deer	.30-06 Springfield*
Red Deer	.30-06 Springfield*
138 Lion, Antelope	.465 DB, .360 DB Fraser*
139 Elephant, Lion, Rhino, Buffalo, Antelope, Gorilla	.405 Win.,* .30-40 Win.
140 Moose, Deer, Bear	.45-90, .38-40, .30-30 Win., .303, .250 Sav., .32 Rem. A., .256 Mannl.*
141 Lion, Rhino, Buffalo, Antelope	.400 DB Jeffery,* .303 Lee Metford
142 Tiger, Bear, Deer, Boar	.256 Mannlicher*
Tiger, Goral, Serow, Gazelle	.256 Mannlicher*
Elk, Sheep	.250-3000 Sav.,* .256 Mannl.
Gazelle	.250 Savage*
143 Moose, Caribou, Bear, Sheep	8mm Mannlicher*
144 Elephant, Lion, Rhino, Buffalo, Antelope	.405 Win.,* 10.75 Mauser, .32 Win., 8mm Rival

* The asterisk indicates the favorite rifle.

1906-1946—High-Velocity Small Bores

	NAME	WHEN	WHERE
145	A. B. Hepburn	1913-1914	East Africa
146	Arthur H. Carhart	1915-1945	N. America
147	Harold McCracken	1916-1942	Alaska
148	C. E. Hagie	1916-1946	N. America
149	Commander David E. Blunt	1919-1933	East Africa
150	Edison Marshall	1920-1928	N. America
	"	1929-1930	East Africa
	"	1931-1946	Indo China-India
151	Elmer Keith	1920-1936	U. S.-Canada
	"	1936-1937	Alaska
	"	1938-1946	United States
152	Herbert E. Bradley	1920-1924	Central Africa
	"	1928-1929	Malaya
153	Mary Hastings Bradley	1920-1924	Central Africa
	"	1928-1929	Malaya
154	Major James E. Corbett	1920-1940	India
155	Martin Johnson	1921-1935	East Africa
156	Osa Johnson	1921-1935	East Africa
157	Monroe H. Goode	1921-1937	N. America
158	Dr. Richard L. Sutton	1923-1924	East Africa
	"	1925-1926	Indo-China
	"	1929-1930	Africa-Indo China
	"	1931-1932	Spitzbergen
	"	1933-1946	North America
159	John M. Holzworth	1923-1929	Canada-Alaska
160	Vivienne de Watteville	1923-1927	East Africa
161	William J. Morden	1923-1925	India
	"	1926-1927	Central Asia
162	Martin Stephens	1924-1925	India
	"	1933-1934	N. America
	"	1935-1936	East Africa

1906-1946—High-Velocity Small Bores

ANIMALS HUNTED	RIFLES USED
145 Lion, Rhino, Buffalo, Antelope	.450 DB, .256 Mannl., .35 Rem. Auto.*
146 Elk, Bear, Deer	.25-35 Win.*
147 Moose, Bear, Caribou, Sheep	.303 Savage, .30-40 Win.*
148 Moose, Elk, Bear, Sheep, Deer	.25-35 & .30-30 Win., .303 & .250 Sav., 7.9 Mauser,* .30-06 Spr., .270 Win.
149 Elephant, Buffalo, Hippo, Antelope	12 bore DB, .416 Rigby,* .318 Westley R., .303 Lee Metford
150 Moose, Caribou, Bear	.35 Remington
Lion, Rhino, Antelope	.470 DB, 9.5mm Mannl.*
Seladang, Bison, Tiger	.404 Gibbs Mauser, .404 DB Gibbs,* 9.5mm Mannlicher
151 Elk, Bear, Sheep, Goat, Caribou, Deer	.38-55 Win., .30-06 Spr., .400 Whelen,* .35 Whelen
Bear, Sheep	.35 Whelen*
Elk, Bear, Goat, Deer	.280 Dubiel, .300 H&H Magnum*
152 Elephant, Lion, Rhino, Buffalo, Antelope	.475 DB Jeffery, .30-06 Springfield*
Tiger, Rhino	.475 DB Jeffery, .30-06 Springfield*
153 Elephant, Lion, Buffalo, Antelope	.30-06 Springfield*
Tiger	.30-06 Springfield*
154 Tiger, Panther, Bear, Goral	.450 Martini, .400 DB,* .275 Mauser
155 Elephant, Lion, Rhino, Buffalo, Antelope	.470 DB Bland, .405 Win.,* .30-06 Springfield
156 Elephant, Lion, Rhino, Buffalo, Antelope	.405 Win., .30-06 Springfield*
157 Moose, Elk, Bear, Deer, Sheep	.30-06 Spr., .315 Hoffm., .300 H&H, .270 Win.*
158 Elephant, Lion, Rhino, Buffalo, Antelope	.577 DB Westley R., .465 DB Purdey,* .30-06 Win.
Elephant, Tiger, Seladang, Banteng, Sambur	.465 DB Holland, .400 DB Jeffery, .375 Hoffm., .300 H&H
Lion, Rhino, Antelope, Tiger, Bantung	.577 DB Westley R., .465 DB Holland, 9.3 Mauser
Walrus, Seal, Polar Bear	9.3 Mauser
Moose, Caribou, Bear, Elk, Sheep	.348 Win., .300 H&H, 9.3 Mauser
159 Caribou, Bear, Sheep, Goat	.405 DB Griffin & Howe, .30-06 Mauser
160 Elephant, Lion, Rhino, Antelope	.416 Rigby Mauser, .318 Westley Richards
161 Markhor, Ibex, Ammon	.30-06 Springfield
Poli, Burrhel, Yak, Gazelle	.30-06 Springfield
162 Tiger, Markhor, Ibex, Ammon, Shapoo	.375 M Holland*
Goat, Sheep	.375 M Holland*
Elephant, Rhino, Lion	.450 DB Holland,* .375 M Holland

* The asterisk indicates the favorite rifle.

1906-1946—High-Velocity Small Bores

	NAME	WHEN	WHERE
163	Capt. E. T. L. Lewis	1924-1928	East Africa
	"	1929-1931	India
	"	1932-1934	N. America
164	Count Vasco da Gama	1925-1930	Central Africa
165	John P. Holman	1925-1931	Alaska-Canada
166	Paul L. Hoefler	1925-1929	Central Africa
167	Theodore Roosevelt, Jr.	1925-1926	India-C. Asia
	"	1927-1928	China-Indo China
168	A. R. Siedentopf	1926-1941	East Africa
169	Mrs. John Borden	1927-1928	Alaska
170	John W. Eddy	1927-1928	Alaska

1906-1946—High-Velocity Small Bores

ANIMALS HUNTED	RIFLES USED
163 Elephant, Lion, Buffalo, Antelope	.465 DB Holland,* .375 H&H Magnum, .303 Lee Metford
Tiger, Bear, Sambur	.465 DB Holland,* .375 H&H Magnum, .303 Lee Metford
Bear, Deer, Sheep	.375 H&H Magnum,* .303 Lee M.
164 Elephant, Lion, Rhino, Buffalo, Antelope	.465 DB Holland, 9 Mannl., 7.9 Mauser, .275 Rigby Mauser*
165 Moose, Bear, Sheep	.45-90 Win., .30-06 Springf.,* .256 Mannl.
166 Lion, Buffalo, Antelope	.505 Gibbs, .30-06 Rem., 7mm Mauser*
167 Sambur, Poli, Burrhel, Yak	.375 M Hoffman, .30-06 Springfield*
Wapiti, Sambur, Serow, Takin, Panda	.375 M Hoffman, .30-06 Springfield*
168 Elephant, Lion, Rhino, Buffalo, Antelope	9mm Mauser, .30-06 Springfield,* 7mm Mauser
169 Sheep, Bear, Walrus	.30-06 Springfield*
170 Bear	.35 Whelen,* .405 Winchester

* The asterisk indicates the favorite rifle.

1906-1946—Summary of The High Velocity Small Bores

Large Bore Muzzle Loaders

LARGE BORES	USED BY	TOTAL
10 bore Paradox	116	1
12 bore Paradox	121	1
12 bore DB	149	1
Total		3

Medium Bore Muzzle Loaders

MEDIUM BORES	USED BY	TOTAL
.577 DB	118, 119, 133, 135, 158	5
.505 M	166	1
.500 DB	114	1
.500 SS	119	1
.50-110 M	118	1
.475 DB	122, 127, 152	3
.470 DB	119, 129, 131, 132, 134, 150, 155	7
.465 DB	131, 138, 158, 163, 164	5
.450 DB	115, 120, 123, 124, 125, 129, 130, 145, 162	9
.450 SS	154	1
.45-90 M	140, 165	2
11.2 M	118	1
10.75 M	144	1
.416 M	133, 149, 160, 170	4
.405 DB	159	1
.405 M	118, 124, 125, 133, 139, 144, 155, 156	8
.404 DB	150	1
.404 M	150	1
.400 DB	115, 116, 119, 121, 135, 141, 154, 158	8
.400 M	151	1
Total		62

Small Bore Breech Loaders

SMALL BORES	USED BY	TOTAL
.38-55	130, 151	2
.38-40	140	1
.375 M	122, 124, 157, 158, 162, 163, 167	7
9.5 M	150	1
93mm M	115, 158	2

Small Bore Breech Loaders

SMALL BORES	USED BY	TOTAL
.360 DB	138	1
9mm M	113, 119, 123, 125, 127, 128, 164, 168	8
.35 Whelen	151, 170	2
.35 Rem.	145, 150	2
.348 Win.	158	1
.32 Win.	144	1
.32 Rem.	140	1
.318 M	113, 121, 129, 131, 132, 134, 149, 160	8
8 x 60mm M	115	1
8 x 60 SS	115	1
8 x 56mm M	123, 143, 144	3
7.9 x 57mm M	119, 131, 148, 164	4
.303 M Lee	136, 141, 149, 163	4
.303 DB	115	1
.303 SS	114, 115	2
.303 Sav.	140, 147, 148	3
.300 H & H	151, 157, 158	3
.30-06 M	124, 126, 131, 137, 148, 151, 152, 153, 155, 156, 157, 158, 159, 161, 165, 166, 167, 168, 169	19
.30-06 DB	115	1
.30-40 M	139, 147	2
.30-30 M	140, 148	2
.280 M	113, 134, 151	3
.280 SS	135	1
7mm M	120, 126, 154, 164, 166, 168	6
.270 M	126, 148, 157	3
.256 M	117, 118, 119, 127, 129, 130, 135, 137, 140, 142, 145, 165	12
.250 Sav.	140, 142, 148	3
.25-35 M	146, 148	2
.22 Sav.	129	1
Total		114

SUMMARY	
Rifles Large bore	3
Rifles Medium bore	62
Rifles Small bore	114
Total	178

Hunters 58—Rifles per hunter, 3.1

APPENDIX F

Grand Summary of Big Game Hunting Rifles

LARGE BORES	USED BY	TOTAL
ML 4 bore SS	4, 5, 18, 26	4
8	5	1
10	26	1
12	4	1
24	20	1
ML 6 bore DB	13	1
7	10	1
8	2, 5, 6, 14, 15, 23, 34	7
9	10	1
10	1, 3, 5, 6, 10, 11	6
12	3, 4, 7, 14, 19	5
14	7, 8	2
17	7	1
18	9	1
BL 4 bore SS	17	1
6	21	1
BL 4 bore DB	33	1
8	11, 17, 27, 29, 41, 47, 52, 75, 86	9
10	21, 22, 47, 50, 70, 77	6
12	6, 9, 13, 14, 16, 17, 18, 19, 29, 33, 40, 52, 63, 71, 87, 112, 149	17
14	14	1
16	17	1
Paradox 8 bore DB	46, 69, 73	3
10	50, 64, 68, 75, 77, 85, 116	7
12	36, 46, 55, 57, 61, 69, 71, 74, 79, 121	10
Total		90

MEDIUM BORES	USED BY	TOTAL
ML .577 DB	12	1
.450 DB	12	1
BL .600 DB	57, 62, 69	3
.577 DB	5, 22, 27, 41, 46, 59, 76, 98, 112, 118, 119, 133, 135, 158	14
BL .577 SS	9, 30	2
.505 M	166	1
.500 DB	13, 16, 24, 28, 31, 33, 37, 40, 42, 47, 48, 50, 57, 68, 71, 72, 75, 77, 85, 86, 87, 114	22

APPENDIX F

Grand Summary of Big Game Hunting Rifles

MEDIUM BORES	USED BY	TOTAL
.500 SS	14, 45, 119	3
.50-110 M	23, 31, 55, 63, 90, 94, 118	7
.50-70 SS	24, 25	2
.475 DB	77, 78, 122, 127, 152	5
.470 DB	73, 78, 103, 119, 129, 131, 132, 134, 150, 155	10
.465 DB	49, 56, 60, 82, 102, 131, 138, 158, 163, 164	10
.450 DB	17, 20, 22, 23, 29, 31, 36, 44, 56, 57, 59, 74, 75, 83, 88, 93, 96, 100, 105, 108, 110, 115, 120, 123, 124, 125, 129, 130, 145, 162	30
.450 SS	18, 20, 26, 31, 45, 46, 47, 52, 70, 80, 86, 101, 104	13
.45-100 SS	25, 35, 39, 43	4
.45-90 M	44, 54, 58, 63, 90, 95, 140, 165	8
.45-90 SS	35	1
.45-75 M	24, 38, 44	3
.44-40 M	30, 43, 49, 53	4
.44-100 SS	30	1
11.2mm M	118	1
11mm DB	85	1
10.75mm M	76, 80, 144	3
.416 M	98, 106, 133, 149, 160, 170	6
.405 DB	159	1
.405 M	27, 34, 44, 49, 90, 103, 118, 124, 125, 133, 139, 144, 155, 156	14
.404 M	64, 70, 150	3
.404 DB	150	1
.400 DB	5, 37, 48, 57, 59, 69, 73, 77, 84, 86, 115, 116, 119, 121, 135, 141, 154, 158	18
.400 SS	71	1
.400 M	151	1
.40-90 SS	25, 44	2
.40-82 M	39, 51	2
.40-75 SS	38, 39, 65	3

Grand Summary of Big Game Hunting Rifles

MEDIUM BORES	USED BY	TOTAL
.40-65 M	51	1
.40-60 M	32, 53	2
.40-70 SS	34	1
Total		206

SMALL BORES	USED BY	TOTAL
.38-55 M	53, 130, 151	3
.38-40 M	140	1
.375 DB	75, 85, 86	3
.375 SS	26	1
.375 M	26, 82, 106, 122, 124, 157, 158, 162, 163, 167	10
9.5m M	150	1
9.3m M	108, 115, 158	3
.360 DB	12, 15, 96, 138	4
.9m M	63, 78, 85, 88, 102, 106, 113, 119, 123, 125, 127, 128, 164, 168	14
.350 DB	110	1
.350 M	23, 63, 64, 97, 98	5
.35 Newton	51, 103	2
.35 Whelen	65, 151, 170	3
.35 Rem.	95, 145, 150	3
.348 Win.	155	1
.333 M	64	1
.33 Win.	90	1
.32 Win.	144	1
.32 Rem.	140	1
.32-55 SS	38	1
.318 M	70, 73, 76, 84, 93, 113, 121, 129, 131, 132, 139, 149, 160	13
8 x 60 M	115	1
8 x 60 SS	115	1
8m M	102, 104, 123, 143, 144	5
7.9m M	70, 106, 109, 119, 131, 148, 164	7
.303 DB	41, 48, 75, 115	4
.303 SS	25, 26, 61, 70, 114, 115	6
.303 M	22, 27, 40, 46, 50, 52, 59, 61, 66, 68, 70, 74, 76, 77, 81, 82, 83, 87, 98, 101,	

Grand Summary of Big Game Hunting Rifles

SMALL BORES	USED BY	TOTAL
	105, 106, 108, 136, 141, 149, 163	27
.303 Sav.	34, 61, 92, 140, 147, 148	6
.300 M	151, 157, 158	3
.30-06 DB	115	1
.30-06 M	44, 49, 56, 58, 60, 65, 78, 82, 89, 90, 95, 124, 126, 131, 137, 148, 151, 152, 155, 156, 157, 158, 159, 161, 165, 166, 167, 168, 169	30
.30-40 M	49, 53, 58, 88, 89, 91, 94, 139, 147	9
.30-40 SS	65, 91	2
.30-30 M	43, 44, 49, 51, 82, 99, 140, 148	8
.280 M	48, 66, 113, 134, 151	5
.280 SS	135	1
.276 M	78, 95	2
7mm	53, 59, 60, 70, 84, 87, 95, 97, 99, 102, 120, 126, 154, 164, 166, 168	16
.270 M	65, 95, 126, 148, 157	5
.256 Newton	95	1
.256 Mannl.	22, 23, 26, 27, 28, 29, 37, 42, 64, 66, 67, 69, 70, 77, 78, 81, 93, 96, 97, 100, 102, 104, 106, 111, 117, 118, 119, 127, 129, 130, 135, 137, 140, 142, 145, 165	36
.250 Sav.	79, 92, 95, 99, 103, 140, 142, 148	8
.25-35 M	146, 148	2
.22 M	92, 95, 129	3
Total		262

SUMMARY	
Large bores	90
Medium bores	206
Small bores	262
Total	558

Hunters 170—Rifles per hunter, 3.3

APPENDIX G

APPENDIX G—The Most Popular Rifles (Used by 5 or more hunters)

Caliber (Bore)		Rifle Type	Rifle Weight Lbs.	Powder Charge Grains	Bullet Weight Grains	Muzzle Velocity F.P.S.	Muzzle Energy Ft. Lbs.	Recoil Energy Ft. Lbs.	Number of Hunters Using
Large Bore	8 Bore	Double Barrel	18	B 273	1257	1500	6280	92	9
	10 Bore	Double Barrel	15	B 218	875	1550	4650	61	6
	12 Bore	Double Barrel	12	B 190	750	1550	3980	57	17
	10 Paradox	Double Barrel	9	B 150	850	1150	2480	44	7
	12 Paradox	Double Barrel	8	B 120	750	1200	2400	40	10
Bore	.577 BP	Double Barrel	14	B 164	590	1660	3610	36 }	14
	.577 SP	Double Barrel	14	S 100	750	2050	6990	92 }	
	.500 BP	Double Barrel	12	B 138	440	1780	3100	28 }	22
	.500 SP	Double Barrel	12	S 80	570	2125	5700	50 }	
	.50-110 BP	Magazine	8	B 110	300	1600	1700	17	7
	.470 SP	Double Barrel	11.5	S 75	500	2125	5000	57	10
	.465 SP	Double Barrel	10.8	S 75	480	2125	4800	56	10
	.450 BP	Single Barrel	10	B 85	540	1350	2180	23	13
	.450 BP	Double Barrel	10.5	B 110	320	1780	2250	18 }	30
	.450 SP	Double Barrel	10.5	S 70	480	2050	4470	44 }	
	.45-90 SP	Magazine	8	S 40	300	1890	2370	23	8
	.405 SP	Magazine	8.5	S 52	300	2200	3210	30	14
	.400 SP	Double Barrel	10	S 60	400	2150	4100	39	18

Small	.375	9	Magazine	S	57	270	2570	3950	35	10
Bore	9mm	7.5	Magazine	S	54	280	2250	3140	33	14
	.318	8.3	Magazine	S	48	250	2340	3050	25	13
	7.9mm	7.5	Magazine	S	48	227	2050	2120	16	7
	.303 Lee	8	Magazine	S	38	215	2000	1910	15	27
	.303 Sav.	7	Magazine	S	30	190	2000	1690	12	6
	30-06	8	Magazine	S	50	180	2700	2910	21	30
	.30-40	8	Magazine	S	42	150	2560	2180	14	9
	.30-30	7	Magazine	S	33	170	2200	1820	12	8
	.280	8	Magazine	S	50	140	3010	2820	17	5
	7mm	7.8	Magazine	S	40	173	2300	2060	13	16
	.270	8	Magazine	S	50	130	3160	2880	16	5
	6.5mm	7	Magazine	S	38	156	2380	1950	15	36
	.250	7	Magazine	S	36	87	3000	1740	9	8

NOTES: Rifle weight from Burrard's *Notes on Sporting Rifles*, 3rd Ed., 1932. Black Powder BP or B. Smokeless Powder SP or S.

$$\text{Recoil in ft. lbs.} = \left\{ \frac{\text{Bullet weight} \times \text{Velocity} + \text{Powder weight} \times 4700}{\text{Rifle weight} \times 7000} \right\}^2 \times \frac{\text{Rifle Weight}}{64.4}$$

APPENDIX H

Big Game Species of the World [1]

The Pachyderms	Continent	Occurrence
Elephant	India, Indo China	Limited—protected
Elephant	Africa	Numerous
Rhino	India, Burma	Scarce
Rhino	Africa	Numerous (White Rhino-Rare)
Hippo	Central Africa	Numerous

General habitat well watered, flat or rolling, forest or jungle where there is sufficient vegetation for food. Temper is unpredictable, and because of size these animals are always dangerous:

The Bison	Continent	Occurrence
Buffalo	North America	Scarce—protected
Aurochs	European Russia	Rare—protected
Gaur	India, Indo-China	Limited
Yak	Tibet	Limited
Gayal	Burma	Limited
Muskox	Arctic	Limited

These are in general grazing animals and frequent plains or open jungle, where grass is available. The yak and the muskox are adapted to cold, one on the high steppes of Asia, and the other on the Arctic tundra.

The Buffalo	Continent	Occurrence
Buffalo	Central Africa	Numerous
Water Buffalo	India, Burma	Limited
Banteng	Malaya	Fairly Numerous
Carabao	Philippines	Limited—domesticated

Grazing animals, frequenting open bush and grass jungles that are well watered. All are dangerous when wounded.

The Elk	Continent	Occurrence
Elk	Norway, Sweden	Scarce
Moose	North America	Limited

These animals frequent rocky pine barren lake country. The moose is America's largest game animal and is rapidly disappearing.

---

[1] These family divisions may not be strictly scientific as certain animals such as the gaur and the muskox are at variance with the characteristics of the group in which represented, but the grouping is essentially correct.

The Wapiti	Continent	Occurrence
Wapiti	Central Asia	Limited
Elk	North America	Limited
Maral	Asia Minor	Limited
Stag (Red deer)	Scotland	Limited

These animals frequent open and wooded mountain lands in the temperate zone. Comparatively easy to hunt and kill and so require protection.

The Reindeer	Continent	Occurrence
Reindeer	Arctic Europe	Limited
Caribou	Canada, Newfoundland	Numerous
Woodland caribou	Nova Scotia	Scarce

The European reindeer, wild and domesticated, are a smaller animal than the American caribou, but frequent the same open tundra wastes. The woodland caribou was a forest animal, once frequenting the northern United States and eastern Canada.

The Deer	Continent	Occurrence
Roedeer	Central Europe	Limited
Sambur	India	Limited
Barasingh	India	Limited
Swamp	India	Limited
Musk	Asia	Limited
Whitetail	Eastern No. America	Numerous
Mule	Western No. America	Numerous
Blacktail	Western No. America	Scarce

The Mule Deer and Sambur are found in open mountain country but the rest of the deer family are generally forest animals and browsers. Because of their acute senses of sight, hearing and smell, the deer family will be one of the last of the big game animals to be exterminated.

The Antelope	Continent	Occurrence
Eland, Giant	Sudan	Rare
Roan	Sudan	Limited
Sable, Giant	Tanganyika	Rare
Kudu	South Africa	Rare
Nyala	Abyssinia	Rare
Springbuck	South Africa	Numerous
Waterbuck	South and Cent. Africa	Numerous
Oryx	Sudan	Rare
Addax	Sudan	Rare
Sitatunga	Central Africa	Uncommon
Bongo	Kenya	Rare
Beisa	Somaliland	Limited
Reedbuck	South Africa	Numerous
Kob	Uganda	Numerous
Gazelle	North Africa, Asia	Limited
Pronghorn	North America	Limited

Grazing animals of the open plain or open jungle or forest, with few exceptions such as Bongo, Nyala, Kudu, etc., which live in the denser jungles, and Sitatunga and Waterbuck in the swamps.

Mountain Antelope	Continent	Occurrence
Chamois	Europe	Limited
Serow	Tibet	Limited
Goral	Himalaya	Numerous
Takin	China	Limited
Rocky Mountain Goat	North America	Scarce

Animals resembling the goat family in appearance and habitat but grazers like antelopes. Mountain ledges, nullahs, plateaus, and grassy, steep slopes are their natural habitat.

The Goats	Continent	Occurrence
Ibex	Abyssinia, India, Spain	Rare
Markhor	India, Persia	Rare
Goat	Spain, Asia Minor	Rare
Thar	India	Limited

Goats both browse and graze, but their habitat is usually the most precipitous mountain slopes, gullies and ledges, at an altitude from 2,000 to 10,000 feet.

The Sheep	Continent	Occurrence
Moufflon	Sardinia, Corsica	Rare
Barbary Sheep	North Africa	Rare
Ammon	Mongolia	Limited
Poli	Tibet	Limited
Burrhel	Himalayas	Limited
Oorial	India	Limited
Shapoo	Himalayas	Uncommon
Bighorn	North America	Scarce

Of the above only the oorial and the bighorn are ever found much below 1,000 feet. Mountain meadows and grassy ledges and nullahs form their usual habitat. Their hunting is difficult because of their fine sense of sight and the precipitous nature of the hunting ground.

The Cats	Continent	Occurrence
Tiger	India, China	Numerous
Lion	Persia, Africa	Numerous
Panther	India	Numerous
Leopard	Africa	Numerous
Cougar	North America	Limited
Jaguar	South America	Numerous
Snow Leopard	Tibet	Rare

With the exception of the lion, in open country, and the snow leopard in high mountains, these cats live in wooded hill or plain jungles where there is plenty of animal life for food.

The Bears	Continent	Occurrence
Black	Europe, No. America, Asia	Numerous
Brown	Alaska	Limited
Grizzly	North America	Scarce
Polar	Arctic	Numerous
Sloth	India	Limited

Only in the North temperate zone, these are creatures of their habitat, the brown and the polar in treeless country preying on salmon and seal in addition to small animals, berries, roots, and nuts. The other three are forest or mountain animals, feeding on rodents, grubs, acorns, grass, etc.

INDEX

A.

261

G.

H.